Gerald Lionel Joseph Goff

Historical Records of the 91st Argyllshire Highlanders

Gerald Lionel Joseph Goff

Historical Records of the 91st Argyllshire Highlanders

ISBN/EAN: 9783337165727

Printed in Europe, USA, Canada, Australia, Japan

Cover: Foto ©ninafisch / pixelio.de

More available books at **www.hansebooks.com**

HISTORICAL RECORDS

OF THE

91st ARGYLLSHIRE HIGHLANDERS.

DEDICATED TO

THE OFFICERS OF THE REGIMENT,

PAST, PRESENT, AND FUTURE.

CONTENTS.

	PAGE
CHRONOLOGICAL TABLE OF EVENTS	xiii

CHAPTER I.

Raising of Regiment — List of Officers — Services at the Cape of Good Hope—Return to England—Guernsey — Second Battalion raised — Second Battalion go to Holland — Bergen-op-Zoom—Reduction of Second Battalion—First Battalion to Hanover—England—Ireland 1

CHAPTER II.

Peninsular War, August, 1808, to Retreat of Corunna—England—Walcheren Expedition—England ... 27

CHAPTER III.

Peninsular War, 1812, to affair at Aire, February, 1814   44

CHAPTER IV.

Peninsular War—Toulouse—End of War—England—Ireland—Ostend 57

CHAPTER V.

Waterloo—Cambray—Army of Occupation round Paris
—England—Ireland 69

CHAPTER VI.

Ireland—Jamaica—England—Ireland—St. Helena—
Grahamstown, South Africa 78

CHAPTER VII.

Detachment at St. Helena—Removal of Napoleon's
body—Reserve Battalion formed 88

CHAPTER VIII.

Wreck of the *Abercrombie Robinson* 100

CHAPTER IX.

Kaffir War, 1846–47—Part taken therein by First
Battalion 113

CHAPTER X.

Kaffir War, 1846–47—Part taken therein by the
Reserve Battalion 139

CHAPTER XI.

Kaffir War, 1851–53—Reserve Battalion ... 173

CHAPTER XII.

Redistribution of the Regiment—The name " Reserve Battalion" discontinued—Depôt companies' history to their absorption in 1857 208

CHAPTER XIII.

First Battalion—England—Ireland—Malta—Greece— Ionian Islands 213

CHAPTER XIV.

India 232

CHAPTER XV.

Dover — Aldershot — Princess Louise's Wedding — Scotland—Ireland 243

CHAPTER XVI.

England—Natal—Causes of Zulu War 259

CHAPTER XVII.

Zulu War, April to September, 1879—Cape Town— Mauritius—St. Helena—Loss of Regiment's Number 273

APPENDICES.

		PAGE
A.	Colours	299
B.	Dress	301
C.	Succession List of Colonels	307
D.	Succession List of Lieutenant-Colonels	308
E.	List of Campaigns and Battles the Regiment has taken part in	309
F.	List of Battles inscribed on the Regimental Colour	311
G.	The Waterloo Roll	312
H.	The Regimental Record Book	314
I.	Sergeant-Major's Walking-stick	315
K.	Table showing Duration of Stay of the Regiment in Different Quarters	317
Alphabetical List of Officers		319

FORT AT EKOWE, MARCH, 1879.

LIST OF ILLUSTRATIONS.

	PAGE
THE COLOURS OF THE REGIMENT ...	*Frontispiece*
FORT AT EKOWE, MARCH, 1879	xi
THE UNIFORM OF THE REGIMENT WHEN RAISED *To face*	1
DUNCAN CAMPBELL ... ... ,,	2
THE CASTLE, CAPE TOWN ... ... ,,	7
TOULOUSE, 1814. *From an old print* ... ,,	63
DRESS OF THE REGIMENT IN 1822 ... ... ,,	78
THE LADDER AT JAMES TOWN (TO THE FORT AT TOP OF CLIFF). *From an old drawing* ,,	83
NAPOLEON'S TOMB, ST. HELENA ... ... ,,	92
REMOVAL OF NAPOLEON'S BODY FROM ST. HELENA. *Being a fac-simile reproduction of a very old plate* ... ... ,,	95
MAP SHOWING SCENE OF WARS 1845–46, 1851–53 ,,	113

LIST OF ILLUSTRATIONS.

	PAGE
GRAHAMSTOWN, 1845	*To face* 117
THE MARQUESS OF LORNE	,, 252
THE MARCHIONESS OF LORNE	,, 252
EMBARKATION OF REGIMENT AT SOUTHAMPTON *	,, 261
PORT NATAL	,, 262
CETYWAYO	,, 267
MAP OF EAST ZULULAND	,, 273
FORT PEARSON	,, 275
RELIEF FORCE CROSSING A RIVER *... ...	,, 277
GINGINHLOVO, 2ND APRIL, 1879. *From a sketch by the Author*	,, 280
PORT DURNFORD (FROM THE ANCHORAGE) * ...	,, 289
EMBARKATION OF CETYWAYO AT PORT DURNFORD *	,, 291

* From sketches which appeared in the *Illustrated London News* in 1879, reproduced by permission of the proprietors of that paper.

CHRONOLOGICAL TABLE OF THE CONTENTS OF THE RECORDS OF THE XCI. HIGHLANDERS.

1794. Regiment raised and numbered 98th.
1795. Proceeded to the Cape. Assisted at the capture of Cape Town, and the rest of the Dutch possessions.
1796. Expedition to Saldanha Bay.
1798. Number of regiment changed to 91st.
1799. Quelled a mutiny of the garrison in Cape Town.
1801. The colours of the regiment altered on the occasion of the union between Great Britain and Ireland.
1802. The Cape given back to the Dutch. Part of the regiment embarked for England.
1803. Remainder of the regiment, after delivering over the Cape, proceeded to England, leaving again in September for Guernsey.
1804. Regiment returned to England. A second battalion raised.
1805. First Battalion ordered to Hanover.
1806. First Battalion returned to England. Inspected by H.R.H. the Duke of York. Embarked for Ireland in December.
1807. Landed at Cork. Quartered at Mallow and Cashel.
1808. Quartered at Cashel, Enniscorthy, Dublin, and Bandon. Embarked for the Peninsula. Battles of Roleia and Vimiero. Retreat to Corunna.

1809. Battle of Corunna. Return to England, leaving one company under Captain Walsh, which was engaged at Talavera. The regiment took part in the expedition to Walcheren, returning to England in December.
1810. Stationed at Canterbury, Ramsgate, and Ashford.
1812. Embarked for the Peninsula, and joined the army at Villafranca.
1813. Battle of Vittoria. Affair at Pampeluna. Battles of Nivelle and Nive. Second Battalion went to Holland, and was present at attack on Bergen-op-Zoom.
1814. Battles of Orthes and Toulouse. Returned to Ireland in June.
1815. To Belgium. Battle of Waterloo. Affair at Cambray. March to Paris.
1816–17. Remained in France.
1818. Returned to England in November. Proceeded to Ireland in December.
1819. Quartered in Dublin.
1820. To Enniskillen.
1821. To Scotland *en route* for Jamaica.
1822–31. In Jamaica.
1831. To England. Stationed at Portsmouth and Oxford.
1832. At Bolton, Manchester, and Mullingar.
1833–34. Naas and Fermoy.
1835. To St. Helena.
1839. To Algoa Bay, leaving three companies at St. Helena.
1840. Outpost duties in Kaffirland. St. Helena detachment took part in disinterment of the body of the Emperor Napoleon.
1841. Outpost duties in Kaffirland.
1842. Reserve Battalion formed at home and sent to the Cape. Wreck in Table Bay of the *Abercrombie Robinson*. St. Helena detachment rejoined headquarters.

1843. Reserve Battalion joins First Battalion in Kaffirland. Detachments of both battalions proceed on the expedition against Tola.
1844. In detachments on Kaffir frontier.
1845. New colours presented First Battalion by Colonel Hare.
1846. Kaffir War. Block Drift.
1848. First Battalion to England. Stationed at Gosport. Reserve Battalion at Boem-plaats.
1849. Reserve Battalion at head-quarters, Grahamstown. First Battalion at Gosport.
1850. Beginning of second Kaffir War. First Battalion moved from Gosport to Dover.
1851. Second Kaffir War. Various actions. First Battalion —Preston, Liverpool, Manchester to Belfast.
1852. Second Kaffir War continued. Loss of the *Birkenhead*. First Battalion to Enniskillen.
1853. Second Kaffir War concluded. To Fort Beaufort.
1854. First Battalion to Dublin. Reserve Battalion, head-quarters, Fort Beaufort. First Battalion to Cork. Embarked for Malta in December.
1855. Reserve Battalion to England. Redistribution of the regiment. First Battalion to Greece.
1856. Kaffir War medals presented for 1846, 1847, 1850, 1851, 1852. Reserve Battalion reviewed by Queen Victoria. First Battalion to Greece.
1857. Reserve Battalion merged into First Battalion, which went from Greece to the Ionian Islands.
1858. To India. A wing employed against the insurgent Rohillas.
1859–63. At Kamptee.
1863. Kamptee to Jubbulpoor.
1864. Restoration of Highland name and dress.
1866. Jubbulpoor to Dumdum.
1867. Dumdum to Hazareebagh.
1868. To Kamptee. To England. Quartered at Dover.
1869. New colours presented.
1870. To Aldershot.

1871.	H.R.H. Princess Louise's marriage; a detachment present at the ceremony. To Aberdeen and Fort George.
1873.	To Edinburgh.
1874.	To Newry.
1875.	To the Curragh.
1876.	To Enniskillen and Londonderry.
1877.	To Belfast. Old colours burnt at Inverary.
1878.	To Dublin.
1879.	To Aldershot. Embarking for Zulu War in February. Zulu War. Battle of Ginginhlovo. Cape Town, with detachments at Mauritius and St. Helena.
1880.	Head-quarters at Cape Town, with detachments as in 1879.
1881.	Mauritius detachment rejoined head-quarters. Zulu medals presented. South Africa added to names on the colour.

HISTORICAL RECORDS

OF THE

91st ARGYLLSHIRE HIGHLANDERS.

CHAPTER I.

Raising of Regiment—List of Officers—Service at the Cape of Good Hope—Return to England—Guernsey—Second Battalion raised—Second Battalion go to Holland—Bergen-op-Zoom—Reduction of Second Battalion—First Battalion to Hanover—England—Ireland.

IN the year 1794 George III. expressed a desire to the Duke of Argyll, and several other Scotch noblemen and gentlemen, to raise an Argyllshire regiment.

1794.

A letter of service, dated the 10th of February, 1794, was granted, the chief terms of which were as follows :—

The regiment to be completed within three months.

1794. The corps to consist of one company of grenadiers, one of light infantry, and eight battalion companies; the establishment being 1102 officers and men, not including field officers. Levy-money to be allowed to the Duke of Argyll at the rate of five guineas per man, for 1064 men.

Recruits to be engaged for unlimited service; minimum height, five feet four inches; age between eighteen and thirty-five years.

The letter also contains other details as to the seniority of officers, etc.

On the 4th of March the establishment was altered to 1112, which included two lieutenant-colonels. The first lieutenant-colonel commandant of the new regiment was Duncan Campbell, of Lochnell, an Argyllshire man, who had served as captain in the Foot Guards. He assumed command at Stirling on the 15th of April, 1794. The following is the list of officers taken from the Army List of the 1st of January, 1795:—

Lieut.-Colonel Commandant	Duncan Campbell.
Major	Archibald Campbell.
,,	Henry M. Clavering.
Captain	Archibald Campbell.
,,	James Stuart.

DUNCAN CAMPBELL.

Captain	Donald Campbell.	1794.
,,	Colin Campbell.	
,,	John McDougall.	
,,	John Campbell.	
,,	Archibald Campbell.	
Captain-Lieut. and Captain	James Campbell.	
Lieutenant	Allan McPherson.	
,,	Hugh Campbell.	
,,	Robert McNab.	
,,	Archibald Campbell.	
,,	James Ferrier.	
,,	D. MacNeal.	
,,	John Campbell.	
,,	John MacNeal.	
,,	Duncan Campbell.	
,,	Lorne Ferrier.	
,,	Angus Campbell.	
,,	James Phillips.	
,,	William H. Crawford.	
,,	Colin Campbell.	
Ensign	Allan McLachlan.	
,,	William Munro.	
,,	Mark Anthony Bozon.	
,,	Donald Gregorson.	
,,	John M. Campbell.	
,,	Robert Guthrie.	
Chaplain	P. Fraser.	
Adjutant	Allan McPherson.	
Quarter-Master	Duncan Campbell.	
Surgeon	James Campbell.	

The names of the officers, as shown in the above list, gives an idea of how distinctively it was a clan regiment, as it will be observed there were seventeen bearing the name of "Campbell," and there must have been some confusion among so

1794. many having the same name, which was made further puzzling by many of their number having the same christian name; there being four Archibalds, three Duncans, three Jameses, two Johns, and two Colins. Any person who has attempted to trace the careers of these several officers in the army in subsequent years, has found it a very difficult task, as the plan of numbering officers of the same name (1), (2), (3), which is done in later Army Lists, was not carried out in books of that period.

On the 26th of May the first inspection of the battalion was made by General Lord Adam Gordon, who highly complimented the regiment on its soldierlike appearance. There were on parade over 700 men who had only been raised as a battalion within four months; they were therefore either men who had had some previous training, or were marvellously apt pupils to be considered worthy of being complimented on their military bearing by the general officer inspecting.

The regiment remained at Stirling until the middle of June, when it marched to Leith, to be embarked on the 17th and 18th of that month *en route* for Netley.

On the 9th of July the king was pleased to approve of the list of officers, and the regiment was numbered 98. 1794.

In November the regiment was at Chippenham, and on the 19th of January, 1795, they received orders to hold themselves in readiness to proceed on foreign service at the shortest notice. 1795.

On the 28th of January they moved to Poole, arriving on the 2nd and 3rd of February, and proceeded to Fareham on the 20th and 21st, arriving at Gosport on the 22nd and 23rd of April.

On the 5th of May they were ordered to join the expedition under Major-General Alured Clarke to the Cape of Good Hope, the object of which was to assist the force of some 4000 men which had been sent in a fleet, under command of Admiral Elphinstone, to take possession of the Cape Colony. They embarked at the Mother-Bank, near Spithead, on board the following East India ships: *General Coote*, *Deptford*, *Osterley*, and *Warren Hastings*.

These ships touched at Saint Salvadore, in South America, on the 6th of July, the strength of the battalion then being, 1 lieutenant-colonel, 1 major, 7 captains, 15 lieutenants, 5 ensigns, 3

1795. surgeons, and 815 non-commissioned officers and men. The expedition arrived at Simon's Bay on the 3rd of September, where they found that General Craig, who was in military command, had already fought the battle of Muysenberg without the reinforcements; having waited for them for more than three weeks, he at length decided to proceed with the operations against Cape Town with the small force which he then had at his disposal, consisting of about 1600 men, composed of 450 of the 78th Highlanders, and 350 marines, together with 800 seamen from the *Rattlesnake* and *Elcho* sloops-of-war.

The position of affairs there, when the 98th arrived, was: the English were encamped at Muysenberg, and the Dutch were in the neighbourhood of Wynberg, under command of Major Buissine. On the 4th of September the 98th landed and, with the rest of the reinforcements, marched on the 9th to Muysenberg to join General Craig, who now had a force of about 5000 men to complete the subjugation of the Cape Colony.

The road from Simon's Town to Wynberg runs along the sandy shore on the west of False Bay until beyond the pass of Muysenberg, which

THE CASTLE, CAPE TOWN.

is merely a narrow passage between a steep mountain and the sea; after this the road crosses a sandy plain, which forms part of the isthmus which divides Table Bay from False Bay.

1795

On the 14th the English troops struck their camp, and began their advance on Wynberg; little resistance being met with from the enemy, as the burghers deserted in such numbers that soon any further chance of a fight was gone. The battalion companies of the 98th, under Colonel Campbell, formed the centre of the British line, while the grenadier company formed part of the grenadier battalion under Lieutenant-Colonel Ferguson, and the light company, part of the light battalion, under Major King, both of the 84th Regiment. The casualties of the 98th on this occasion were four men wounded.

The Dutch now retreated towards Cape Town, and hostilities were suspended for twenty-four hours to arrange terms of surrender. On the 16th of September the 98th entered Cape Castle, and relieved the Dutch garrison by capitulation, the latter, however, marching out with all the honours of war. Sir James Craig was installed governor; and in this manner was ended the rule of the Netherlands East India Company

1795. in South Africa, after an existence of 143 years. Upon the surrender of the Cape of Good Hope and its dependencies, the following general order was issued: "Head-quarters, Castle, Cape Town, 19th of September. All forts and batteries in Cape Town and its dependencies being now in possession of his Majesty, agreeably to the articles of capitulation signed on the 16th inst., the Commander-in-Chief feels great satisfaction in expressing the high sense he entertains of the merits of Major-General Craig, and the officers, soldiers, seamen, and marines who composed the army, through whose spirited exertions and cheerful perseverance through every hardship this great object has been so successfully accomplished, and for which he begs they will accept of his warmest thanks. At the same time, he assures them he will not fail to represent their gallant conduct in the warmest terms to their most gracious sovereign at the earliest opportunity, and that he shall be happy to avail himself to contribute to their ease and prosperity." The flank companies were also thanked by a general order issued during that month.

The records of the regiment mention that a

new mode of drill was introduced in October of this year, "wherein the several times of march were regulated by the plummet, and the length of the pace fixed."

For more than a year the 98th remained in Cape Town, and during that time nothing of special importance to the regiment occurred. Cape Town at this period contained about 1100 or 1200 houses, inhabited by some 5000 whites and free people of colour, and about 10,000 slaves. Besides the castle, forts, and barracks, its principal buildings were: the Government House, the Dutch Reformed Church, the Lutheran Church, the town hall, the hall of the court of justice, a theatre, and a large building used as a government slave-pen. Many of the residents in the town were persons who had estates in the country, and who, through their slaves, retailed farm produce. The free people of colour were mostly fishermen. Food was plentiful and cheap; but firewood was very dear, as all the forests in the vicinity had been cut down. During the occupation of the English the Dutch language continued in use in the courts and churches, as well as in the farm-houses.

In August, 1796, the grenadier and light com-

1796. panies were engaged in the operations against the expedition sent from Holland under Admiral Lucas, for the purpose of again obtaining possession of the colony of the Cape of Good Hope. A fleet had been fitted out, consisting of the *Dordrecht*, 68; *Van Tromp*, 64; *Revolutionnaire*, 64; *Castor*, 40; *Brave*, 40; *Syren*, 24; *Havre*, 24; *Bellona*, 24; and the *Maria*, transport.

On board this fleet, 2000 soldiers, principally German mercenaries, were embarked, this number being considered sufficient for the purpose; as it was anticipated that before their arrival the British fleet, with a large portion of the land forces, would have left for the East Indies, and that the expedition would be joined off the Cape by a French squadron, with troops from Mauritius and Java. It was expected also that the colonists would join the Dutch army as soon as a landing was effected. The expedition was placed under the command of Admiral Lucas, who accepted the charge with reluctance, as he believed the force to be too small and too poorly fitted out to accomplish the end in view. So ill-supplied was he, that his provisions were nearly exhausted before he reached the colony, and he therefore put into Saldanha Bay, with the double purpose of procuring supplies and arming the colonists. On an island lying in the entrance to the bay he landed his sick, and began to construct fortfications. Here he learned that success was hopeless unless the French fleet joined him quickly; for none of the colonists came to his assistance, nor could he obtain those stores of food, of which he was so greatly in need.

On the 5th of August, 1796, information reached Cape Town that a Dutch fleet had left Europe, and might be expected at any moment. On receipt of this intelligence, Admiral Elphinstone, who was then in Simon's Bay, put to sea with a fleet, consisting of the *Monarch*, 74; *Tremendous*, 74; *America*, 64; *Ruby*, 64; *Stately*, 64; *Trident*, 64; *Jupiter*, 50; *Crescent*, 36; *Moselle*, 20; *Sphinx*, 20; *Rattlesnake*, 16; and *Echo*, 16. After cruising about some days without seeing the enemy, the British admiral put back to Simon's Bay, and was informed where the Dutch fleet was. He again set sail on the 14th, and on the 17th arrived at Saldanha Bay. The garrison of Cape Town at this time consisted of the 28th Light Dragoons, a corps of artillery, and the battalion companies of the 78th, 84th, 95th, and 98th Regiments of foot; the grenadiers of these

1796. regiments garrisoned Muysenberg, and the light companies, with the Hottentot regiment, were cantoned as a reserve corps at Wynberg. But just at this critical moment a fleet of East Indiamen, having on board the 25th and 27th Light Dragoons, the 33rd and 80th Regiments of foot, and five companies of the 19th Regiment, put into Simon's Bay for fresh stores. All of these troops were at once landed, and a re-distribution of the different garrisons took place. General Craig had now a strong army at his disposal, and leaving Major-General Doyle in command at Cape Town, he marched to Saldanha Bay, throwing out before him detachments of dragoons and light troops, which picked up several parties the Dutch admiral had sent to reconnoitre. So well-timed was General Craig's march, that he arrived in Saldanha Bay just two hours before the English fleet hove in sight. On descrying the fleet, the Dutch were in great joy, imagining the ships to be those of their friends the French; but they were soon undeceived when, to their great surprise, the English drew up in line of battle across the entrance to the bay. They now perceived that they were completely shut in, and that no chance was left for escape. The Dutch officers had some idea of running their vessels ashore to prevent them falling into the hands of the English in a perfect state, and of attempting to make their own escape into the country. General Craig, however, suspecting that they might have such intentions, sent an officer with a flag of truce to inform the Dutch admiral that if the ships were injured he would allow no quarter. The next morning (August 18, 1796) Admiral Elphinstone sent a flag of truce to Admiral Lucas, requiring him to surrender without delay. Resistance or escape was equally impracticable, and therefore, after an ineffectual request for one of his frigates to convey him and his officers to Europe, he surrendered at discretion. So the entire force of ships and men, comprising an expedition from which the Batavian Government expected nothing less than the recovery of the colony, fell into the hands of the English without a shot being fired, or a drop of blood spilt.

General Craig, in his despatch of the 19th of August, 1796, specially mentions the intelligence and action with which McNab of the 98th, and about twenty mounted men, performed the service of watching the enemy and preventing any communication with them from the land from the first

1796. moment of the fleet entering the bay. During the expedition the battalion companies of the 98th, together with the 95th, garrisoned Cape Town.

After the surrender of the Dutch fleet the troops marched back to Groenekloof, about half-way to Cape Town, and remained encamped there for three or four weeks.

The following general order was issued on the 19th of August, announcing the success at Saldanha Bay :—" Major-General Doyle has the happiness to make known to the troops the brilliant success that has attended his Majesty's army in the expedition to Saldanha Bay. The whole of the enemy's fleet and all the land forces destined to attack this colony have been obliged, by the masterly movements of the admiral and general, to surrender at discretion."

Nothing more of interest is recorded for some time of the movements of the regiment.

1797. On the 19th of June, 1797, the 98th was reviewed by General Dundas, who afterwards issued the following complimentary order :—
" Major-General Dundas is perfectly satisfied with the attention of the officers, and the steadiness of the men of the 98th Regiment, as well as with

the general appearance of the regiment at the review this morning, and returns his thanks to Brigadier-General Campbell and Lieut.-Colonel King for the attention that they appear to have shown on this occasion, as well as at all other times, in disciplining and perfecting their regiment."

On the 9th of October the regiment marched from Muysenberg to Simon's Town to protect the latter place from some seamen of the fleet who had mutinied. They returned to Muysenberg three days later, and encamped there for some time previous to again taking up their quarters in Cape Town on the 2nd of the following January.

On the 27th of October orders were received that the establishment of the regiment should be reduced to 600 rank and file, which was accordingly done; but in August of the following year it was again raised to 950 rank and file, with full complement of officers and non-commissioned officers.

In October, 1798, the number of the regiment was changed from the 98th to that of the 91st.

The names of the officers on the change of numbers was as follows :—

1798.

	Colonel	Duncan Campbell.
	Lieut.-Colonel	Fielder King.
	,,	James Catlin Craufurd.
	Major	Berkenhead Glegg.
	,,	James Campbell.
	Captains	Archibald Campbell.
	,,	Donald Campbell.
	,,	John McDougall.
	,,	Archibald Campbell.
	,,	James Orde.
	,,	John Robertson.
	,,	William Douglas.
	Captain-Lieut. and Captain	James Campbell.
	Lieutenant	Allen McPherson.
	,,	Robert McNab.
	,,	Archibald Campbell.
	,,	D. MacNeal.
	,,	John Campbell.
	,,	John MacNeal.
	,,	Duncan Campbell.
	,,	Colin Campbell.
	,,	Alexander Campbell.
	,,	Allan McLachlan.
	,,	William Munro.
	,,	Mark Anthony Bozon.
	,,	Donald Gregorson.
	,,	Henry Lindsay.
	,,	John Campbell.
	,,	John Campbell.
	,,	Phineas McIntosh.
	,,	Hugh Stewart.
	,,	Samuel Cooper.
	,,	John Campbell.
	,,	Charles Clinch.
	Ensign	Duncan Stuart.
	,,	John Cole Cooper.
	,,	James McLean.
	,,	Duncan McArthur.

Ensign	John Baumgardt.	1798.
,,	Robert Lowrie.	
Adjutant	Allan McPherson.	
Quarter-Master	Robert Cooke.	
Surgeon	James Campbell.	

In May, 1799, a regimental school was established for the first time for the non-commissioned officers and men. The terms were fixed at one shilling per month. 1799.

In the beginning of 1799, a strong attempt was made by a number of the soldiers in the garrison at Cape Town to organize a mutiny, their purpose being to destroy the principal officers, and to establish themselves in the colony. Not only did the 91st not take any part in this diabolical attempt, but the papers containing the names of the mutineers and their plans were discovered and seized by the aid of Private Malcolm McCulloch and others, the first soldiers of the regiment who were requested by the mutineers to enter into the conspiracy. Lieut.-Colonel Craufurd, in a regimental order dated 7th of August, specially commended the conduct of McCulloch, and declared that he considered himself fortunate in being the commander of such a regiment. For some little time after this, nothing more exciting occurs in the annals of the 91st

1799. than their encampments in the neighbourhood
1800. On the 2nd of April, 1800, the regiment marched from Cape Town to Wynberg, returning on the 21st of the following month. Ten days later we find the regiment again encamped in the same quarter of Wynberg. On the 14th of September the regiment encamped with the rest of the army at Rondebosch and Wynberg, and for the remainder of that year nothing of special interest
1801. is recorded. In 1801 the regiment passed from Brigadier-General Fraser's to General Vandeleur's division, and in parting with them, the former officer issued a general order, expressing his entire approval of the conduct of the men while under his command. On the 14th of February the regiment re-occupied the quarters in Cape Town, and on the 21st of March again elicited a complimentary general order from General Dundas for their efficiency and general discipline.

In June, 1801, the colours of the regiment were altered, on the occasion of the union between Great Britain and Ireland.

1802. On the 27th of May, 1802, the treaty of Amiens was signed.

"Europe," says Mr. Theal, in his history of

the Cape, "was exhausted, and required breathing time in order to prepare for still greater struggles than those she had just gone through. One of the conditions of peace insisted upon by France, and agreed to by England, was that the Cape Colony should be handed over to the Batavian Republic. In accordance with this agreement a force was despatched from Holland to relieve the British garrison and occupy the forts of the colony. The 1st of January, 1803, was fixed for the evacuation; and the English troops had actually commenced to embark when, on the 21st of December, a vessel arrived, which had left Plymouth on the 31st of October, with orders to delay the cession, as it was probable that war would break out again immediately. The Dutch troops were, therefore, cantoned at Wynberg, where they remained until February, 1803, when fresh orders from England were received, and the colony was given up." Meanwhile, however, the 91st had returned from their camp at Rondebosch to Cape Town, and in November, 1802, the first division of the regiment embarked at Table Bay for England, arriving at Portsmouth in February, 1803, and marching from thence to Hilsea Barracks. On the 28th of that month

1803. the second division of the 91st assisted at the delivering over of the Cape of Good Hope to the Dutch, which duty having been performed, they also embarked for England on the 2nd of March, and arrived at Portsmouth in May, rejoining the first division at Bexhill, to which place they, the latter, had moved from Hilsea. Thus ended the share taken by the 91st in the first occupation of the Cape of Good Hope by the English.

In June, 1803, a general order was published directing that each company throughout the army should have an effective captain, and consequently that field officers should no longer command a company, which up to this date they had done. The rank of captain-lieutenant was also abolished. The regiment had been reduced to a peace establishment on their arrival in England.

In September the 91st were ordered to Guernsey, at which place they did not remain very long, leaving it again for England in the following 1804. April; first to be quartered at Shoreham, and afterwards at Lewes.

Directly after the return of the regiment to England, it was notified that an additional force was required by his Majesty, and that the levy should be undertaken by officers selected, and who might be desirous of raising men, promotion being given to such officers if they raised a given number of men. Captains William Douglas and Donald MacNeal, and Lieutenants Duncan Stuart and Robert Lowrie, were selected, and came forward on this occasion.

1804.

In August of this year his Majesty was pleased to direct that a second battalion should be forthwith formed from the men to be raised in accordance with the Act of Parliament known as the "Defence Act," from the counties of Perth, Argyll, and Bute; the recruiting officer's headquarters to be at Perth. The 1st battalion was to be kept up to strength through this new battalion.

In March, 1805, the 2nd battalion was still at Perth. It will be as well to record at once the short history of this battalion before continuing that of the 1st or original one.

1805.

On the 7th of April, 1809, the Highland dress was discontinued to be worn. In 1811 this battalion was stationed at Canterbury, and two years later was again in Scotland, quartered at Ayr. In July of the same year, it embarked for Germany under command of Major-General

1809.
1811.
1813.

1813.   Samuel Gibbs, sailing to Stalsund with the troops under Brigadier-General Gore, which expedition shortly returned, and the battalion again sailed from Yarmouth in December to join
1814.   the army in Holland. On the 2nd of March, 1814, they were brigaded with the other regiments under Lieut.-General Sir Thomas Graham, and were present at the unfortunate attack upon the strong fortress of Bergen-op-Zoom.

On the 8th of March Sir Thomas Graham collected about 4000 British troops, for an attempt to carry the place by storm. They were formed into four columns, two to attack the fortifications at different points, one to make a false attack, and the fourth to attempt an entrance by the mouth of the harbour, which is fordable at low water. The attack at first was quite successful, as the two first columns established themselves on the ramparts; but when there, unforeseen difficulties arose which made it necessary to alter the point of attack, and resulted in a number of men being killed and wounded. Finally, this attempt was abandoned, and the troops retired, leaving over 300 dead.

Napoleon, when at St. Helena in 1817, is reported to have observed that the storming of

Bergen-op-Zoom was a most daring attempt, 1814. but that it ought not or could not have succeeded, the number of the garrison being greater than that of the assailants. He added that the idea that the failure of the attack was in part attributed to one of the British generals not having taken the precaution to communicate the orders which had been given him to any one else, so that when he was mortally wounded the troops did not know how to act, made no difference, as an attempt of that kind ought never to succeed unless the party attacked becomes panic-stricken, which sometimes happens.

The 91st's casualties, according to the official returns, were—

Ensign—	Hugh McDugald.*
Sergeants killed—	John Banks.
	Dugald Campbell.
	Robert Howell.
	Malcolm McDonald.
	Duncan McInnes.
	Charles Peters.
Ditto, died of wounds—	Thomas Dougleby.
Corporals killed—	W. Porter.
Ditto, died of wounds—	Alex. Burns.
	John Halley.

* As Ensign Hugh McDugald's name appears as a lieutenant in 1815–16, he must have been reported killed in error; probably he was wounded and left for dead.

1814.

Corporals died of wounds—	George Liddle.
	Alex. McPherson.
	Christopher White.
Drummer died of wounds—	W. McBirnie.
Privates killed—	29
Ditto, died of wounds—	4

In this affair the name of Sergeant-Major Patrick Cahil was brought into notice, on account of his conspicuous conduct in securing and carrying off one of the battalion colours, when the officer who was in charge was wounded; for his bravery on this occasion, he was recommended and promoted from the ranks, receiving a commission as ensign.

In September this battalion returned to England, arriving at Deal from Ostend, and proceeding to Canterbury, to be quartered there for a month, when it embarked at Gravesend for Ayr; and on the 25th of December, 1815, it was reduced at Perth.

The above history of this battalion is all that can be found out about it, as the records of the 1st battalion do not mention any details of its existence, and probably for most of the period in which it was formed it was only used as a recruiting depôt for the 1st battalion, which during most of these years was employed in the Peninsular War.

We will now return to follow the history of the 1st battalion, which we left in Lewes in 1804.

In October, 1805, the regiment was reviewed with other troops of the brigade, consisting of the 42nd and 92nd, by the Commander-in-Chief at Bexhill, and were noticed for their appearance and discipline.

In December the order came for it to embark for Hanover, where it was brigaded with the 26th and 28th Regiments, under the command of Major-General Mackenzie Fraser, arriving at Beverstadt on the 3rd of January, and Hanbergen on the 8th. However, the general orders, dated Bremen, 27th of January, stated that the king had been pleased to recall the troops from North Germany, and that they were to be embarked immediately to return to England, which was done, and the 91st disembarked at Ramsgate on the 20th of February, and marched to Faversham, where it was inspected on arrival by Lieutenant-General Sir John Moore, whose satisfaction with its appearance is noted in the regimental orders of that date.

On the 17th of March the 91st moved to Ashford, and at the end of July they were at Shorncliff. On the 10th of August, H.R.H. the Duke of

1806. York reviewed the regiment, and expressed his satisfaction; and on the 24th of October a move was made to Hythe, where they remained till the 21st of December, proceeding then to Dover, to
1807. be embarked for Ireland on the 24th of January. Arriving at Cork on the 27th, they marched to Fermoy. After that the head-quarters were stationed at Mallow, moving to Cashel on the
1808. 27th of November. In January, 1808, they marched *viâ* Enniscorthy, arriving at Dublin on April the 6th and 7th; there they only remained till the 21st of May, when they moved to Bandon.

CHAPTER II.

*Peninsular War, August, 1808, to Retreat of Corunna—
England—Walcheren Expedition—England.*

On the 13th of June, 1808, the regiment embarked at Monkstown, to take part in the Peninsular expedition.

Sir Arthur Wellesley decided that the expedition should land at the mouth of the Mondego river, which was the only locality on the Portuguese coast where there was any chance of a safe place for a disembarkation, there being the little fort of Figueras, occupied by British marines guarding it. The landing commenced on the 1st of August, and although the weather was favourable, it was not before the 5th that it was completed, and the army encamped at Lavaos.

On the 9th the advanced guard marched towards Leiria, the main body following the next day, arriving there on the 11th, where they were joined by the Portuguese force.

1808. The people at Lisbon at this time were panic-stricken, and were equal to believing anything the French told them. They were under the impression that the British had brought with them a Moorish force, and the belief was confirmed by the appearance of the Highlanders, whose dress was immediately pronounced not to be Christian; and for a time no doubt was entertained but that these were the Moorish auxiliaries.

In the mean time the French general, Laborde, arrived at Candeiros on the 9th, and Loison entered Abrantes. On the 10th Laborde sought for a position near Batalha, which is about eight miles south of Leiria; but, being unable to select an advantageous one, he fell back on the 12th to Obidos, a town with a castle built on a gentle eminence in the middle of a valley. This place he occupied with his picquets, and retired on the 14th six miles southward, to Roleia, a place which overlooked the whole valley of Obidos.

Loison at the same time fell back on the 13th to Santarem, and on the 15th Sir Arthur's advanced guard reached Caldas, and drove Laborde's picquets from Obidos. This placed the French general in a dilemma, as he had either to risk a battle alone (as Loison was only at Alcoentre) or he had to retire, leaving the road to Lisbon open; he determined, therefore, to abide the assault, with a hope that Loison might arrive during the action.

The 91st, during these operations, had been brigaded with the 45th and 50th Regiments under Catlin Craufurd, forming part of the main body of Sir Arthur's army, and on the morning of the 17th the allied troops, consisting of about 14,000 of all arms, issued from Obidos, and broke into three distinct columns of battle. The 91st were attached to the centre column, under the direct command of Sir Arthur, the left column being commanded by Ferguson, the right consisting of Trant's Portuguese. The centre column was composed of Hill's, Nightingale's, Fane's, and Catlin Craufurd's brigades of British infantry, besides cavalry and artillery.

The three first-mentioned brigades, on approaching the French position at Roleia, formed for attack, while Craufurd's, with most of the guns, were kept as a reserve. Laborde's position was soon driven in, and he had to retire to the heights of Zambugeira, about three-quarters of a mile to the rear. Fresh dispositions had now to be made to dislodge him. Ferguson and Fane were directed to turn his right, Trant to do the same to his left, while Hill and Nightingale advanced against his front; Craufurd still remaining in reserve.

For some time Laborde held his own, but at length he was forced to retire, which he did by alternate masses, protecting his movements with short, vigorous charges of cavalry, retreating through the pass of Runa, and by an all-night march gained the position of Montechique, leaving three guns on the field, and the road to Torres Vedras open.

The French casualties were 600 killed and wounded, including Laborde himself; while the English, who had not had more than 4000 men actually engaged, lost about 500 killed, missing, or wounded.

Sir Arthur, hearing after the action that Loison was only five miles distant at Bombaral, took up a position in an oblique line to that which he had just forced, so as to face the fresh army.

Next day, the 18th of August, the army marched to Lourinham, about ten miles south of Roleia, and took up a position at Vimiero, a village near the sea-coast. Here Anstruther's brigade joined the allied troops, having been landed on the morning of the 19th at Paymayo. On the 20th the army was still further strengthened by the arrival of Acland's brigade, which was disembarked at Maceira Bay.

1808.

Sir Arthur, estimating that he had the advantage in numbers over the French, determined to bring Junot, who was now in command, to an action. This, however, he was stopped doing by the arrival of Sir Harry Burrard, who was senior to him, and who determined to await the arrival of Sir John Moore's troops. In the mean time the French general had decided to do exactly what Sir Arthur proposed forcing him to do, and on the morning of the 21st attacked the allies' position.

The English brigades were formed along the top of a line of hills running north-east from Vimiero, which was on the right centre of their position, with Hill's brigade on the extreme right. The 5th brigade (in which were the 91st, together with the Portuguese troops) were on the extreme left, and some distance to the rear of the allied position.

Junot had quitted Torres Vedras, which was about nine miles distant, on the evening of the 20th, with 14,000 men, intending to fall on

1808. the British troops at daylight, but he found the difficulties of the road did not allow him to reach their position before 9 o'clock, and it was not till 10 o'clock that he commenced the action by two connected attacks, one against the centre and the other against the left of the allies' army.

The centre attack was repulsed with heavy loss; and on the left, where he had expected a weak flank, he found Ferguson's brigade, and in the distance, threatening his rear, the 5th brigade (in which was the 91st) was to be seen marching by a distant ridge towards Lourinham. Ferguson's brigade made a vigorous counter-attack, and drove back the enemy, taking prisoner Brennier, who commanded one of the French brigades.

By this time the French army was in confusion, and at 12 o'clock Sir Arthur determined to take the offensive; but he was again stopped by Sir Harry Burrard, who had arrived on the battle-field, and now assumed chief command, ordering further operations to cease, and resolving to await the arrival of Sir John Moore. Junot now retreated with order and celerity to the pass of Torres Vedras, and when evening came the relative position of the two armies was the same as the day before. The French loss was estimated at over 2000. 1808.

On the 23rd the French demanded a cessation of arms, and proposed the basis of a convention to evacuate Portugal. This was listened to by the allied commanders, and eventually, on the 30th, a definite treaty was concluded. By the 30th of September, all the French (except the garrisons of Elvas and Almeida) were out of Portugal.

In the beginning of September, by a new distribution of the army, the 91st were brigaded with the 6th and 45th Regiments, under Major-General Beresford. On the 20th of this month the regiment was encamped at Quillos; and on the 19th of October marched with the rest of Sir John Moore's army into Spain, arriving at Albrantes on the 25th; Castello Branco, the 30th; Cavellos, November the 3rd; Belmonte, the 8th; Guarda, the 9th; Morillo, the 10th; Ciudad Rodrigo, the 11th, and Salamanca on the 18th.

On the 28th of the same month the 91st was placed in brigade with the 20th, 28th, 52nd, and 95th Regiments, under command of Major-General the Hon. Edward Paget, under whose command the regiment remained during the rest of its stay in the Peninsula.

1808. In consequence of the time of year and the difficulties of marching large bodies of troops on indifferent roads, through a country which could supply next to nothing in the way of food, the army of Sir John Moore was scattered over a great front of country; his artillery being far away to his right, and the length of his column such that, although the head of it reached Salamanca on the 13th of November, the centre portion did not arrive there until the 23rd.

Sir John's instructions on arrival, were "to open communication with the Spanish authorities, for the purpose of framing the plan of campaign;" but he found that the Spanish forces, with which he was to co-operate, had been thoroughly routed, and that Napoleon, with an army of unknown strength, was already near Madrid.

His first object, therefore, was to unite the scattered divisions of his army. Sir David Baird had landed at Corunna, and had marched his troops towards Astorga; but was still sixteen days distant, and it would take him more than twenty days to reach Salamanca with the main body.

The defeat of the Spanish troops at Tudela on

the 23rd was only made known on the 28th, and Sir John saw that under the circumstances he had no option but to fall back on Portugal. Baird was to regain Corunna or Vigo, and go by sea to Lisbon. 1808.

On the 13th of December, by intercepting a despatch of Napoleon's addressed to Soult, Sir John ascertained that Madrid was in the hands of the French, and that corps of the French army had been despatched in directions which would eventually lead to their surrounding him; he accordingly moved his head-quarters to Toro, and ordered Hope, who was at Tordesilla, to pass the Duero and go towards Villepando, Baird's head-quarters being at Benevente.

The retreat of Sir John's army, which consisted of only 19,000 men fit to fight, commenced on the 16th, the head-quarters being at Castro Nuevo on the 18th. On the 22nd Napoleon placed himself at the head of his army, but reached Valderas twelve hours too late to stop the English troops, who had crossed the Esla. Soult, however, was in full pursuit. Moore, knowing the line of the Esla could not be maintained, retired towards Lugo. Napoleon entered Astorga on the 1st of January, 1809, and had 1809.

with him an army of 70,000 French infantry; he, however, had personally to relinquish command, as his presence was required in France, and the command devolved on Soult, who continued the pursuit to near Lugo, where, on the 5th of January, he found that Moore had halted, and prepared to resist his advance. A fight commenced with the French advanced guard and the English reserve, who, commanded by Paget, maintained the post until nightfall, and then retired to Lugo.

On the 8th the two armies were still in front of each other, ready for battle; on the French side about 22,000 fighting men, and on the English, 18,000 men of all arms.

The state of the English army at this crisis was desperate; even if they won a battle, they had no means of taking advantage of it, as they were without transport, having no draught cattle, no magazines, hospitals, provisions, or second line; and if defeated, had nothing but the sea behind. In Lugo, they had only enough bread left for one more day; the men were dispirited by fatigue and bad weather, but still anxious to fight, and therefore each moment of delay increased their difficulties. Moore, therefore, determined, as the enemy did not seem willing to attack, to retire to a position nearer, and covering Corunna; this was attempted on the night of the 8th, with most unfortunate results, as the column lost its way in a fall of sleet, and everything became disorganized. The reserve, commanded by Paget, remained in position during the night of the 9th a few miles from Betanzos, the rest of the army being quartered in that town.

Moore now assembled his army in one solid mass, and moved towards Corunna, arriving on the 11th. Three divisions occupied the town and suburbs, and the reserve was posted between the village of El Burgo and the road of St. Jago de Compostella.

For twelve days these hardy soldiers under Paget had covered the retreat, during which time they traversed eighty miles of road in two marches, passed several nights under arms in the snow of the mountains, were seven times engaged, and now took the outposts, having fewer men missing from the ranks, including those who had fallen in battle, than any other division in the army; an admirable instance of the value of good discipline.

Moore caused the land front of the town to

1809. be put in a state of fortification, destroyed the magazine, which was full of powder, and caused all the horses, which were useless on account of the nature of the ground, to be shot.

On the 16th, the ships having arrived, all encumbrances were shipped, and it was intended to have embarked the men that night; but it was found that the French proposed to fight.

The order of battle of the English, therefore, was—Baird's division on the right; Hope's, forming the centre and left, with Paget's reserve behind the centre of the position; but Paget was ordered, shortly after action commenced, to carry the whole of the reserve to turn the French left, and menace the great battery which Soult had placed on the left of his line, on some rocks. Fraser was ordered to form support to Paget.

The troops in the centre and right having become engaged, a most furious action ensued along the whole line, and in the valley between the two armies. It was at this period that Sir John Moore was mortally wounded. The reserve, overthrowing everything in the valley, forced the French dragoons to retire, and thus turning the enemy's left, approached the eminence where the big battery was posted. Night coming on put an end to the battle, which had resulted in the English favour all along the line.

Hope, who was now chief in command, determined to embark his army, which he managed to do; for when morning dawned the French found the British position abandoned. Hill embarked at the citadel, which was held until the 18th by a rear-guard under Beresford.

When the wounded were all on board, the remaining troops embarked, and the fleet sailed for England, the ships carrying the 91st arriving at Plymouth on the 28th.

The officers and men who were left sick in Portugal, when the regiment embarked for England, were formed into a company under Captain Walsh, and attached to the first battalion of detachments, which was under command of Colonel Bunbury, of the 3rd Foot, and composed part of the army under Sir Arthur Wellesley.

On May the 10th, 11th, and 12th, 1809, this company was actively employed in the affairs of the days above mentioned, which led to the capture of Oporto, and it afterwards advanced with the army which drove the French into Spain, with the loss of all its artillery, ammunition, and baggage. On the 27th and 28th of

1809. July they took part in the hard-fought battle of Talavera, in which engagement the company lost one officer, Lieutenant McDougall, and nine men killed; one officer, Captain Walsh, and nineteen men missing; and thirty-one rank and file wounded, out of a total strength of three officers and ninety rank and file.

Captain Walsh was taken prisoner in a charge, and, with many other officers similarly situated, was marched under a strong escort towards France; but he managed to effect his escape at Vittoria on the night of the 20th of August, by swimming the river Jago, and after suffering the utmost privations and hardships, he joined the allied army and reported himself personally to the commander-in-chief.

Captain Thomas Hunter Blair of the 91st, who was acting major of brigade in the action of Talavera, was also wounded and taken prisoner, and was not released until 1814.

After the arrival of the main body of the regiment in England, they were quartered at Deal, and afterwards at Margate, when they were brigaded with the 6th and 50th Regiments under Major-General Dyott, in the second division under Lieutenant-General the Marquis of Huntley. On the 15th of July they marched to Ramsgate to be embarked at that port as part of the expedition under Lord Chatham, and sailed with the fleet from the Downs to South Beverland, where they disembarked on August the 9th, and entered Middleburg, in the island of Walcheren, on the 2nd of September. This island, which is one of the four principal islands of Zealand, on the West Scheldt, is about ten miles in length and eight in breadth, and contains a larger population than any of the others at the mouth of the river, and was deemed perfectly secure from hostile attacks at the time of the expedition. The inhabitants were principally Dutch and English, the trade being notoriously smuggling. Like the rest of the islands of Zealand, Walcheren had in former times been at the bottom of the sea, until the industry of man succeeded in pushing the sea back and ramparting the reclaimed land with high dykes. The island therefore had the appearance of being scooped out and fenced round in the bed of the ocean. The principal towns in Walcheren are, Campveer, Flushing, and Middleburg. The latter, in which the 91st were stationed, was a fortified place, and had been recently strengthened, having eight gates and twelve bastions to defend

1809.

the walls and ramparts, with large deep ditches, and the situation was such as to enable the inhabitants to lay the country about the town under water when they pleased, by merely cutting a sea-dam.

The object of the expedition was to drive the French from the mouth of the Scheldt, and prevent them from making docks to build a fleet, the well-known object of which was to attack England. Lord Chatham, however, finding that it was useless to proceed, gave up the idea of pushing up the Scheldt to reduce the French fleet, and on the 4th of the month returned to England, taking the greater number of his troops with him, leaving the remainder to keep possession of the island of Walcheren for the purpose of blockading the Scheldt. The 91st was part of the force left behind, where they remained until the 23rd of December, on which date the island was completely evacuated by the British army, nearly one-half of whom, according to a return rendered to the House of Commons, were either dead or sick. The 91st itself lost over sixty men during its stay there, from the deadly fever which ravaged the place, and the parade state in September showed that, out of 636 men, 205 were in hospital.

The 91st arrived in England at Deal on the 26th of December, and proceeded to Shorncliffe, and were from 1810 to 1812 quartered successively at Canterbury, Ramsgate, Ashford, and Chatham; nothing of any importance happening during that period.

1809.

1810-1812.

CHAPTER III.

Peninsular War, 1812, to affair at Aire, February, 1814.

1812. IN September the 91st were for a second time under orders to take part in the Peninsular War, and on the 18th and 19th of that month they embarked at Chatham in small craft, which dropped down to the Nore, where the men were transhipped to the transports *Malabar*, *Diomede*, and *Success*, which set sail on the 20th; but being dispersed by a gale, they arrived at Corunna on the following dates: the *Diomede* on the 6th, the *Success* on the 9th, and the *Malabar* on the 12th of October, and the troops were landed on the succeeding days. The *Malabar* conveyed 300 men of the Guards in addition to the men of the 91st.

On the 14th the regiment set out to join the grand army under the Duke of Wellington, arriving at Villafranca, about twelve miles from Benevento, on the 1st of November. Here information was received, on the following day, that the enemy was in force at the last-named place; and the 91st, with a detachment of Guards, the whole being under the orders of Major MacNeal (91st), moved in the direction of Braganza, on the frontier of Portugal, where they arrived on the 5th, and occupied the place and its forts, despatching couriers to find out where the grand army was, and obtain orders as to their future movements.

1812.

The 91st, on joining the Duke's army, was placed in the sixth division in the Highland, or General Pack's brigade, then under command of Colonel Stirling of the 42nd Highlanders. On going into winter quarters, the regiment was removed to San Remo, where it remained for five months.

In April the army was collected together, and Wellington prepared to advance northward, the 91st starting on the 14th of May with the rest of the troops, and on the 26th the advanced guard of the allied troops came in contact with the French under Vellatle, and drove him across the Torneo river. Two days after this, the main body arrived in the country between Zamora and Toro, and on the 31st a junction was formed with Graham's troops, which formed the left wing of Wellington's army.

1813.

1813. The allied army was now composed of 90,000 men, with more than 100 guns, while the French only numbered some 55,000; Wellington therefore marched forward without much opposition. The French had proposed to stop the allies' advance on the elevated plain of Burgos; but, as that place was found to be untenable, on account of there being no store of provisions and the new defensive works being unfinished, they determined to cross the Ebro and take up a position near Vittoria, where a heap of baggage and stores, with a number of fugitive families, had accumulated.

Meanwhile the allies crossed the Carrion on the 7th of June, and on the 12th drove the remaining French out of Burgos. The French general had caused part of that town to be undermined; but by some error in the haste of retreat, the mine was fired before all his troops had retired; the consequence being that over 300 of the French were blown to pieces.

After passing Burgos, Wellington moved on the 15th, by his left, to the mouth of the Ebro, masking his front with cavalry, gaining the seacoast, and providing his army with a new base of operations. His connections with Portugal were accordingly cast off, and all the posts on the road to Lisbon and the places where troops were left on the march were abandoned, and the men were transferred by sea to the coast of the Bay of Biscay.

Wellington now moved the army to the right, to break up the French force which was lying in the plain through which the river Zadora flows, at the upper end of which is Vittoria. The allies were halted on the 20th, to allow scattered units to be picked up, and also to enable the French position to be thoroughly examined. The sixth division, in which were the 91st, was left at Medina de Pomar, and only 80,000 of the allies moved forward to fight. The strength of the French was about 60,000; they were, however, stronger in artillery than the allies.

The next day, the 21st of June, the battle of Vittoria was fought, resulting in a victory for the allies, who drove the French off the field, took all their guns, treasure, and stores, but did not kill many men, as the French retired before they were half beaten. The following day the sixth division, under Packenham, came up and assisted at the taking possession of Vittoria, while the main body, under Wellington, followed up the French towards Pampeluna. On the 25th this division, together

1813. with the fifth and D'Urban's Portuguese, marched in the direction of Logrono to cut off any stragglers escaping that way. By the 7th of July, the whole line of the Spanish frontiers, from Roncesvalles to the mouth of the Bidassoa river, was occupied by the allies.

Wellington now determined to reduce the fortresses of San Sebastian on the sea, and Pampeluna. He therefore placed his troops to effect this object, the fifth and sixth divisions being told off to the latter place; the sixth, however, only remained until the 15th of July, when they were again moved on to the front and quartered at St. Estevan.

On the 12th of July Soult, who had taken supreme command of the French forces in Spain, found himself at the head of an army of about 77,000 men, whose front extended from the mouth of the river Bidassoa on the right, to St. Jean Pied de Port on the left.

On the 25th the combats of Roncesvalles and Maya took place, in consequence of which Wellington ordered a general retirement to cover Pampeluna. A position being taken up on the heights of Sauroren, Soult, who followed, did not offer to engage seriously on the 27th, which gave time for the allies to get up the sixth and seventh divisions. The former did not leave St. Estevan until daylight on that morning, and had halted from 10 o'clock till 4, having had to make a detour to gain the Marcalain road, on account of Soult having got between them and Sauroren. This caused a delay in their arrival of some eighteen hours.

About midday on the 28th the French commenced their attack with Clausel's division, who at once turned Coles' left (which was the left of Wellington's line); at the same time the main body of the sixth division appeared on the battlefield from behind a ridge, and formed in order of battle at an angle to the French front, by which means the enemy's flank was turned, and they were driven back fighting fiercely, strewing the ground with their enemy's bodies as well as their own. All along the line a furious and nearly hand-to-hand conflict raged, until the French were forced to give way.

During this action the 91st's casualties were: one sergeant and eleven men killed, and six officers (Lowrie, Maclean, Marshall, Ormerod, Ormiston, and MacFarlane) and ninety-seven rank and file wounded.

The following day both armies rested without

1813. firing a shot; but on the 30th Wellington attacked the French, holding the village of Sauroren with a brigade under Byng, while the sixth division, under Packenham, was sent to the left of that place. Byng, after a sharp engagement, was entirely successful, taking 1400 prisoners, and driving the French back into the mountains in their rear.

The allies had 1900 killed and wounded in the actions of the 28th and 30th, while the French loss was enormous. On the latter day the 91st lost one private killed, while Major MacNeal and eight rank and file were wounded. Of those wounded in the regiment in these two actions, it is recorded that at least forty died subsequently of their wounds.

The following day the sixth division was ordered to march *viâ* Eugui to join Picton in the neighbourhood of Roncesvalles, at which place the 91st bivouacked on the night of the 1st of August. The allied troops were now occupying the same position as they had previous to the retreat on Pampeluna on the 27th of July, with the exception of the sixth division, who were on this occasion ordered, with the third division, to guard the Bastan and Col de Maya. In this district the 91st remained until November.

In the meanwhile Wellington was engaged in laying siege to San Sebastian, which did not fall until the 9th of September. Soult was in the neighbourhood of the mouth of the Bidassoa, and had several engagements with the allies.

On the 7th of October the allies on the left of the line crossed the river Bidassoa, and the sixth division was ordered forward to make a demonstration in the direction of Urdax, which they did, making a false attack on the French troops under D'Erlon; but Soult soon found out that the real object was the passage of the Bidassoa on his extreme right.

In the beginning of November the position of the allied troops was the line of mountains which divide the Nivelle river from the Bidassoa, stretching from the sea to opposite St. Jean Pied de Port. Wellington had intended to fight a battle on the 8th, but had to abandon the idea, as the Spanish troops under Freyre were declared not to be ready to move. On the 10th, when this difficulty was surmounted, the allied army of 90,000 men and ninety-five pieces of artillery descended to attack the French, who could only muster about 80,000 of all arms.

The sixth division, together with other troops,

in all about 26,000 men, were collected under Hill, with orders to attack D'Erlon. They moved off during the night of the 9th by the different passes of the Col de Maya, the sixth division being ordered to assault the works covering the bridge at Amotz over the Nivelle river, either on the right or left bank, according to circumstances.

Day broke on the 10th with great splendour, and as the first ray of light showed, the signal-gun for action was fired. The French were taken by surprise, and hastily rushed to their defences, Soult having, during the weeks previous, thrown up many works to defend the north bank of the river.

The allied troops, by their impetuosity, swept everything before them. The sixth division crossed the river about 7 o'clock some distance above Amotz, and by the right bank threatened the bridge, driving the French out of the partly finished fort covering the bridge, and then, turning to the right, drove D'Armagnac's troops through his hutted camp towards Helbacen de Borda; D'Erlon was by this means nearly cut off from the rest of Soult's army, and had to retreat to save himself. Darkness coming on found the allies in possession of most of the right bank of the river. The troops were exhausted, especially the sixth division, which had been marching and fighting for nearly twenty-four hours.

The 91st's casualties during the action were: Captain David McIntyre and three men killed, two sergeants and four men wounded; while Macneil, the adjutant, had two horses shot under him.

On the 11th the allies advanced, and found that Soult had retired to take up a new position with his right near Arylet, on the sea-coast, and his left in the entrenched camp of Bayonne. The rain, which fell heavily in the mountains on the 11th, rendered the fords impassable, and as the French in their retreat had broken down the bridges at Ustaritz, the advance of the allies was checked. It was not until the 9th of December that active operations were again commenced. Wellington, finding that the enemy held the river Nive at Cambo, which was on his right when he wished to advance on Bayonne, determined to clear the French away. He accordingly detailed Hill to cross the river and turn the enemy's left flank with his division. Beresford was ordered to take the third and sixth divisions, to cross at Ustaritz with pontoons at the same time as Hill

1813. crossed at Cambo. Early on the morning of the 9th the sixth division crossed and drove the French back, while Hill's troops did the same at Cambo, and, marching up the right bank, joined Beresford's troops at about 1 o'clock.

For the next four days the sixth division was kept in reserve, and did not take part in any of the hard fighting in which the casualties were so heavy. The 91st had five men wounded at the crossing of the Nive. The French, being driven back, retired within the fortifications of Bayonne. The weather now became too severe to keep troops in tents, so they were cantoned in the houses in the environs of Bayonne, and were employed fortifying their positions and preparing for the spring campaign.

1814. Soult was now trusting the winter would drive the allies back into Spain, while Wellington was aiming at making the French either abandon Bayonne, or so reduce their force that the place might be stormed.

December and January were thus passed, but February saw Wellington at work again. In the second week of that month he had his army on the move, leaving the fifth division and some Spanish troops to blockade Bayonne, whose garrison had been reduced by Napoleon's wants to about 45,000 men.

On the 12th the sixth division was at Mousserolles, and on the 24th part of the allied troops crossed the Adour. Meanwhile the sixth division was marching towards Orthes, crossing the Gave d'Oleran without opposition at Montfort, above Sauveterre. On the 25th this division together with the second and light division were massed in front of Orthes, and two days later at daybreak they crossed the Gave, near Berenx, by a pontoon bridge thrown over in the night, and reached the great road of Peyrehorade, which runs parallel to the river. The light division was then sent to connect the fourth division with Picton's (the third), while the sixth were ordered to reinforce them. At 9 o'clock the third and sixth divisions won, without much difficulty, the lower part of the ridges which were held by the French under D'Armagnac, and at 12 these divisions were turned to their left, and thrown in mass on Foy's left flank, which movement was successful, the French being driven back, and their general (Foy) wounded; a battery was then established on a commanding position, from whence their shot ploughed through the French masses from one

1814. flank to another. The enemy now abandoned Orthes, and a general retreat commenced along the whole line, the French troops yielding step by step without confusion, while the allies advanced with incessant musketry and cannonade.

The allies' casualties during this action were about 2000 men, among the wounded being Wellington, while their adversaries lost nearly 4000. The 91st's casualties were Gunn, Alexander, Campbell, Marshall, Taylor, and twelve rank and file wounded.

The next day the pursuit was continued; Wellington crossed the Adour by 10 o'clock, and on the 2nd the French were attacked and driven from Aire, the 91st losing one man killed, whilst Colonel Douglas, Ensign Macdougall, one sergeant, and fourteen men were wounded.

CHAPTER IV.

Peninsular War—Toulouse—End of War—England—Ireland
—Ostend.

EXTREMELY perilous now and disheartening was the situation of the French marshal. His army was reduced by losses in battle and desertion.

Wellington's head-quarters were fixed at Aire, his army being in position on each side of the Adour. All the bridges were repaired. Frequent actions took place between small bodies of the troops, and on the 20th of March, after fighting at Tarbes, Soult retreated in two columns on Toulouse; but, owing to the slowness with which Wellington followed him, he was able to place himself in an excellent position in rear of that city, on the far side of the river Garonne.

Toulouse was surrounded by a wall with towers, the bridge across the river being protected by an ancient *tête-de-pont*. The canal of Languedoc joins the Garonne about a mile below the town;

1814. its course is about a thousand yards distant from the river, and less than half that distance from the city wall from the point at which it approaches the town. Toulouse, therefore, was not only protected by its walls, but by the river Garonne on one side, and by the canal on two others. Soult augmented and extended the works of the *tete-de-pont*, and also formed bridge heads to all the approaches across the canal, fortifying the houses in their neighbourhood.

The French marshal judged that the allies could not attack him in front, but would have to try and turn his flanks. This is what Wellington found he would have to do, and though in a strategic view the passage of the river should be made below the town, he resolved to cast a bridge across at Portet, six miles above Toulouse, designing to throw his right wing into the open country between the Garonne and the canal.

With this object, Hill on the 27th commenced a bridge, but found that, in consequence of the swollen state of the river, his pontoons would not reach across, so the attempt had to be abandoned.

Wellington therefore changed his project. A new bridge was laid further up the river, and on the 31st 13,000 men crossed; but the roads and country were found impracticable owing to the rains, so the troops recrossed.

The rest of the allies remained inactive until the 3rd, on account of the river not subsiding until that date. That night a bridge was thrown over the river at Grenade, about fifteen miles below Toulouse, and the third, fourth, and sixth divisions under Beresford immediately passed.

Meanwhile, events in France were happening that were to bring the war to a close. Soult is said to have heard on the 7th that the allied sovereigns had entered Paris, but probably he determined not to let slip an opportunity of having another engagement with the allies, in which he hoped by a success to wipe off the disgrace of his recent defeats. He accordingly made no attempt to ascertain the truth of the report of Napoleon's abdication.

On the 8th the waters, which had again risen in the river after the crossing of Beresford's troops, subsided, and another bridge was placed across the Garonne some distance nearer the town. Wellington, with the Spanish and Portuguese artillery, now crossed, and commenced an advance on both banks of the river, determining to attack on the 9th; but this he was unable to do, as the

1814. light division had not crossed; he was, therefore, forced to defer his battle until the 10th.

Soult, who had now had seventeen days to prepare for attack, had strengthened his position as above related, which was on ground naturally adapted for defence, and matters looked as if he was sure of success. His army was placed on a ridge about five hundred yards from the canal, well fortified with a number of redoubts, connected by earthworks about two miles in length, having in front marshy ground, and rendered nearly impassable by artificial inundations.

Wellington's disposition of his troops was as follows :—Hill to menace St. Cyprien; the third and light divisions to advance against the northern front of Toulouse; the fourth and sixth divisions (which included the Scotch brigade) to move round the left to the Pugade, and along the low ground below the French position, until the rear had crossed the Lavour road, when they were to wheel to their right and attack the platform of St. Sypiere. These divisions were under the command of Marshal Beresford.

At 6 o'clock on the morning of the 10th, Easter Sunday, the whole army moved to their assigned positions; the 91st, which formed part of the Highland brigade under Major-General Pack, was brigaded with the 11th Regiment and the 42nd and 79th Highlanders. Marshal Beresford's division had to march between the redoubts to the right of the French position and the river Ero, the width between these points being not greater than a mile at any part, and in some places only five hundred yards. The distance to be marched was not less than two miles, being under fire the whole time. The operation therefore took a long time, as it was necessary to cover and protect by a heavy fire of artillery the advance of this division.

An officer of the 42nd, in his reminiscences of that day, says, "Early on Sunday morning our tents were struck, and we moved with the other regiments of the sixth division towards the neighbourhood of Toulouse until ordered to halt on a level ground, from whence we had a distinct view of the enemy's position on a ridge of hills. Major-General Pack came up, and, calling the officers, non-commissioned officers, and men of the brigade around him, addressed them to this effect: 'We are this day to attack the enemy; your business will be to take possession of these fortified heights which you see towards the front.

1814. I have only to warn you to be prepared to form close column in case of a charge of cavalry, to restrain the impetuosity of the men, and to prevent them from wasting their ammunition.' Our division (the sixth) approached the foot of the ridge of heights on the enemy's right, and moved in a direction parallel to them until we advanced to the point of attack. We advanced under a heavy cannonade, and arrived in front of a redoubt which protected the right of the enemy's position, where we were formed into two lines—the first consisting of some Portuguese regiments, and the reserve of the Highland brigade. Darkening the hill, flanked by clouds of cavalry, and covered by the fire of their redoubt, the enemy came down upon us like a torrent, the generals and field officers riding in front and waving their hats amidst shouts of the multitude resembling the roar of an ocean. Our Highlanders, as if actuated by one instinctive impulse, took off their bonnets, and, waving them in the air, returned their greeting with three cheers."

It was about half-past two in the afternoon when Beresford made his final attack with Pack's Scotch brigade. The men scrambled up the steep banks under a wasting fire of cannon and musketry. The 42nd and 79th, who were in advance, rushed the Colombette and Calvinet redoubts; they were, however, driven out again with great slaughter.

Brown, in his account of Pack's brigade in this action in "Highland Clans," says, "Two of the redoubts on the left were occupied by the 42nd, the one on the right by the 79th, the 91st being in rear of a farmhouse. The left redoubt by some oversight had not been properly occupied, and the enemy in great strength rushed it, overpowering the 42nd, who were compelled to retire to the farmhouse; but, being promptly supported by the 91st, they again attacked the enemy and drove him back."

In a conversation between General Hill and General Stewart a few days after the battle, the former, alluding to the above-mentioned attack, said to General Stewart, "I saw your friends the Highlanders in a most perilous position, and had I not known their firmness I should have trembled for the result; as it was, they could not have resisted the force brought against them if they had not been so instantaneously supported."

After this repulse, a fresh column of the

1814. French arrived to attack the redoubts. They made a most desperate attempt, but the firmness of the British troops forced them to retire and abandon their position. During the action Major-General Pack was wounded, but was able to remain on the field.

The division now halted in order that Beresford should reform his order of battle, the sixth division having been hardly handled. Soult, however, seeing how matters stood, and deeming further resistance useless, withdrew the whole army behind the canal at 5 o'clock.

The French that day had lost 5 generals and 3000 men killed and wounded; while the allies lost 4 generals and 4600 men. The 91st had 1 sergeant and 17 men killed, and 7 officers—namely, Colonel William Douglas, who commanded the brigade after Pack was wounded; Meade, Walsh, Callander, J. Macdougall, Hood, and Colin Macdougall—and 98 men wounded: a lamentable spilling of blood, and useless, as Napoleon had already abdicated.

On the 11th Soult was again ready to fight, but Wellington was not prepared to go on until the 12th. In the interval the French general changed his mind, and in a surprising manner left the city and made a forced march of twenty-two miles to Villefranche, leaving all his wounded to the care of the conquerors. The allies entered Toulouse in triumph; but in the afternoon messengers arrived from Paris making known officially the abdication of Napoleon.

On the 19th of April the 91st was directed to break up its encampment and go into cantonments. On the following day the regiment cantoned near Auch. A general order was on that same day issued, announcing the suspension of hostilities between the allied armies and the French army, and congratulating the British troops upon the prospect of an honourable termination to their labours.

In an order of the 19th of May, General Clinton took farewell of the sixth division in the following terms:—"Being called upon to another service, Lieutenant-General Sir Henry Clinton takes leave of the sixth division. He does not without regret give up the command of troops who, in their meeting with the enemy, have not failed honourably to distinguish themselves; while their orderly and generally soldier-like appearance have often attracted the notice and approbation of the great commander of the forces.

1814. The Lieutenant-General is desirous of acknowledging how highly he feels indebted to the valour so often displayed by the brave sixth division. He cannot better mark the interest he feels in the future reputation of those regiments, than by reminding their commanding officers how entirely their good order depends upon a prompt obedience to the orders, and a steady and continued observance of the regulations framed for the government of the army; that no regiment can continue essentially in order unless the qualifications of its officers for the performance of their duties be provided for, and rigidly required; and that the capacity for the instruction of the soldier ranks foremost in the qualifications of regimental officers. Sir H. Clinton returns his thanks to Major-Generals Pack and Lambert, and to Colonel Douglas, for the support which they have afforded at the head of their respective brigades; to the commanding and other officers for their assistance in the field, as well as the maintenance of discipline; and to the whole of the troops for their general good conduct."

There is a story told in "Stewart's Sketches," that a soldier of the regiment deserted in 1814, and emigrated to America, where he settled. Several years after, a letter was received from him, enclosing a sum of money for the purpose of procuring one or two men to supply his place, as the only recompense he could make for breaking his oath to God and his allegiance to the king, which preyed on his conscience in such a manner that he could not rest.

1814.

On June the 1st the Highland brigade marched from Auch, and on the 7th encamped at Blanque Fort, where, on the 11th of June, it was reviewed by the Duke of Wellington.

On the 24th of June the first detachment of the 91st sailed for home, the second detachment following on July the 1st, and both arriving at Cork towards the end of the latter month.

After this the regiment proceeded to Athlone, Limerick, and Clonmel, where they remained until March the following year, when orders were received that it was to be attached to the force then assembling under orders of Major-General Johnstone at Middleton. After marching to this place and being embarked, fresh orders arrived countermanding the destination of the expedition, and directing they should sail to Carlingford Bay; but on reaching that place the destination was

1815.

1815. again changed, and the transports sailed for the Downs, where they arrived at the beginning of April. The other troops who formed part of this force were the 42nd, 71st, and 92nd Highlanders.

The 91st were next transhipped to small craft, which sailed to Ostend, at which place the greater number arrived the same day; the smacks conveying the head-quarters and one company, however, were driven back to Dover, and did not reach Ostend until three days after the rest of the regiment.

CHAPTER V.

Waterloo—Cambray—Army of Occupation round Paris—
England—Ireland.

BEFORE proceeding with the future movements of the 91st, it will be necessary to glance briefly at what had been taking place in Europe since the return of the regiment from the Peninsula. The record of the regiment has already shown that the Peninsular War was brought to a conclusion by the battle of Toulouse. In 1814, after an absence of five years, the Duke of Wellington returned to England, and for a while was engaged in diplomatic duties. Having been a short time ambassador at the restored Bourbon court at Paris, he attended, in 1815, the General Congress of European powers at Vienna. The deliberations of that assembly were broken up by the news that Napoleon had not only quitted Elba, but was in the Tuileries with a large army flocking to his standard, while the Bourbon king was flying to

1814.

1815.

Ghent. Upon the receipt of this intelligence, the representatives of the eight powers at Vienna drew up a paper, in which Buonaparte was denounced as a disturber of the peace of the world, and the Duke of Wellington was nominated commander-in-chief of the army to be concentrated in the Netherlands. In the month of April, 1815, the "Iron Duke" was at Brussels preparing for the impending contest, which resulted in the great battle which brought the continental war to an end.

It had been arranged that the allied troops should be mustered on the Rhine, and it was in order to cover this general gathering, and also to protect Belgium, that Wellington decided to fix his head-quarters at Brussels. The 91st, having started for the seat of war, arrived at Ostend on the 11th of April, and were transhipped into lighters, in which they were conveyed up the canal to Ghent. On the 24th the regiment marched into Oudenarde, and was placed in the 6th British brigade, composed of the 35th, 54th, and 59th Regiments, commanded by Major-General Johnstone, and in the fourth division, employed as a corps of observation under the command of Lieutenant-General the Hon. Sir C. Colville,

forming part of the second army corps, commanded
by Lieutenant-General Lord Hill, K.G., C.B. On
June the 16th (the same day that the French
attacked Blucher at Ligny, and Wellington repulsed Marshal Ney at Quatre-Bras), the enemy
having attacked General Colville's outposts, the
division marched to join the army, which it did
on June the 17th, at Braine-le-Compte. On the
following day, June the 18th, the memorable
battle of Waterloo was fought. Early in the
morning, the fourth division, in which the 91st
were placed, together with a division of the
troops of the Netherlands, were sent to cover the
Genappe road to Brussels, which was threatened
by a column of the French. Thus the 91st escaped
taking part in the great action itself, although
its services were so efficient as to secure for the
regiment full participation in all the honours,
grants, and privileges which were granted to the
army on that occasion. Major Thomas Hunter
Blair, of the 91st, was wounded during the action
when serving as brigade-major to Major-General
Lord George Beresford, on the staff of Field
Marshal the Duke of Wellington, and for which
he received the brevet rank of lieutenant-colonel.

The names of the officers who were present on

1815. the 18th are given in Appendix G., under the head of "The Waterloo Roll."

In the *London Gazette* of the 21st of June, 1817, a notification is published respecting the grant by Parliament to the army that served under the command of Field Marshal his Grace the Duke of Wellington, in the battle of Waterloo and capture of Paris. The share of the 91st, which was to be paid at 18, Suffolk Street, Charing Cross, between the 25th of August and the 24th of September, 1817, was—

	£	s.	d.
Field officers and colonels	433	2	4½
Captains	90	7	3½
Subalterns	34	14	9½
Sergeants	19	4	4
Corporals, drummers, and privates ...	2	11	4

This distribution was also given to the Dutch, Belgic, Hanoverian, and Brunswick troops.

The whole of the officers and men who served with the regiment on the 18th of June were presented with Waterloo medals, but the honour of carrying "Waterloo" on the colours was not granted them. It may be noticed here that the medals for the Peninsular War were not issued for many years after, and it was not until 1847 that sanction was given to strike medals for the various actions which were enumerated in a general order dated "Horse Guards, June 1st, 1847," calling for a list of the names of officers and men who had served in these actions.

1815.

On the 19th of June the 91st proceeded, with the rest of the army, in pursuit of the flying enemy, and on the 24th of that month sat down at Cambray, a strongly fortified town seventeen miles from Valenciennes. Having refused to capitulate, the town was carried by assault, one column being commanded by Colonel Douglas; and the whole of the garrison surrendered the next day. The casualties of the 91st in this attack were two lieutenants (Andrew Cathcart and James Black) and six privates wounded, and one private killed. On the 26th of June the division proceeded *en route* to Paris, and on the 1st of July arrived at Autel-de-Dieu, where Private Johnson of the 91st was killed at his post by some of the French picquets.

On the 4th of July a suspension of arms was agreed to under the walls of Paris. In the *Irish Times* of the 17th of January, 1879, we read of the death of William Ballantine of the 91st, who was present at Waterloo, and shared in the advance on Paris, and who was the first man to

1815. enter the French capital, having been one of the escort sent with the flag of truce.

The 91st removed on the 5th of July from Autel-de-Dieu to St. Denis, and two days later marched to and encamped in the Bois de Boulogne near the town of Neuilly. Here they remained until the 31st of October, when the regiment marched for Aspalzon, and arrived there on the 2nd of November, and went into cantonments. On the 20th of November a general order was issued from Field Marshal the Duke of Wellington, returning thanks to the general officers and troops, on his breaking up of the army he had had the honour to command, and referring to the uniform good conduct of the troops. On the 30th of November the regiment was placed in the third brigade of the second division under Major-General Sir H. Clinton. On the 11th of December the 91st marched to Sèvres and Meudon, arriving there on the 15th, and marching again on the 27th for Gorveau and adjacent villages, where they arrived on the 28th, and went into cantonments.

1816. On the 23rd of January, 1816, the regiment marched for St. Pol, and in February the head-quarters were fixed at that place, while detachments were sent out to occupy thirty-nine different villages. On the 6th of August the regiment encamped on the heights near St. Omer, and on the 15th of October moved with the rest of the army to the plains of Denain. During the same month the regiment, together with the rest of the army, was reviewed by the Duke of Wellington and several foreign princes, after which the 91st returned to St. Pol and the adjacent villages. Here they remained until the 13th of March, 1817, when they were transferred to the third brigade, and marched on the 6th of April to join the brigade at Valenciennes, where they arrived on the 9th. On the 18th of September the regiment moved with the division and encamped on the glacis of Cambray; and on the 2nd of October they proceeded to the plains of Denain, and were again reviewed on the 15th by the Duke of Wellington and foreign princes, returning on the following day to the barracks at Valenciennes.

On the 9th of August, 1818, the division at Valenciennes moved and encamped on the glacis of Cambray, and on the 18th moved to the plains of Denain, where the 91st took part in a review for the third time by the Duke of Wellington and foreign princes.

On the 23rd of August Sir William Douglas

1818. died at Valenciennes, where his remains were buried, and a monument was erected over his grave by the officers, non-commissioned officers, and men of the 91st. The officers also placed a tablet in St. John's Episcopal Church at Forfar (he was born at Brigton, his father's place in Forfarshire), which bears the following inscription:—

"Jamais arrière.

"In memory of Colonel Sir William Douglas, K.C.B. This monument is erected by his brother officers of the 91st, or Argyllshire Regiment, as a tribute of their respect and esteem for his distinguished services in the field, and amiable qualities in private life. He fell an early victim to the duties of his profession at Valenciennes, in France, on the 23rd of August, 1818. Aged 42 years. Universally regretted by the army, and all who knew him."

On the 11th of September the 91st were again present at the fourth review by the Duke. The regiment returned to Cambray on the 24th of October, and, the allied forces being ordered to evacuate French territory, the division marched for Calais on October 27th, and encamped there on the 1st of November. On the following day the 91st embarked in small craft for England. The head-quarters disembarked at Dover on the 3rd of November; but, some of the smacks having been dispersed in a gale, the troops in them were disembarked at Ramsgate on the 9th of that month. The regiment next marched for Bexhill Barracks, and arrived there on the 8th of November. Early in December they moved to Haslar Barracks, and on the 17th embarked on board transports at Gosport, and sailed the same day for Ireland, disembarking at Cork on the 24th, and finally marching on the 27th and 28th, in two divisions, for Dublin, which place was reached on the 6th and 7th of January, 1819.

CHAPTER VI.

Ireland — Jamaica — England — Ireland — St. Helena — Grahamstown, South Africa.

1820. The 91st remained in Dublin until July, 1820, when it proceeded to Enniskillen, furnishing detachments to the counties of Cavan, Leitrim, and Donegal. Orders having been received in June,
1821. 1821, that the regiment should prepare to proceed to Jamaica from the Clyde, the 91st embarked on the 18th at Donaghadee for Port Patrick, and marched to Glasgow, where it arrived on the 27th and 28th. The regiment was here inspected by Sir T. Bradford, and on the 5th of November the first division, consisting of the grenadiers, 2nd, 3rd, and 4th companies, with part of the 6th company, embarked at the Broomielaw on board steamboats, which conveyed them to Greenock, where they were transhipped into the transport brigs *Brilliant* and *Loyal Briton* for
1822. Jamaica. On the 9th of January, 1822, the second

ments being sent out to various towns. During this period the regiment was several times called upon to assist the civil authorities at the elections, and often had to perform the most harassing duties. Notwithstanding this, no irregularity took place on their part, nor was the slightest complaint ever preferred against them. For this creditable conduct the regiment was highly complimented. In 1833 the 91st was at Naas and Fermoy, and nothing appears to have occurred during the remainder of its stay in Ireland.

In this year the names of the battles of Roleia, Vimiero, and Corunna were ordered to be put on the regimental colours.

In 1835, the regiment having received instructions to hold itself in readiness to embark for St. Helena, a regimental depôt was formed, and on the 29th of October head-quarters, consisting of four companies under the command of Major Lamont, moved to Cork, occupying the barracks there until the necessary arrangements were made for embarkation.

In November the regiment embarked in two detachments from the Cove of Cork, sailing on the 1st of December, and arriving at the island of St. Helena on the 26th of February, 1836.

1836.   This island, which has an area of only forty-seven square miles, was, at the time the regiment landed there, considered of great importance, as a port to water and obtain fresh vegetables for ships to and from India *viâ* the Cape. Its appearance from the sea is gloomy and forbidding; masses of volcanic rock, with jagged peaks, rise up round the coast, and form an iron girdle which seems to bar all access to the interior.

The whole island appears to bear evidence of having been formed by the agency of fire, but so gigantic are the strata of which it is composed, and so disproportioned to its size, that it has been thought by some to be the relic of a submerged continent. The highest point in the island is Diana's Peak, which is about six hundred miles distance from Ascension (the nearest land), and twelve hundred miles from the Cape of Good Hope.

James Town, the only town the place can boast of, is situated in the bottom of a wedgelike ravine, enclosed on each side by barren and overhanging precipices. It consists of a long straggling street running up a valley, with steep hills on each side. The houses are built in the same style as those of small towns in England, generally of one, but

THE LADDER AT JAMES TOWN (TO THE FORT AT TOP OF CLIFF).

sometimes of two stories, with a balcony to each. Lime being scarce, the stone of which the houses are chiefly built is cemented with mud. There were a church, botanical gardens, a hospital, a tavern, and barracks. The latter, where the 91st were quartered, are at the top of the street, about half a mile from the landing-place, and are built on an artificial terrace overlooking a little stream which flows through the town. The terrace is nearly in the shape of an oblong, lying lengthways to the valley, and divided into two parts by a range of two-storied buildings, built of stone, and designed to hold six companies of infantry, as well as officers' quarters. The military hospital lies still further up the valley, and is placed in a pleasant and salubrious position.

On the west of the mouth of the valley a battery is surmounted, called the "Ladder Hill Battery;" here is also accommodation for two companies of infantry. The companies stationed here at the time the 91st went to the island were relieved every six months, by which time the officers and men must have been tolerably well inured to mountain-climbing, as the place where the barracks stand is over seven hundred feet above the town, which lies immediately below it,

1836. and the companies had to attend all drills and parades at the barracks in the town. There are two means of ascent to the battery, one by a traverse road about a mile in length, and the other by a ladder of six hundred and ninety-nine steps, which leads direct from the town to the battery.

It may be easily imagined that St. Helena cannot be called a lively quarter for either officers or men; the scenery of course is beautiful, but after a few visits to the most favoured spots it must cease to interest. The island is also subject to extreme and sudden changes of temperature, often occurring several times in a day, which is one of the chief causes of its unhealthiness. It is singular that thunder and lightning are unknown in St. Helena, probably owing to the electric fluid being attracted by Diana's Peak and other conical hills, and conducted into the sea.

There was very little sport to be had, and that was the reason that cock-fighting was a great source of amusement. There is a racecourse on the north-west part of the island near Longwood, which owed a great deal of its prosperity to Admiral Rous, who, in his younger days, was a supporter of racing at St. Helena. Horses from fourteen to fifteen hands high were brought over from the Cape for the purpose. The best record for a mile in the time when the 91st was there was two minutes seven seconds, performed by a Cape horse, the property of an officer of the regiment.

The only duties, besides the usual regimental routine, were those of the main guard, stationed inside the sea gate, which was under command of a subaltern who always mounted in full dress, the climate being moderate owing to the sea-breeze.

Officers of all ranks had an extra allowance of three shillings a day on account of the dearness of provisions. The men received salt rations five days a week, which had no bad effect on their health, owing to the abundance of fresh vegetables obtainable.

Nothing of importance occurred during the time the head-quarters of the 91st was stationed at St. Helena; but, as an instance of their feelings at being quartered there, we find that the troop-ship *Athol*, arriving in England in July, 1837, reports, "The officers and men of the 91st were getting reconciled, as well as circumstances would admit, to the discomforts and privations of the island of St. Helena." In the same year, 1837, the regiment was on the roster for India.

1838. During their stay the regiment lost a few of their number, who were buried in the church-yard close to the main guard; among others, in 1838, a promising officer named McMurdo. A St. Helena correspondent of that date writes, "Lieut. Charles Baird McMurdo, 91st Regiment, died on the 30th of July, having just completed the 26th year of his age, when an injury in the knee, received as he was returning to his quarters at Ladder Hill on the Sunday week previous, terminated fatally in lock-jaw two days after the symptoms had manifested themselves. The high estimation in which this lamented officer was held was evinced by the attendance at his funeral of H.E. Major-General Middlemore, C.B., and staff, together with the whole of the military and civil establishment of the island. A monument to his memory is about to be erected by his brother officers in the church of James Town."

1839. On the 2nd of June, 1839, the garrison was surprised to see H.M.S. *Melville*, 74 guns, sail into anchorage at James Town and immediately land despatches for the governor, ordering the head-quarters (then commanded by Major Burne) and three companies of the regiment to embark immediately for service on the eastern frontier of the Cape. Accordingly, on the 4th the head-quarters, grenadiers, No. 2, and light infantry companies embarked for the Cape of Good Hope, leaving three companies behind under the command of Captain Blackwell. The transport with the head-quarters on board anchored in Algoa Bay on the 28th of June, but the men were unable to land, on account of the surf, until the 3rd of July, when they encamped near Port Elizabeth. The head-quarters marched to the Zwaitkops River the next day, and encamped, arriving on July 8th at Grahamstown. Nothing of note occurred in connection with the regiment for the first two years of its stay at the Cape. It was regularly employed in detachments in the performance of duty at the various outposts on the Fish River, Blinkwater, Double Drift, Fort Peddie, and other places, the detachments being relieved at regular intervals.

CHAPTER VII.

Detachment at St. Helena—Removal of Napoleon's body—Reserve Battalion formed.

1840. In 1840 the detachment which was left at St. Helena in 1839 took part in the disinterment of the body of the Emperor Napoleon.

Before describing this event, a short account of Napoleon during the six years of his life at St. Helena may not be entirely foreign to the history of a regiment which had served in armies opposed to him.

He was brought to the island on the 15th of October, 1815, and at first resided at the Briars, which was about a mile and a half from James Town, the accommodation at Longwood, his future residence, being at that time quite inadequate for himself and his suite, the house only consisting of five rooms on a ground floor. The Briars was preferred by Napoleon as a temporary residence, to being located in the town. He remained there till the 9th of December, when the alterations and enlargement of Longwood were completed.

The owner of the Briars (Mr. Balcombe) and his family did all in their power to make the emperor happy, and lessen the discomforts of his situation. Mrs. Abell (Mr. Balcombe's daughter), in her " Recollections of the Emperor," says, "The emperor's habits during the time he stayed with us were very simple and regular. His usual hour for getting up was eight, and he seldom took anything but a cup of coffee until 1 o'clock, when he breakfasted. He dined at 9, and retired about 11 to his own rooms. His manner was so unaffectedly kind and amiable, that in a few days I felt perfectly at ease in his society, and looked upon him more as a companion of my own age than the mighty warrior at whose name 'the world grew pale.' His spirits were very good, and he was at times almost boyish in his mirth, not unmixed at times with a tinge of malice."

During the time he was at the Briars he only left the grounds once, but frequently walked for hours in the shady paths and shrubberies, where every care was taken to prevent his privacy being interfered with. When at Longwood, a square of about twelve miles in circumference was allowed him, within which he might ride or walk without being accompanied by a British officer. A subaltern's guard was posted at the entrance of Longwood, about 600 paces from the house, and a cordon of sentinels and picquets was placed round the limits. At 9 o'clock in the evening they were drawn in, and stationed in communication with each other, and after that hour until daybreak Napoleon was not at liberty to leave the house except in the company of a field officer.

When he first came to the island he generally, when the weather allowed of it, either rode or drove for an hour or two in the afternoon, accompanied by all his suite; but during the last four years of his life he hardly went out at all. He very much disliked the situation of Longwood, which was bleak and dreary in the extreme, and begged that his new house might be built at the other side of the island, which was a much more sheltered position. This request, however, was not acceded to, and towards the end of the year 1818 the foundations of the new building were laid in the garden of Longwood; but it was never inhabited by Napoleon, whose death occurred before it was finished. The building he lived in was in a most ruinous state of repair, the roof being chiefly of wood, covered with brown paper, smeared with a composition of pitch and tar.

In November, 1819, the doctor being anxious that Napoleon should leave the house more frequently and take more air, he (Napoleon) turned his attention to gardening, and Colburn, in his "History of the Captivity of Napoleon," says, "It was a picture worthy of being represented by an artist, to see the conqueror of so many kingdoms, who had dictated laws to so many sovereigns, at dawn of day, spade in hand, a broad straw hat on his head, and his feet clad in red morocco slippers, directing our labour, and those more useful still of the Chinese gardeners."

A favourite occupation of Napoleon's was writing and dictating papers on the subject of defensive operations by fieldworks, and the depth and formation of troops, and it is said he would often get up several times in a night to write notes on the question. In the day he would demonstrate his ideas to his officers and attendants in his garden, tracing out his plans and fieldworks.

His health suffered much from want of fresh air and exercise, and failed rapidly the last few months of his life, and finally, on the 5th of May, 1821, he died.

Napoleon expressed a wish in his will that he should be buried in France; or, if there was any difficulty about that, that he should be placed by the fountain in the grounds of Longwood, where he was finally laid to rest with the honours of a military funeral. His other wish was also fulfilled nineteen years later, when his country reclaimed his body, and it was at its disinterment that the 91st assisted.

The French Government having requested that the remains should be moved to France, a squadron, commanded by H.R.H. the Prince de Joinville, consisting of *La Belle Poule*, frigate, and two corvettes, *La Favorite* and *L'Oreste*, were despatched to the island, where they arrived on the 8th of October.

The arrangements for the disinterment were entrusted to the Count de Charbot on the part of the French, and Captain Alexander, C.R.E., on the part of the English.

It was determined to commence at 12 o'clock on the night of the 14th, which was the twenty-fifth anniversary of Napoleon's arrival at St. Helena. This allowed ample time for the crews

NAPOLEON'S TOMB, ST. HELENA.

of the French ships to make pilgrimages to the spot, where their eagerness to carry away relics produced some devastation of the willow trees around the grave, and such a consumption of the water of Napoleon's favourite spring as would gladden the heart of a "total abstinence" man; and even the earth was carried away in handfuls.

An officer's guard of the 91st was mounted over the tomb. The night was wet and dark, and the work was carried on by the light of numerous lanterns fixed to the trees. A strong party of workmen were employed, and very few minutes sufficed to remove the iron railings and stone slabs, which exposed a square vault filled with clay and stones, under which the body was deposited. By half-past three in the morning this tamping, which was seven feet deep, was entirely cleared out, and the solid masonry reached. It took nearly five hours to get through this, so strongly was it put together, and it was long past daybreak when the actual sarcophagus was reached.

The coffin had been deposited in a water-tight cell, of which each side consisted of a single slab of freestone, a similar slab sealing the top. At half-past eight this slab was removed, and the coffin was found to be sound and dry.

1840. L'Abbé Coquereault then performed an appropriate service, after which, the necessary medical precautions having been taken, the party of the 91st on guard raised and bore the coffin into a tent erected close by, where another service was gone through, the "Levée du Corps."

The body was deposited within four coffins, one of tin, one of lead, and two of mahogany; these were all found perfectly closed, but it was thought necessary to open them to ascertain the actual condition of the remains. The coffins were therefore opened, and the satin cloth which covered the body, when removed, disclosed the remains in a state of preservation almost perfect.

Captain Ward of the 91st, who had been at St. Helena with the 67th Regiment in 1821, at the time of the emperor's death, and had been permitted to see the body as it lay in state, had then taken a pencil sketch of the face. Strange to say, he was again on the island, and was present at the exhuming of the body, and had the opportunity of comparing the sketch taken twenty years previously. He found it a perfect likeness (a copy of it appeared in one of the illustrated papers some years ago).

The coffins were closed again, after remaining a

REMOVAL OF NAPOLEON'S BODY FROM ST. HELENA.

minute or two open, with the exception of the outer one, which was exchanged for a beautiful ebony sarcophagus which had been brought from France.

By 3 o'clock in the afternoon, the funeral-car was loaded and arrangements completed for the procession. Some apprehensions were entertained as to whether the carriage would perform the journey safely with its enormous load, the sarcophagus with its contents weighing about twenty-four hundredweight. The garrison, headed by 300 militia followed by the 91st, led the way; then came the priests, preceding the hearse drawn by six horses, with artillerymen at the head of each, the governor and the rest of the officers being on foot in the rear. Minute-guns were fired during the whole time occupied by the procession in getting to the landing-place.

None of the officers of the French squadron took part in the proceedings on shore, but awaited the body at the wharf, headed by the Prince de Joinville. Here the office and responsibility of the English officials terminated. The coffin was lowered, under a royal salute from the fort, into the prince's barge, which he steered himself, and was rowed to the *Belle Poule*, where it remained

1840. in state in a small chapel erected on the main-deck, permission being given to every one from the island to visit the vessel.

The squadron sailed on the 18th of October for Ascension. A considerable number of medals in silver and bronze were distributed on this occasion; the prince also gave a donation of £200 to the workmen employed in moving the body, and left £800 to the charitable funds of the island.

One relic of Napoleon was in possession of the 91st for many years, viz. a large crystal lamp, which was generally suspended in the officers' mess. There is also a picture of the regiment formed in line in the square of James Town, with the procession passing between the ranks.

In March, 1875, the Director of the Mint in Paris addressed a letter to Major Battiscombe, at that time in command of the 91st, of which the following is a translation :—

"I hasten to inform you that the Director of the Mint is happy to place at your disposal a specimen, in bronze, of the medal which he desires to be offered to the officers of the 91st Regiment, in remembrance of the memorable event which it commemorates, and in which the regiment took part. I have therefore the honour to inform you that I have given the necessary instructions to have the medal placed at your disposal at the office of the Mint."

This medal (which is kept in the officers' mess) has on one side, in relief, a head, with the words, " Ludov. Philippus I., Francorum Rex;" and on the other is represented the dome of the Invalides, and classical figures of France receiving the *cortége*, and the words, " Reliquis Receptis Napoleonis funus, Triumphale xv. Dec. MDCCCXL."

In 1842 Government decided upon the formation of reserve battalions for the purpose of facilitating the relief of regiments abroad, and shortening their periods of foreign service. In April of that year, in order to carry this arrangement into effect, the establishment of the four company depôts of certain regiments was changed, and they were formed into battalions of six skeleton companies by volunteers from other corps.

The 91st, whose depôt companies were then stationed at Naas, was selected as one of the regiments to be thus augmented, and the strength of the battalion was ordered to be—1st battalion, 540 men; reserve ditto, 540 men; depôt, 120 men;—total, 1200.

1840.

1842.

1842. The lieutenant-colonel, whose post was to be with the 1st battalion, had general charge and superintendence of the whole regiment, assisted by an additional major. The reserve battalion had the usual proportion of officers and non-commissioned officers appointed to it, but had no flank companies. The senior major was to have immediate command of this battalion.

The three companies of the 91st which had been left in St. Helena in 1839, under Captain Blackwell, were ordered to rejoin the headquarters of the battalion on the 6th of December, 1842. On leaving the island, Captain Blackwell was presented with the following address by the inhabitants:—" We, the undersigned inhabitants of St. Helena, cannot permit her Majesty's 91st Regiment to take their final departure without expressing our satisfaction at the uniform good order and moral conduct they have manifested during the six years they have been on this station. Those of us who witnessed the transfer of the government from the East India Company— a measure affecting various interests and involving very important and, to a considerable part of the community, very painful consequences—cannot but remember the high expectations created by the considerate conduct of the regiment, which arrived at this crisis under the command of Lieutenant-Colonel Anderson; and all of us have seen with pleasure the fulfilment of these hopes in their orderly disposition under the command of that efficient officer and his successor, Major Burne, and also during the last three years in the detachment under your command. In thus recording the last impression left by the friendly disposition of the officers, non-commissioned officers, and privates, we beg, sir, to express our regret at your departure, to present our best wishes for the welfare of yourself and your brother officers, and to convey to you our honest conviction that wherever their duty to their country may call the regiment, their colours will be preserved untarnished."

CHAPTER VIII.

Wreck of *Abercrombie Robinson.*

1842. THE reserve battalion, having been reported fit for service, was ordered to proceed to the Cape. Leaving Naas, where it had been collected, it arrived at Kingstown on the 27th of May, 1842, and embarked on board the transport *Abercrombie Robinson*, of 430 tons.

On the 2nd of June the transport sailed for the Cape of Good Hope, the strength of the regiment on board being seventeen officers and 460 men, Lieutenant-Colonel Lindsay being in command. The ship also contained drafts of the 27th Regiment, and the Cape Mounted Rifles.

The *Abercrombie Robinson*, having touched at Madeira, arrived at Table Bay on the 25th of August, 1842. Here the battalion was warned for service on the north-eastern frontier of the colony, relieving the 1st battalion of the regiment, which was to be stationed at Cape Town.

In consequence of this arrangement Lieutenant-Colonel Lindsay and Major Ducat disembarked on the 27th, for the purpose of joining the 1st battalion, to which they belonged. All the other officers not on duty obtained permission to go on shore, and all landed except six, the command of the troops on board devolving on Captain Bertie Gordon. During the voyage out, several men were carried off by typhus fever, and one man was lost overboard. But the most exciting part of the story of the *Abercrombie Robinson* has to be told. During the night of the 27th the ship parted from her anchors, and was driven ashore about a mile below Cape Town, near the mouth of Salt River.

The narrative is thus graphically given in the records of the regiment:—

At 11 o'clock p.m. on the night of the 27th, it was blowing a strong gale, and the sea rolling heavily into the bay. The ship was pitching much, and began to feel the ground, but she rode by two anchors, and a considerable length of cable had been served out the night before. Captain Gordon made such arrangements as he could, warning the officers, the sergeant-major, and the orderly non-commissioned officers to be in readiness.

1842. From sunset on the 27th the gale had continued to increase until at length it blew a tremendous hurricane, and at a little after 3 o'clock on the morning of the 28th the starboard cable snapped in two. The other cable parted a few minutes afterwards, and away went the ship before the storm, her hull striking with heavy crashes against the ground as she drove towards the beach, three miles distant under her lee. About the same time the fury of the gale, which had never lessened, was rendered more terrible by one of the most awful storms of thunder and lightning that had ever been witnessed in Table Bay.

While the force of the wind and the sea was driving the ship into shallower water, she rolled incessantly and heeled over fearfully with the back set of the surf. While in this position the heavy seas broke over her side and poured down the hatchways. The decks were opened in every direction and the strong framework of the hull seemed compressed together, the beams starting from their places. The ship had been driven with her starboard bow towards the beach, exposing her stern ports and tearing up the cabin floors of the orlop deck. The thunder and lightning ceased towards morning and the ship seemed to have worked a bed for herself on the sand, for the rolling had greatly diminished, and there arose the hope that all on board might get safe ashore.

1812.

At daybreak (about 7 o'clock), it was just possible to distinguish some people on the beach opposite the bank.

Owing to the fear of the masts, spars, and rigging falling, as well as to keep as much top weight as possible off the ship's deck, the troops had been kept below, but were now allowed to come on deck in small numbers. An attempt was made to send a rope ashore, and one of the best swimmers (a Krooman) volunteered the trial with a rope round his waist; but the back set of the surf was too much for him. A line fixed from a cannon also failed: one of the cutters was then carefully lowered, and her crew succeeded in reaching the shore with a hauling-line. Large surf-boats were shortly afterwards conveyed in waggons to the place where the ship was stranded, and the following orders were given by Captain Gordon for the disembarkation of the troops: 1. The women and children to disembark first (of these there were above ninety). 2. The sick

1842. to disembark after the women and children. 3. The disembarkation of the troops to take place by the companies of the 91st Regiment drawing lots; the detachment of the 27th Regiment and the Cape Mounted Rifles to take precedence. 4. The men to fall in on the upper deck, fully armed and accoutred, carrying their knapsacks and greatcoats. 5. Every officer to be allowed to take a carpet-bag or small portmanteau.

The disembarkation of the women and children, and the sick, occupied from 8.30 until 10 o'clock a.m. Among them was Mrs. Ward, wife of Captain Ward, and her daughter Isabel (afterwards Mrs. Savage). The detachment of the 27th Regiment and the Cape Mounted Rifles followed. The disembarkation of the 91st was arranged by the wings drawing lots, and then the companies of each wing.

At 10.30, one of the surf-boats, which had been employed up to this time in taking the people off the wreck, was required to assist in saving the lives of those on board the *Waterloo* convict ship, which was in still more imminent peril about a quarter of a mile from the *Abercrombie Robinson*. There was now but one boat to disembark 450 men, the wind and sea beginning again to rise, and the captain was apprehensive that his ship might go to pieces before sunset.

It became necessary, in consequence, that the men should abandon their knapsacks, as they not only filled a greater space in the surf-boat than could be spared, but took a long time to hand over the ship's side. Officers were also ordered not to take more than each could carry on his arm. The disembarkation of the men went on regularly but slowly from 11 a.m. until 3.30 p.m., the boat being able to hold only thirty men at a time. At 3.30 the last boat-load left the ship's side. It contained those of the officers and crew who had remained to the last—Captain Gordon of the 91st, Lieutenant Black, R.N., agent of transports, the sergeant-major of the reserve battalion of the 91st, and one or two non-commissioned officers who had requested permission to remain.

Nearly 700 souls thus completed their disembarkation after a night of great peril, and through a raging surf, without the occurrence of a single casualty. Among them were many women and children, and several sick men, two of whom were supposed to be dying. Although

1842. it had been deemed prudent to abandon the men's knapsacks and the officers' baggage, the reserve battalion of the 91st went down the side of that shattered wreck fully armed and accoutred, and ready for instant service.

It would be difficult to praise sufficiently the steady discipline of that young battalion, thus severely tested during nearly seventeen hours of peril, above eight of which were hours of darkness and imminent danger. Nor did that discipline fail when the apparent hopelessness of the situation might have led to scenes of confusion and crime. The double guard of sentries which had at first been posted over the wine and spirit stores, were found unnecessary, and these stores were ultimately left to the protection of the ordinary sentries.

Although the ship was straining in every timber, and the heavy seas were making a fair breach over her, the companies of the battalion fell in on the weather side of the vessel as their lots were drawn, and waited for their turn to muster at the lee gangway; and so perfect was their confidence, their patience, and their gallantry, that, although another vessel was going to pieces within a quarter of a mile of the transport ship, and a crowd of soldiers, sailors, and convicts were perishing before the eyes of those on board, not a murmur arose from their ranks when Captain Gordon directed that the lot should not be applied to the detachment of the 27th Regiment and Cape Mounted Riflemen, but that the 91st Regiment should give the precedence in disembarking from the wreck.

The officers who landed with the battalion were—Captain Gordon, 91st (in the year 1854, the last remaining officer in the regiment present at that fearful wreck), Captain Ward, Lieutenant Cahill, Ensign McInroy (sold out in 1845), Ensign Lavers, and Assistant-Surgeon Stubbs (retired in 1844). If among the ranks of men who all behaved so well it were allowable to particularize any, the names may be mentioned of Acting Sergeant-Major Murphy (appointed a yeomen warder of the Tower by the Duke of Wellington at Major Gordon's request), Colour-Sergeant G. Phillips (transferred to the Cape Mounted Rifles, and killed by the Kaffirs), Sergeant P. Murray (promoted to the rank of quarter-master of the regiment from the 2nd battalion of the 19th Regiment, at Colonel Bertie Gordon's urgent recommendation, in March, 1861,

1842. he having been appointed quarter-master sergean[t] of the 2nd battalion of the 19th Regiment fro[m] colour-sergeant of the 91st in 1857), Corpora[l] F. Nugent (discharged in Africa). It wa[s] through the first-named that Captain Gordo[n] communicated his orders and carried them int[o] execution. Every order he received was obeye[d] during the confusion of the wreck with th[e] exactness of the parade ground. He never le[ft] the spot where he had been stationed during th[e] darkness and terror of the night, although a wif[e] and child seemed to claim a portion of hi[s] solicitude; and when he received permission t[o] accompany them into the surf-boat, he petitione[d] to be allowed to remain with Captain Gordon ti[ll] the last.

The two sergeants were young lads, barel[y] twenty-two years of age. They had marrie[d] shortly before the battalion embarked at King[s]town, and their wives, quite girls, were clingin[g] to them for support and comfort when the shi[p] parted from her anchors. The guards we[re] ordered to be doubled, and additional sergean[ts] were posted to each. This brought Sergean[ts] Phillips and Murray on duty. Without [a] murmur, they left their wives and joined th[e] guards on the lower deck. Their example of perfect obedience and discipline was eminently useful. Corporal Thomas Nugent was of great service in helping to encourage the men of the four companies whom it was considered necessary to keep below on the orlop deck, which was a position of the greatest danger. He assisted in silencing some, whose fears were beginning to be expressed too loudly for the general good, and he also requested to be allowed not to disembark with his company, as it was his wish to stand by Captain Gordon to the last. And if any officer's name may be mentioned, the conduct and assistance of Assistant-Surgeon Stubbs well deserves notice. He was in wretched health, but on the first announcement of danger he retired to the sick bay, and never left his charge until they were all safely landed.

And, although last in the narrative, the calmness and resignation of the soldiers' wives ought to be ranked amongst the first of those ingredients of order which contributed to safety. Confusion, terror, and despair, joined to the wildest shrieks, were spreading their dangerous influence from the women's quarters when Captain Gordon first descended among the people on the lower deck. A few words sufficed to quiet them, and from that moment their patience and submission never faltered.

By 3.30 p.m. the bilged and broken wreck was abandoned, with all the stores and baggage (public and regimental), to the increasing gale and to the chances of the approaching night.

The above graphic description of the wreck was submitted to Field Marshal the Duke of Wellington, who wrote upon it words of the highest commendation on the conduct of officers and men. "I have never," the Duke wrote, "read anything so satisfactory as this report. It is highly creditable, not only to Captain Bertie Gordon and the officers and troops concerned, but to the service in which such an instance has occurred of discretion and firmness in an officer in command, and of confidence, good order, discipline, and obedience in all under his command, even to the women and children. Captain Bertie Gordon, and all concerned, deserve the highest approbation, and I will not forget their good conduct.

"I wish that I had received this statement after this misfortune occurred.*

* This refers to the fact that the Duke of Wellington did not see the narrative of the wreck till 1844.

"The approbation of the public which must have been given to this remarkable instance of good conduct in all, and of the beneficial effects resulting from it, would have been satisfactory to the feelings of all, and of their friends. As it is, I will take an early opportunity of laying before her Majesty this most interesting narrative, and I will not fail, as opportunities offer, to draw her Majesty's gracious attention to those whose conduct is the subject of it."

Assistant-Surgeon Stubbs, who was in medical charge, states, in a letter subsequently written, that the exact number of the troops on board the ship when she stranded was—

Reserve Battalion 91st	... ...	450 men.
Detachment of the 27th ...	... ...	31 ,,
Cape Mounted Rifles ...	... ...	11 ,,
Women	...	43
Children	...	63

The convict ship *Waterloo*, which went aground soon after the *Abercrombie Robinson*, had on board 219 convicts, under a guard of about thirty men of the 99th Regiment, making with the crew about 300 souls on board; of these 143 convicts and fifteen soldiers were drowned.

In consequence of this disaster the reserve battalion remained stationed at Cape Town until

1842. February, 1843. In October, 1842, Lieutenant-Colonel Lindsay took command of the 1st battalion at Grahamstown, and Major Ducat assumed command of the reserve.

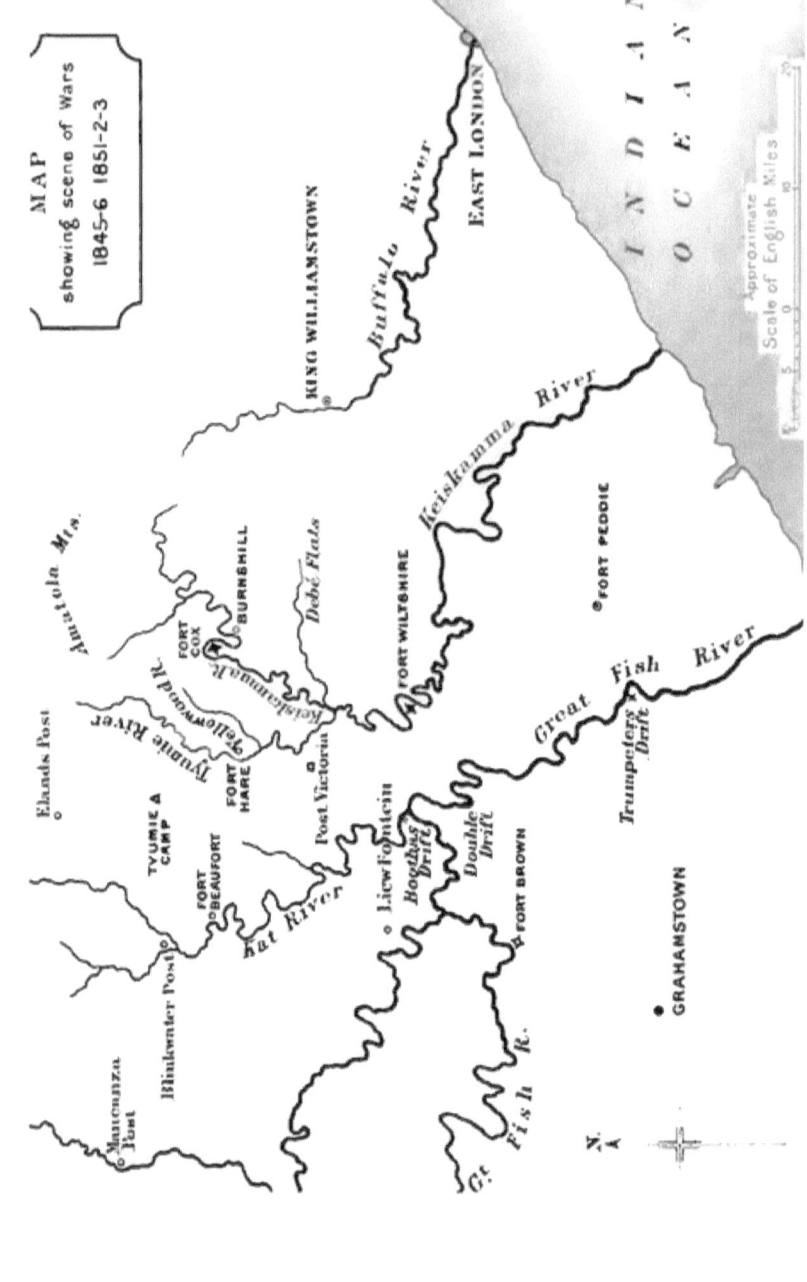

CHAPTER IX.

Kaffir War—Part taken therein by 1st Battalion.

IN the beginning of December, 1842, a force consisting of 800 men (of whom 400 belonged to the 91st Regiment) was ordered to proceed from the eastern frontier to the northern boundary, an insurrection of emigrant farmers having been expected in that quarter. The force was commanded by Colonel Hare, the lieutenant-governor, and arrived at Colesberg, near the Orange River, about the end of the month. No active operations, however, were found necessary, and in the beginning of the February following the troops were ordered to return to their quarters, leaving 300 men of the 91st in cantonment at Colesberg. A general order was issued complimenting the men upon the manner in which they had performed the fatiguing march, and on their general good conduct and discipline.

In June, 1843, nearly all the available troops

1843. on the eastern frontier were ordered on a special service to Kaffirland. The first and reserve battalions of the 91st furnished detachments for this service, the object of the expedition being to drive a refractory Kaffir chief named Tola from the neutral territory, and to dispossess him of a number of cattle stolen from the colony. The third division, commanded by Lieutenant-Colonel Lindsay of the 91st Regiment, during the performance of this duty, encountered some opposition from a body of armed Kaffirs, in a skirmish with whom one man of the battalion was severely wounded. The force returned to the colony in the beginning of the following July, having captured a considerable number of cattle.

In December, 1843, the Dutch Boers in the district of Colesberg, on the northern frontier about 300 miles from Grahamstown, began to give serious trouble to the authorities. Accordingly a force of 400 men, consisting of 100 of the 27th Regiment, 200 of the 91st, and 100 of the Cape Mounted Rifles, were ordered from Grahamstown *via* Somerset and Craddock to Colesberg, under command of Lieutenant-Colonel Johnstone of the 27th Regiment, Major Lamont of the 91st being second in command. A like force of the reserve battalion, with two guns, under command of Major Forbes, was ordered from Fort Beaufort to join at Colesberg, a march of about 300 miles *viâ* the Winterberg mountains, where the whole force would be under command of Colonel Hare, C.B., who on arrival issued a proclamation ordering all loyal subjects to appear and swear allegiance, which the Dutch farmers thought wiser to do when they had seen the force sent to put down any rebellion on their part; therefore no hostilities took place, and the main part of the troops returned to their previous quarters, leaving three companies of the 91st under Major Lamont, who was succeeded by Major Ducat on being appointed to command the reserve battalion. Major Ducat, however, caught a severe cold which ended in his death, when Captain Campbell took command.

1842.

1844.

The emigrant farmers beyond the Orange River, or north-east boundary of the colony, early in 1845, committed aggressions on the Griquas or Bastards, by attacking their villages or kraals, and carrying off their cattle, etc.; the Griquas claimed the protection of the British Government, the Boers having assembled in large bodies. Accordingly a detachment of the 91st stationed

1845.

1845. at Colesberg, composed of the grenadiers, No. 2, and light companies under Major Campbell, was ordered to the Orange River, about fifteen miles from Colesberg.

The garrison of this place consisted of 200 men of the 91st under the above-named officer, and one company of Cape Mounted Rifles under Captain Donovan. Gordon Cumming, in his "Five Years' Adventures in South Africa," says, "The men of the 91st used to practise ball-firing at a large granite stone above the town. Campbell, Yarborough, Bailey, and Patterson, officers of the regiment, challenged any four Dutchmen of Graaf Reinet or the Colesberg district, to shoot against them; the challenge was accepted, and the Dutchmen got 'jolly well licked.'"

The detachment, together with a company of the Cape Mounted Riflemen, crossed the river at Bootha's Drift on the night of April the 22nd, and marched to Philippolis, a village of the Griquas. Information having been received that the Boers were encamped in force at Touw Fontein, about thirty-five miles from Philippolis, the detachment marched on the night of the 24th for their camp, within four miles of which the Boers and Griquas were found skirmishing, the

GRAHAMSTOWN, 1845.

former, 500 strong, being mounted. Dispositions were made to attack the camp, but when the troops of the 7th Dragoon Guards and the company of the Cape Rifles pushed forwards, the Boers fled in all directions, after offering a very slight resistance. The detachment remained encamped until the 30th of June, when it was ordered to Grahamstown to rejoin head-quarters.

That town at this time was a very small place, containing a population, including the military, of about 2000. It lies in a valley encircled by low hills, and watered by little streams which run into the Cowrie River. It was built in the form of an irregular square, with one broad main street, from either side of which several smaller streets branched off at right angles.

The garrison consisted of the head-quarters of the 27th and 91st Regiments and Cape Corps, under the command of Colonel Somerset (afterwards commander-in-chief at Bombay), and there was also a company of sappers. The 27th occupied the Drostdie Barracks, and the 91st the old thatch-roofed barracks at Fort England, which lie above the town, the remainder of the troops being in the new barracks.

On the 25th of November new colours were

1845. presented to the regiment by Colonel Hare, C.B. The ground on this occasion was kept by a troop of the 7th Dragoon Guards, under command of Captain Schonswar, the 91st being drawn up in hollow square. The ceremony commenced with an exhortation from the minister, Mr. Locke, who, after reminding them of their duty to their sovereign, their country, and their God, pointed out to them the honourable profession of the British soldier, his high achievements in the cause of freedom, and the lofty position to which he had raised the British name among the nations of the earth. At the termination of this address the old and new colours were unfurled, the former literally in shreds, soiled, weather-worn, and tattered, contrasting strongly with the brilliancy and freshness of those about to be presented. The lieutenant-governor then addressed the corps, commending highly the regiment for its good soldier-like conduct through its long and arduous service in Cape Colony, and enumerated with great animation its gallant achievements while forming part of the British army in the Peninsular War. He then referred to the country which had given birth to most of the soldiers of the 91st as the country celebrated for the gallant deeds of her sons, and also for their intelligence and high moral character. The lieutenant-governor terminated his address by heartily wishing them prosperity wherever they might be called by their country, and he felt persuaded that they would never disgrace the colours he was about to have the high gratification of presenting to them. He then presented the Queen's colour to Lieutenant Patterson, and the regimental one to Lieutenant Cole.

Lieutenant-Colonel Lindsay returned thanks in the following terms: "Sir, in the name of the 91st, I beg to thank you for the honour you have done us in presenting us with the new colours, and it must ever be a source of pride and gratification to us that they have been put into our hands by one who has served his country so long and so honourably as our lieutenant-governor, under whom we have served with so much satisfaction during our sojourn on the frontier.

"Soldiers of the 91st, in receiving these sacred ensigns of your country, remember that your allegiance is not only to be displayed in the excitement of the battle, but by your obedience to your superiors, and by your attention to the discipline of the service to which you

1845. have the high honour to belong, you may prove your devotion to your sovereign and your country as though you died fighting in defence of those very colours. Owing to the blessed interval of peace long enjoyed by our native country, there are none here who have fought under the banners from which you are about to part. Should, however, the God of armies call you forth to battle, let the memory of the honours earned by those who long since bore your number on their caps stimulate you to keep the brave name for which the 91st Regiment has ever been distinguished. To the minister who has consecrated these colours our united thanks are due. For many years you have received the benefit of his kind and able ministry, and I am well aware of the interest he has in your spiritual welfare. May the wholesome effects of his ministry be felt long after you shall be parted from him and each other! His address has left me little to say on the subject of consecration, but, in reminding you of your duty to these standards and yourselves, bear in mind that the sovereign whom you serve is the delegate of that God to whom, as Christian soldiers, your first obedience is due. Next to God, then, and your Queen, remember that these colours claim your most devoted affection and allegiance."

On the conclusion of Colonel Lindsay's address the band struck up, "Should auld acquaintance be forgot?"

At the end of the year orders were received from England to hold the first battalion of the 91st in readiness to return to England, to be relieved by the 45th Regiment, whose arrival they were to await. This latter regiment, however, was detained in Monte Video, assisting the authorities there to quell an insurrection, in consequence of which the 91st were still at Grahamstown when the Kaffir War of 1846–47 broke out.

The men of the regiment at this time, after ten years abroad, were according to all accounts a very fine body. Munro, who was then one of the surgeons, says in his book, "Service in Many Lands," that their average height was five feet eight inches, and that they were well-set-up, powerful fellows, with great powers of endurance, although they had a great capacity for strong drink—a habit which had grown on them from having nothing else to do when they were quartered at St. Helena. They were quite aware of the fact

1845. themselves, and acknowledged that "they were jist a set o' drunken old deevils." However, they could carry their liquor well, and, when they did feel the worse, went quietly to bed. The ranks were filled mostly with Lowland Scotch, having a few Gaelic-speaking * Highlanders among them.

It will be best now to indicate briefly the causes which led to the outbreak of the Kaffir War of 1846. 1846-47. In the early part of the year 1846 the Kaffirs began to manifest symptoms of a restless and aggressive spirit, their marauding incursions into the colony becoming daily more frequent and daring. A meeting of the Gaika chiefs was convened by Colonel Hare at Block Drift on the 29th of January, at which 120 of the reserve battalion of the 91st Highlanders, three troops of the 7th Dragoon Guards, one hundred of the Cape Corps, and one gun were present (a picture of this meeting is now in the officers' mess of the regiment, presented by Major Hollway). This array of British troops was fully equalled or rather exceeded by the Kaffir chief Sandilla, who is said to have had a force of some 4000 horsemen, mostly armed with guns.

* Up to 1839, a squad was always drilled in that language.

When the wily Kaffir saw the troops extended into line, he immediately performed the same movements, his men of course overlapping the British. The conference was brief; the chief acknowledged he had been intemperate in his language (he had defied the British Government, and used personal abuse to the governor), and promised better behaviour in the future.

Matters were brought to a crisis by the following incident, which is thus narrated by Napier in his book on South Africa: "Although symptoms of discontent had long before the last outbreak been manifested by the Gaikas, occasional acts of plunder as usual took place in the colony, and a war at some future period was looked upon as inevitable, and in consequence of the scarcely disguised inimical sentiments of Sandilla, backed as he was by the whole of 'Young Kaffirland,' and further encouraged by more injudicious conduct on our part; still nothing had occurred to warrant a belief of the immediate commencement of hostilities. Macomo, the brother of Sandilla, with his wives frequented the canteen of Fort Beaufort, and was as usual in a constant state of intoxication. However, on the occasion of one of these bacchanalian visits a follower of his

1846. committed a theft, of which no further notice was taken than causing the restitution of the stolen property and driving the offender out of Fort Beaufort. But the thief shortly returned, and, having been again detected purloining a hatchet from out of the commissariat stores, he was made prisoner and despatched under an escort with other malefactors to Grahamstown, to be tried there by the civil power for his offence, which, having been committed within the bounds of the colony, made him amenable to its laws.

"The prisoners thus sent to take their trial were the above-mentioned Kaffir, a Hottentot, to whom for the sake of security he had been manacled, an English soldier, and a Fingoe (the two latter also chained together), and the whole guarded by a small escort. They had not proceeded many miles from Fort Beaufort, when, at the pass known as Dan's Hoek, overlooking the waters of the Kat River, they were suddenly attacked by a strong body of Kaffirs, who liberated their countrymen, and in doing so dreadfully mutilated the poor Hottentot, whose wrist bearing the handcuffs was first severed from his body, after which he was deliberately pierced to death with assegais. Meanwhile the English soldier and the Fingoe, taking advantage of the confusion, managed to creep into the bush, and, in their endeavours to conceal themselves under the bank of the Kat River, were, owing to their fettered condition, nearly drowned in the stream. Such was the event which at last caused the final outbreak of the long-smouldering Kaffir War of 1846-47. On Sandilla's refusal to deliver up the perpetrators of this daring and unprovoked outrage, hostile operations were immediately undertaken on our part, and it was decreed that this ' war of the axe' should be protracted during the space of nearly two years, and at enormous expense to the British public, until the appearance of Sir Harry Smith put an end to the squabble."

At the commencement of the war, the headquarters of the 1st battalion proceeded to Fort Peddie, which stands on the north side of the Great Fish River, between it and the Keiskamma, at a distance of about forty-five miles from Grahamstown. The fort itself was only a very insignificant low-banked earthen fort, with two or three light guns. The commissariat store stood in the centre. The infantry barrack, having accommodation for one company, and a separate barrack with stabling for a troop of

1846. cavalry, were outside the fort proper, being surrounded by loopholed walls. The officers' quarters were also outside, with no protection whatever.

Another portion of the regiment was sent to Post Victoria, where a temporary detachment under Captain Barney was quartered.

The track to Fort Peddie runs through the dense Fish River bush *via* Trumpeter's Drift, where there was a small fortified barrack close to the river (held by a detachment of the 91st under Lieutenant Dickson), ascending from there in an easterly direction through a rough and difficult country, until it reaches Fort Peddie, which is called after Colonel Peddie of the 72nd Regiment, who built it.

A detachment of the regiment had been previously posted here for some time under command of Captain Wright, who had spent his spare time in exploring the neighbouring country, noting its physical peculiarities, and finding out where each path led to. There was little or no game close to the fort, the Kaffirs having destroyed or driven away all large animals, leaving only a few of the smaller varieties of antelope; blue cranes and vultures being the only birds that could be called numerous.

Surgeon-General Munro, in his interesting account of his service during this period, recounts a tale of one of these blue cranes, called "Bobbie," which had been tamed by the soldiers of the 91st detachment. The bird was allowed to be perfectly at liberty, and often absented himself for hours at a time during the day, but always returned towards sunset, and spent the night with the sentry, walking up and down beside him, and retiring into the sentry-box when tired. On one occasion, after an absence of some hours, he returned with a broken leg, and was taken in hand as a patient by Surgeon Munro, who succeeded in mending his fractured limb, after which the bird showed its appreciation by constantly calling at his quarters.

On the 22nd of May a convoy of supplies, consisting of forty-two waggons at Trumpeter's Drift, was ordered to be escorted by sixty men sent from Fort Peddie under command of Captain Colin Campbell; they were to be joined by a detachment under Captain Barney. The latter not putting in an appearance in time, the convoy started without them. After travelling some five miles they were attacked by an immense number of Kaffirs, who compelled them to retire on

1846. Trumpeter's Drift, as it was found impossible to protect such a long line of waggons with so few men. It must be remembered that each waggon had a span of twelve oxen, and, as they could only travel in single file, forty-two waggons covered a great extent of ground. The Kaffirs looted the waggons and burnt them.

On the 27th and 28th of May the head-quarters of the 1st battalion was engaged in protecting the Fingoe settlement at Fort Peddie, when that post was attacked by a very considerable force of Kaffirs. An account of this affair is given in the following despatch from Lieutenant-Colonel Lindsay, of the 91st Regiment, who was in command :—

"I have the honour to report, for the information of his Excellency the Commander-in-chief, that on the 27th inst., about 1 o'clock p.m., the resident agent informed me that his spies had come in to say that there were parties of Kaffirs above the hills north of the post, who would probably try and take off some of the cattle grazing furthest from it. I directed the troop of the 7th Dragoon Guards, with fourteen Cape Mounted Rifles, and the light six-pounder, to patrol round the hills and protect the cattle.

About an hour after this the gun was fired several times from the direction of the north-west hill, about two miles and a half from this. I at once caused the infantry to be turned out, and sent out two companies, amounting together to 100 men, of the 91st Regiment, with the view of affording support to the cavalry and guns if necessary. I ordered Major Yarborough out to take command of the whole. The infantry arrived on the ground where the cavalry were about half-past 3 o'clock, and met the gun returning to the post disabled, in consequence of one of the wheel horses having been shot. The cavalry were then in extended order, engaged with the enemy near a dense bush. The infantry advanced and extended one company, and commenced firing. Major Yarborough, after some time, ordered them to retire so as to draw the enemy more into the open country, which succeeded, and Captain Sir H. Darell, who had retired behind the infantry and closed, had an opportunity of charging with his troops, and reports having sabred from fifteen to twenty of the enemy before they could get to the bush. The infantry then advanced again, and afterwards tried the same plan retiring. The enemy came out a little way, keeping up a brisk

1846. fire, though at a long range. The 91st then halted and ceased firing, waiting for the enemy to come on; but, as they did not do so, and it was getting dusk, the whole came back to quarters. Major Yarborough reports satisfactorily the steadiness of the men and the conduct of the Fingoes, about 100 of whom were skirmishing on the left. He thinks the number of the enemy actually engaged was from 800 to 1000, and considers that from thirty to forty were killed in the skirmish and charge, besides those who must have fallen from the effects of the shells which were thrown into the kloof before he came up, where Captain Sir H. Darell reports the Kaffirs were in great force. The only damage sustained by the force sent from this was one troop sergeant-major, 7th Dragoon Guards, wounded through the shoulder; one charger (Sir H. Darell's) wounded; one troop horse, 7th Dragoon Guards, wounded; and one horse, Royal Artillery, killed. The enemy expended a great deal of ammunition; their skirmishing was perfect—hiding themselves in advancing and retiring behind the smallest ant-heaps and cover. I have further to report that this post was attacked yesterday by about 8000 of the enemy about 10 o'clock a.m. The look-out on the tower reported that there were Kaffirs on the ground where the skirmish took place the day previous; and about half-past 10 o'clock a dense body of Kaffirs made their appearance on the southern hill near the Grahamstown road, with another body some distance to the right, composed of horsemen. These moved a little way down, as if to entice the troops out. I was aware, from the information of Captain McLean, that the enemy were in great numbers all around us, and therefore was not drawn out to leave the post open. All the cattle were driven below the Star Fort, and protected by the Fingoes. The wives and children of the Fingoes were in the ditch of the fort. About half-past 11 o'clock an immense number of Kaffirs, horse and foot, appeared on the south-west hills, arranged in three dense masses, with detached clumps of horses; other large bodies were also on the hills all round. The force at the front was distributed as follows:—The cavalry, with twenty artillery, were at the cavalry barracks and Star Fort, a sergeant's party at Mr. Webb's, and picquets in the officers' and engineers' range. At 12 o'clock the whole of the enemy moved down to the post steadily, preceded by clouds of skirmishers. When they came within range, I directed

1846. Lieutenant King, R.A., to send a round shot at one of the masses, which killed three men. A shell was then thrown, and a twelve-pound rocket. The latter frightened the cattle, which rushed down towards the Kaffirs, and were easily driven off by them. The Fingoes pursued them, and succeeded in re-capturing a good number of them. The enemy, as soon as they found our shot so well directed, scattered, and got into the kloofs and hollows. One party of some hundreds got down the deep trench to Mr. Webb's house, from which the detached party had been withdrawn, and began to plunder what little was left there by the owner; but a shell being pitched into the yard, they quitted it, but got into the ditch and gardens about it, and fired at the barracks and fort without doing any injury, several of their number being shot from the infantry barrack. A large body came down the small kloof on the left of the Beaufort road, but were dispersed by shells from the tower, shells or rockets sent at them generally doing damage. I take this opportunity of saying that Lieutenant King's practice, which was under my own observation in the Star Fort, was much to my satisfaction. The Kaffirs, finding that their attack on the post had failed, except as regarded the capture of cattle, retired to the kloof 1846. about 2 o'clock, when I sent out the cavalry to cut up any stragglers, but they did not succeed in getting near any. The resident agent has reported that 4000 head of cattle were taken off. The attack was by the combined Gaika and T'Slambie, and the numbers who came down, as reported above, are not overrated. The enemy's loss was severe. Ninety-two dead bodies have been reported, and many more must have fallen, as the Kaffirs were seen putting their dead and wounded on horses and bearing them off the field. I should think that their loss may be safely estimated at 200 killed and wounded, most probably more. There has been no casualty on the side of the troops. Two Fingoes were killed and three wounded in the attempt they made to recover their cattle."

Although the Fingoes were the slaves of the Kaffirs until Sir Benjamin D'Urban released them from their bondage, and though the Kaffirs to this day denominate them their "dogs," the Fingoe is in many ways their superior. Fingoe is not their natural appellation, but a term of reproach signifying extreme poverty and misery, a being having no claim to justice, mercy, or life—in fact, an

1846. utter outcast. They are the remains of eight powerful nations who have been driven out of their country by victorious Kaffirs. The mode of warfare between both tribes is in some respects different. The Kaffir goes forth to war besmeared with red clay, and simply arrayed with his kaross, armed with his musket and assegai, and accoutred with his pouch and sack for ammunition, plunder, and provisions.

The appearance of a body of Fingoes, if less terrific, is more imposing. Their heads are ornamented with jackals' tails, ostrich plumes, wolves' teeth, etc. Across their shoulder is flung a skin, and around their waists is girt a kilt of monkeys' tails. The chief, like the Kaffirs, wears a tiger-skin kaross, and their rain-makers, who are alike wizards, doctors, and councillors, are most fearfully grotesque in their costume.

On the 6th of June the battalion furnished to the second division of the army under Colonel Somerset, three companies under a field officer; Major Yarborough was in command of the regular infantry, consisting of 120 of the 91st, which proceeded with the division as far as the Buffalo affluents in Kaffraria, and rejoined head-quarters when the division fell back for supplies on

Waterloo Bay in September. The whole force was under the command of Sir Peregrine Maitland, and after encountering many difficulties, hardships, and privations, successfully effected the object of the expedition, which was to find a place of landing where supplies could more easily be obtained at the front.

1846.

Soon after this, the battalion furnished detachments for the Fish River, from Trumpeter's Drift to Fort Brown, and after the second advance of the second division into the enemy's country, performed a very considerable amount of escort duty in guarding convoys of supplies for the Kei River and other camps.

A small column under Colonel Johnstone of the 27th Regiment, in which was a detachment of eighty men of the 91st, having Lieutenants Bayly and Stein with it, moved at the same time as Colonel Somerset's column to the south-east, to the Amatola Mountains, and assisted the first division to drive the Kaffirs out of the kloofs of those ranges of mountains, but were recalled before any great success was attained. In this march the troops underwent great exposure and fatigue, frequently marching twenty and thirty miles a day; but this did not much affect the men

1846. of the 91st, as an eye-witness of this expedition says—

"They (the 91st) could march from sunrise to sunset, and though without food or other refreshment during all that time, not a man ever fell out of the ranks, so great was their staying power and their endurance; and they never got foot-sore or leg weary, for their feet were hard as horn, and their muscles like whip-cord. The only thing they appeared to dislike was a long halt during a march, for their old muscles got stiff, and would not relax again until they got quickly over a mile or two."

Both battalions at this time were armed with the smooth-bore musket with percussion lock, while the 27th Regiment still had the old "Brown Bess." The new weapon of the 91st does not appear to have been highly thought of; in fact, it was not considered any better in the matter of precise shooting than that carried by the 27th, and used to kick so terribly that the men never put in the full charge of powder.

White cross-belts were worn by the men; the one over the right shoulder secured the bayonet, while the other over the left was attached to the cartouche-box made of black leather. There being no waist-belt to confine these cross-belts, they flapped about when the man doubled, and it required one hand to hold them while the other carried the musket. Knapsacks, fortunately, were not required to be carried during the service in South Africa in those days.

The 27th and 91st (according to an officer of the 74th) were now mere skeletons of their former regiments, approaching their thirteenth year of service in a state of perpetual unrest. Things, however, were looking brighter, and inspections were talked of. Lieutenant-General Sir George Berkeley paid the 91st a high compliment in giving them only two hours' notice for inspection, and the manner in which they turned out did not disappoint his anticipations of their appearance, which was as honourable to the regiment as it was satisfactory to the commander-in-chief.

During the remainder of the time the 1st battalion was at the front, they took no part in active operations.

In January, 1848, the war being over, the 1st battalion marched out from Grahamstown to Port Elizabeth about 360 strong, having discharged such men who had applied to remain in the colony, and having transferred all men under a

1848. certain age, and such as had been only a short time on foreign service, to the reserve battalion— a proceeding not at all appreciated by the men, as they considered that they were leaving their old regiment to go to a new one, although it was numbered the same. On reaching Port Elizabeth, the battalion was embarked on board H.M.S. *Geyser*, arriving at Cape Town after a passage of forty-nine hours, where the head-quarters, under command of Colonel Lindsay, and three companies, embarked for home, on the 23rd of February, in the sailing ship *Acasta*, 350 tons burden, followed on the 10th of March by the other three companies, arriving at Gosport on the 28th of April and 11th of May respectively. The depôt was consolidated with the battalion on the 1st of May. By a memorandum dated Horse Guards, 5th of May, 1846, a second lieutenant-colonel was appointed to the 91st, as well as to all the regiments having reserve battalions; he was to have command of the latter battalion.

CHAPTER X.

Kaffir War, 1846–47—Part taken therein by the Reserve Battalion.

WE must now look back to record the history of the reserve battalion, which we left at Cape Town after their disembarkation from the ill-fated *Abercrombie Robinson*. On their arrival at that station, there were a great number of desertions among the men, who thought they saw an opening to make their fortunes in the interior; and it was principally the young soldiers that went off. One of the officers, Captain Gordon, volunteered his services to stop the men going away, and only stipulated that he should have the help of one of his brother officers, and that he should be allowed one of the Cape Corps soldiers as an interpreter to accompany him. He also asked for an order from the Colonial Office to all field cornets, directing them to give him such assistance in the way of furnishing

1842.

1842. horses for his party, and conveyances for his prisoners, as he might require. Captain Gordon's offer was accepted. He had not the slightest trace or information of the track of a single deserter to guide his course over the districts through which his purpose might lead his patrol. When taking leave of his commanding officer before riding off, Major Ducat (the officer then in command) said to him, "Gordon, if you do not bring them back, we are a ruined battalion!" The patrol was absent from head-quarters for eight days, during which time Captain Gordon rode over 600 miles; and when on the evening of the 16th of November his tired party rode into the barracks of Cape Town just before sunset, after a ride of eighty miles in thirteen hours, sixteen of the men who had recently deserted were lodged in the regimental guard-room as the result of his exertions. Two more deserters, hearing that Captain Gordon was out, had come in of their own accord. The desertions in the reserve battalion ceased from that date.

1843. The reserve battalion embarked on the 22nd of February, 1843, for Algoa Bay, and sailed on the 27th, anchoring there on the 4th and disembarking at Port Elizabeth on the 5th of March.

On the 7th it set out for Grahamstown, which it reached on the 13th, and took up its quarters at Fort England with the 1st battalion of the regiment. In the beginning of January, 1844, it proceeded to Fort Beaufort, which became its head-quarters for the next four years, detachments being sent out to occupy the nine different posts which had been established on the frontier.

The outbreak of the Kaffir War in the early part of 1846 has been already alluded to in connection with the 1st battalion of the 91st. On the 11th of April the head-quarters of the reserve battalion, augmented to 200 rank and file by the grenadier company of the 1st battalion under Captain Ward, marched from Fort Beaufort into Kaffirland with the division under command of Colonel Richardson, of the 7th Dragoon Guards, and on the 14th the detachment joined Colonel Somerset's division near the Debé Flats. On the 15th of April the two divisions encamped with their united forces at Burn's Hill Missionary Station, and on the following morning preparations were made for attacking the enemy, who had assembled in force on the Amatola Mountains.

The country about the Amatola Mountains, in which the operations of the troops were confined,

1846. may be described as a precipitous range of hills, having kloofs of rocky gullies running down from their heights, which served as channels for the deluges of rain which came with the thunderstorms that are so frequent in these districts. The country itself was very wild and picturesque to look upon, and can hardly be likened to any place in the British Isles; for though it had the rugged appearance of the hills of Scotland, it was at the same time covered with rank vegetation, which is met with in semi-tropical climates. The sides of the hills are bold and precipitous, being intersected with ravines and clothed with forest trees of immense size, and apparently of great age. The valleys in the kloofs are of considerable extent, and thickly covered with bushy underwood.

The infantry consisted of 200 of the 1st battalion of the 91st, with the following officers: Captain Scott, reserve battalion; Captain Ward and Lieutenant Cochrane, of the grenadier company, 1st battalion; Lieutenants Howard and Owgan, and Ensigns Fitzgerald and McPherson, reserve battalion, with Assistant-Surgeon Barclay; and 180 Kat River burghers, who had joined the previous day; and were placed under the command of Major Campbell, of the 91st, who was directed to scour the valley of the Amatola. Starting at daybreak for that purpose, the cavalry, upwards of 300 strong, with two guns, making a détour to the left, searched the kloofs and swept away the cattle from the open grounds at the foot of the mountains. Towards evening the troops came into contact with the enemy, and the account of the engagement is given in the following official report by Major Campbell to Colonel Somerset :—

"*Block Drift*, 19*th April*.—I have the honour to acquaint you that in compliance with your order of the 16th inst., I proceeded from the camp at Burn's Hill, with 200 rank and file of the 91st Regiment and 180 burgher Hottentots, across the Keiskamma, and up the Amatola Hoek. The principal part of the way was by a narrow path through a densely wooded valley. After proceeding for about five or six miles without any molestation, the country became more open, and I halted here for a short time. During the time of our halt, I perceived numbers of Kaffirs collecting on the heights all round, but more especially at the only outlet which leads to the flats, where I expected to meet with your division.

1846. In forming a moderate estimate of what we could see of the enemy's numbers, I should compute them at 2000, and all apparently armed with firearms. As their numbers were increasing every moment, and they seemed closing upon us, I determined on ascending the heights without delay, so as to gain the flats and get clear of the bush. The outlet was up a steep, rugged path, about three-quarters of a mile in length, thickly wooded on either side, but more particularly on our left. As soon as we commenced the ascent (the burgher Hottentots skirmishing in our front), the Kaffirs opened a heavy fire upon us from front and both flanks. We continued advancing, steadily firing to both flanks. When about half-way up, the Kaffirs closed on our rear, so that we were entirely surrounded. I then ordered my men to fix bayonets and fire a volley in the thick bush on our left, from which the hottest of the enemy's fire proceeded. This for a short time silenced their fire in that direction, when we again pushed up, keeping up a constant fire to our flanks as before. On gaining the top, I formed the men in line to the rear, and commenced firing on the Kaffirs, who were now emerging from the bush. My men were much done up, owing to the steepness of the ascent; at this moment you arrived with your division to our support.

"With the subsequent occurrences of the day you are acquainted. The casualties of my party on this occasion were—three privates of the 91st killed; one corporal and two privates wounded; one Hottentot burgher wounded, who died on the following morning; and my horse shot during the ascent. I have much pleasure in being able to state that the whole of the party under my command, including the burgher Hottentots, behaved with the greatest coolness and determination." Major Campbell adds in a postscript:—

"On this occasion the Kaffirs acknowledge to have lost 200. (It is well known that the Kaffirs always endeavour to conceal the numbers they lose in war, so the chances are that what even they acknowledge is greatly under the mark.) The conduct of my 200 men was admirable; nothing but coolness and the most determined courage, under a merciful God, brought us through. One poor fellow, after being wounded, shot one and bayoneted two. We were at times muzzle to muzzle."

Colonel Napier, in his "Travels in Southern Africa," says, "It was probably judicious to

1846. advance at once on what the Kaffirs had ever considered their impregnable fastnesses. The great fault, however, consisted in making this movement on the Amatola with a force totally inadequate to the object in view, if resistance were anticipated on the part of the Kaffirs; and, moreover, encumbered by a large train of baggage drawn on waggons, through a broken, wooded, mountainous, and intricate country. But apparently it was never dreamt that the Kaffirs really meant to show fight, or so small a force as 1500 or 1600 men (part of which consisted of heavy cavalry, perfectly useless on such ground) would never have been sent on this expedition. In short, the opening of the campaign was apparently looked upon by many more in the light of a picnic or excursion of pleasure than anything else. Great, however, was their mistake; for now the Kaffirs, on what they considered their own ground, fought on the 16th with the utmost determination. The brunt of the action fell upon the 91st, which, gallantly led up a steep wooded ravine by Lieutenant-Colonel Campbell, was surrounded on all sides by overwhelming numbers of the enemy."

The summit of the pass having been gained,

as above described in Major Campbell's official despatch, that officer was joined by Colonel Somerset and the rest of the force, and a bivouac was formed for the night on the Amatola flats, in the shape of a hollow square, in order to protect the 1800 cattle captured by Colonel Somerset's party.

On the morning of the 17th the force moved towards Burn's Hill, and on approaching the Keiskamma, an advanced party of about eighty men, under command of Captain Scott of the reserve battalion, 91st, was sent to reinforce Major Gibson, 7th Dragoon Guards, who had been left in charge of some waggons at Burn's Hill. The latter officer's despatch recounts the events which led to the party being sent in advance as follows:—

"About 7 o'clock, just as I had diminished the size of my camp, we were attacked by a considerable body of Kaffirs, whom we beat off in six or seven minutes, I am sorry to say, with the loss of four men of the 91st killed, and four wounded."

On the 17th Major Gibson, in compliance with Colonel Somerset's instructions, moved from Burn's Hill at half-past 10 a.m.. From the

1846. number of waggons (125), and the necessity of giving a support to the guns, Major Gibson was only able to form an advance and rear baggage-guard, and could not detach any men along the line of waggons. The advance-guard consisted of Captain Wright's company, a half troop of the 7th Dragoon Guards, and one gun; the rear-guard of Captain Rawstorne's company, one gun, and some troopers. After proceeding about a mile, shots issued from the kloof by the side of the road. Lieutenant Stokes, R.E., ran the gun up to a point some 300 yards in advance, and raked the kloof with shell. When half the waggons had passed, the Kaffirs made a dash upon one of them, firing at the drivers and some of the officers' servants, who were obliged to fly, then took out the oxen and wheeled the waggon across the river. An overpowering force then rushed down from the hills in all directions, keeping up an incessant fire, which was returned by the 7th Dragoon Guards and the 91st with great spirit. The gun was also served with much skill; but owing to the Kaffirs' superiority in numbers, Major Gibson, to prevent his men being cut off, was obliged to retire to Burn's Hill, where he again put his men in position. A short time after this, the company of the 91st, under Captain Scott, advanced in skirmishing order, keeping up a heavy fire; but the waggons completely blocking up the road, the troops were obliged to make a détour, and after considerable difficulty succeeded in getting the ammunition-waggons into proper line, but found it quite impracticable to save the baggage-waggons, the Kaffirs having driven away the oxen. One of the ammunition-waggons broke down, but the ammunition was removed to another. The troops then fought their way inch by inch to the Tyumie Camp, where they were met by Colonel Somerset's brigade, and where they again encamped for the night.

Napier says: "As the savages plundered the waggons at Burn's Hill, scattered abroad their contents, arrayed themselves in the garments of our troops, ate and drank, not only our supplies, but the very contents of our medicine-chests (devouring the blistering ointment, and drinking the laudanum), their ferocious passions were roused to the highest pitch. Cruel tortures awaited such of our people as unfortunately fell into their power. Their bodies were mangled after death, part of their clothes and accoutrements were despatched, in sign of triumph, throughout

1846. the length and breadth of the land, and the Amakosae rose *en masse* to drive the white man into the sea."

On the 18th the camp with the captured cattle was moved to Block Drift, the advance-guard consisting of a détachment of the 91st under Captain Scott, while the rear of the train of waggons was protected by Captain Rawstorne's company of the 91st, assisted by Lieutenant Howard of the 1st battalion. The enemy vigorously attacked the waggons and escort during their march through the bush, killing one and mortally wounding another, while Captain Rawstorne was hit by a musket-ball in the stomach.

On approaching the Tyumie River, the ammunition of Captain Rawstorne's company being all expended, it was relieved from protecting the rear by the grenadier company of the 91st. The waggons crossed the river, the drift being held by the reserve battalion of the 91st and a few dismounted dragoons, the guns of the Royal Artillery firing from the higher ground on the opposite side of the river.

Mrs. Ward, in her book " Cape and the Kaffirs," says, with reference to this incident of the war of 1846, "Thus scarcely 1500, not all regular troops, encumbered with 125 waggons, made their way into the fastnesses of those savages, who were many thousand in number, and although unable to follow up the enemy, of whom they killed at least 300, succeeded in saving all their ammunition, captured 1800 head of cattle, and finally fought their way to the original ground of dispute."

During these engagements Lieutenant Cochrane was wounded three times, and Captain Rawstorne was struck with a spent ball. An officer who was present states that neither he nor any of his division had anything whatever to eat from Thursday, the 16th, at daylight till Saturday night, the 18th, when they reached Block Drift.

During the engagement on the evening of the 18th, Corporal Stuart of the reserve battalion was shot dead. Private Stevenson of the grenadier company proceeded immediately to the spot where the body was lying (which was directly in front of the enemy), and succeeded in carrying off Stuart's firelock, and also attempted to take the ammunition from his pouch; but was obliged to retire in consequence of the Kaffirs making a rush for him. At that moment Corporals Sherrock and Morris, who had

1846. advanced to assist Stevenson, were called to try and bring the body back to the waggons. This they found impossible to do, as the enemy was too numerous, so they were obliged to retire. In doing so, Corporal Morris halted within ten yards of the body, and shot a Kaffir through the head while he was in the act of cutting poor Stuart's throat. Corporal Sherrock also turned and shot another Kaffir through the body, who was trying to extract the ammunition from the pouch.

Among the slain was afterwards discovered a soldier of the 91st, who had probably been burned to death by the savages, as his remains were found bound to the pole of a waggon and horribly defaced by fire. The Kaffirs admit that they tied their victim to a stake and literally flayed him alive; the little children being permitted to assist in torturing him. They said they imagined the grenadiers of the 91st could not be killed, as the balls appeared to glance harmlessly by them.

The result of the fighting on the Amatola Mountains on the 16th, 17th, and 18th of April was, that the Kaffirs poured into the colony, thinking they would carry all before them, and drive every white man into the sea. They consequently attacked, and were repulsed with heavy loss, the following outposts held by the 91st. At the Tyumie post on the 19th of April, under command of Lieutenant Metcalfe, when one private of the 91st was wounded; Lieu Fontein on the 19th, under charge of Ensign Lavers, when two privates of the 91st were killed; at Blinkwater post the 20th of April; Double Drift the 26th of April; Mancazana post on the 1st and 3rd of May; and Trumpeter's Drift the 2nd of May. Concerning the attack on Blinkwater post Colonel Napier says, "The post happened to be at the time occupied by a small party of the 91st, under command of a sergeant. The Kaffirs rushed on as usual in overwhelming numbers to the attack, but were steadily repulsed; and finding all their efforts useless against the gallant little band who so resolutely held their own, were at last fain to retreat, with a considerable loss in killed and wounded, most of whom however they carried off. The brave man who headed this gallant defence was Sergeant Snodgrass of the 91st, and gladly do I record his name."

Among those who were honourably mentioned by Sir Peregrine Maitland in general orders, for their conduct in defending their respective posts when attacked, were Lieutenants Metcalfe and

1846. Thom, and Sergeants Snodgrass and Clarke, of the 91st.

The head-quarters of the reserve battalion remained at Block Drift until July, 1847. On the 12th of May, 1846, it was attacked by the Kaffirs, who were repulsed with the loss of a chief and sixty men killed, whilst the 91st had one man mortally wounded. The following is the official report by Major Campbell, who was in command of the 91st at the post:—

"*Block Drift, May 13th,* 1846.—I have the honour to acquaint you, for the information of his honour the colonel commanding, that yesterday, about 2 p.m., a body of 150 mounted Kaffirs was seen approaching the cattle-slaughter guard (twelve men of the 91st Regiment), which was about 400 yards above Fort Thompson on the slope of the hill, and immediately commenced firing upon them. Considering this to be only a ruse on the part of the Kaffirs to draw the force out of the building, I merely sent a party consisting of one officer and twenty men, to support the cattle-guard, who were retiring on the camp, and got the rest of the men and the gun into position. I then opened a fire with the gun, and after a few discharges, which seem to have been effective, as several Kaffirs were seen to fall from their horses and were afterwards picked up by the others and carried off, the body of Kaffirs retired up the hill out of range; and immediately, as I anticipated, a large force of Kaffirs on foot made a rush from the top and from each side of the wooded hill, about 800 yards in rear of the building, and made directly for it. By this time I had the gun brought to the other flank, so as to fire on the hill, and opened a fire of musketry from the top windows and roof on them as they advanced, which checked them and made them change their direction to the thick bush on our right rear. The gun was then brought to bear on this point, when the Kaffirs retired in various directions behind the hill to our rear. It is impossible to say what may have been the loss of the enemy on this occasion, but on that part of the hill where the gun and musketry fire were directed, there were distinctly seen eight bodies carried away. Our casualty was one man of the cattle-guard severely and dangerously wounded. Whilst these operations were going on, another large body of Kaffirs, both mounted and on foot, carried off the whole of the slaughtered cattle and sheep. This party kept along the ridge to

1846. the south-west, between this and Post Victoria, and shortly fell in with the trek oxen, which were grazing in that direction under their leaders and drivers, and captured the whole of them, killing one of the drivers. Shortly afterwards, I saw the oxen and Kaffirs make a détour to the left and go in the direction of the Amatola Mountains. Having one day's rations of meat only for those on the post, I caused it to be divided into two days' supply, and reduced the forage allowance."

In a second report, also dated May 13th, Major Campbell says, " I may add that the guard which was out yesterday, although nearly a mile distant, escaped in a most remarkable manner, as by the time the relief which I had sent to their aid had reached them, they were completely surrounded by Kaffirs, and this small party deserves the greatest credit for the manner in which they fought their way through a body of attacking Kaffirs so many times more than their number, and to which I was an eye-witness."

The following interesting incidents are re-counted by Mrs. Ward in "Cape and the Kaffirs":—
" When the reserve battalion was holding Block Drift, a very daring act was performed by two private soldiers of the regiment. A despatch

arrived for the governor, Sir Peregrine Maitland, escorted by eighteen mounted burghers, with a request from the commandant at Fort Beaufort, that it should be sent on as soon as possible. The communication between Block Drift and Fort Cox, where the governor was, was completely cut off, and accordingly volunteers were called for to carry the despatch. Two men immediately came forward, Robert Walsh and Thomas Reilly, and to them the despatch was entrusted. They left Block Drift shortly after dark, and proceeded on their perilous journey, dressed in uniform, and with their muskets. All went well for the first six miles, although they found themselves in the vicinity of the Kaffirs. Suddenly, on entering a wooded valley at the foot of the Amatola Mountains, they came right upon a Kaffir encampment, and had hardly time to throw themselves on the ground in the thick underwood, when they found to their horror, that the natives had heard their footsteps, as the latter rushed into the thicket to look for the intruders. Fortunately, a porcupine was sighted, and the Kaffirs, evidently satisfied, returned to their camp, muttering that it was an 'Easterfooke,' *Anglicé* porcupine, that had alarmed them. Walsh and

1846. Reilly, holding their breath, saw the Kaffirs preparing to eat their supper, after which they began to post their sentries. One was put six yards off the gallant fellows, who, not quite discouraged, still kept quiet. The remaining Kaffirs rolled themselves up in their blankets and went to sleep. The sentry stood for a few minutes, looked round, then sat down for a few more minutes, looked round again, and then wrapped himself in his blanket and slept peacefully too. Walsh and Reilly, as may be imagined, did not give them the chance of waking, but made off. They then made a wide circuit, and after numerous escapes from detection, once having been challenged by a Kaffir sentinel who was not asleep, they came to the Keiskamma River, and, knowing that all the fords were guarded by the Kaffirs, they had to cross by swimming, finally reaching Fort Cox shortly before daylight. Here their dangers were not over, for the sentries, not expecting anything but Kaffirs, treated them to some rapid file firing. Again they lay down in shelter until daybreak, when, being recognized as British soldiers, they were warmly welcomed, and delivered their important despatches. Poor Walsh was afterwards killed in action, and Reilly was discharged with a pension, after twenty-one years' service, though it is to be regretted that neither received at the time any public reward of their gallant night's work, which in these days would certainly have been rewarded with the Victoria Cross."

1846.

During the advance of the enemy on Block Drift, at the beginning of the war, and when the post was commanded by Major Campbell, he took up a position on the top of the schoolhouse, rifle in hand; four men were employed in loading his arms for him, and he brought down two of the enemy, successively, in a few minutes. When the third fell dead, a soldier of the reserve battalion, named John Black, could restrain himself no longer; forgetting Major Campbell's rank as an officer, in his delight at his good shooting, he slapped his commanding officer on the back with a shout of delight, and the exclamation "Well done, sodger!" a compliment worth all the praise of an elaborate despatch.

Lieutenant Dickson, of the reserve battalion of the 91st, while commanding at Trumpeter's Drift, frequently obtained the approbation of Sir Peregrine Maitland and Lieutenant-Colonel Johnstone for his zeal and activity. On the 21st

1846. of May, when a convoy of waggons proceeding from Grahamstown and Fort Peddie was attacked and captured by the enemy on Trumpeter's Hill, the gallant conduct of Lieutenant Dickson, who had voluntarily joined the escort, was highly commended by his Excellency the governor in a general order. Mrs. Ward says, "On this occasion, Lieutenant Dickson, 91st Regiment, who had been ordered to assist in escorting the waggon a certain distance till the other escort was met, nobly volunteered to proceed further, and led the advance; nor did he retire till his ammunition was expended. On reaching the rear, he found the commanding officer of the party retreating, by the advice of some civilians, who considered the defile impassable for so many waggons under such a fire. Lieutenant Dickson's coolness, courage, and energy, in not only leading the men, but literally putting his shoulder to the wheel of a waggon to clear the line, were spoken of by all as worthy of the highest praise. His horse and that of Ensign Aitchison were shot under their riders."

On the 5th of June 100 men of the 91st assisted in recapturing from a party of the enemy about 5300 sheep and goats and nine horses, and in bringing them in safely to the post. On the 6th a strong patrol of 250 of the 91st Regiment, a party of Royal Sappers and Miners, with one gun, 40 of the Cape Corps, 400 mounted burghers, and 200 Fingoes, started from Block Drift under the command of Major Campbell, and having scoured all the kloofs and valleys to the foot of the Amatola Mountains, and meeting with no opposition, returned to the post. On the 15th, 200 men of the 91st Regiment, 200 of the 27th Regiment, a company of the Royal Sappers and Miners and two guns, with 43 Cape Corps, and 600 of the burghers and Hottentot and Fingoe levies, under the command of Colonel Hare, again patrolled the Amatola Mountains; but meeting with no opposition, the enemy only appearing on the top of the hills, the force returned to Block Drift early in December, and the 91st proceeded to Fort Beaufort, where they remained until the renewal of hostilities in July, 1847.

On the 27th of July, 1847, the reserve battalion of the 91st, 11 officers and 250 men, formed part of the first division under the command of Colonel Hare, and having left 90 men to maintain Block Drift, proceeded to the Tyumie flats. Captain Ward was appointed commandant of Beaufort in the absence of the lieutenant-governor.

1847

On the night of the 29th of July the Kaffirs made an attack on the camp, but were soon silenced by the fire of the troops, which caused them quickly to retire; and by daybreak next morning the division, more than 2000 strong, with two guns, ascended the summit of the Amatola range, the enemy everywhere fleeing before them. The following day the division proceeded to Fort Cox, with a view of intercepting the retreating foe. This fort is situated about fifteen miles from Block Drift, amongst the rocky and wooded fastnesses of the Amatola Mountains, and was a post of considerable importance, reached by a long and tedious ascent up a wooded acclivity, shortly after crossing the Keiskamma.

On the 4th of August the force again took up the pursuit, and for four days was engaged in scouring the kloofs and hills towards the source of the Keiskamma River, and up to the Buffalo Mountains. Finding that the Kaffirs had eluded their search, and meeting no enemy to contend against, the troops returned to Fort Cox on the 7th of August. On the 16th a patrol of 150 of the 91st, with a party of the 27th Regiment, and 100 Fingoes ascended the Amatola Mountains, and passing into the valley below, returned to camp without seeing an enemy. On the same day eighty-one men of the 91st, under the command of Captain Hogg, 7th Dragoon Guards, started for Tambookieland, to punish the chief Mampassa, who had now joined in the war against the British. The party was thus employed till the 19th of October, when it arrived at Fort Beaufort, having been engaged in several affairs and skirmishes with the enemy during that time, and in one of which the spirited conduct of Ensign Fitzgerald, of the 91st, was particularly noticed. The detachment marched on the 23rd of October to Phoonah's Kloof, and thence to Post Victoria on the 9th of December.

On the 23rd of August a body of Hottentots and Fingoes that had been sent out on two days' patrol, were, when returning to Fort Cox, suddenly attacked on the Amatola Mountains by a superior force of Kaffirs, and were on the eve of being overpowered by them, when the opportune arrival of 100 men of the 91st, hastily despatched to their support, rescued them from their danger, and throwing themselves in the face of the foe, directed such a volley into them as to compel them to beat a precipitate retreat, and the party returned to camp without further molestation.

1847

On the 28th of August the 91st Regiment furnished 160 men as part of a patrol under Captain Durnford, 37th Regiment, which again scoured the bushy kloofs of the surrounding country. On the 5th of September the reserve battalion of the 91st was directed to remain and occupy Fort Cox, with 200 of the Cape Town burghers, all under the command of Major (now Lieutenant - Colonel) Campbell. The division having placed the fort in a state of good repair, then moved towards the Debe River. While at Fort Cox, daily patrols of 100 men, under a captain, were furnished by the 91st Regiment and Cape burghers for the purpose of keeping the surrounding bush clear of the enemy, and reconnoitring the neighbourhood.

On the 17th of September Lieutenant-Colonel Campbell had an interview with the Kaffir chief, Macomo, who said he came in the name of all Kaffirland to sue for peace, and a report of the interview was forwarded to the officer commanding the first division. On the 23rd of October a party of 123 men of the 91st Regiment, an equal number of burghers, and six of the Cape Corps, acting in co-operation with the first division, patrolled under Lieutenant-Colonel Campbell in the direction of Block Drift, and sweeping along the face of the mountain, succeeded in capturing ninety-two head of cattle. On the 1st of December 100 of the 91st Regiment, 100 Cape Town burghers, and six of the Cape Corps, again sallied out of the fort, and co-operating with the first division, as on the previous occasion, captured 106 head of cattle and nine horses, having experienced very trifling opposition.

The head-quarters and two companies entered Kaffirland with Lieutenant-Colonel Campbell's column, and were present in the operations undertaken in the Amatola and Tabudoda Mountains during the months of September and October.

The officers attached to this party were Captains Scott and Campbell, Lieutenants Dickson and Metcalfe, Ensign and Adjutant Gordon, and Surgeon Power.

As a result of these operations, the Kaffir chief Sandilla surrendered at Fort Hare, bringing in about forty head of cattle and several muskets and carbines, taken from the waggons at Burn's Hill on the 17th of April. The 91st had only three men wounded.

Lieutenant-Colonel Campbell and the above column received the warmest approbation of Lieu-

1847. tenant-General Sir George Berkeley, in orders of December 17th, 1847, at the close of the war. At the end of October the two companies above mentioned, under command of Captains Scott and Campbell, with Lieutenants Dickson and Metcalfe, marched to King William's Town to join the force about to proceed to the Kei River, under the commander-in-chief, Sir George Berkeley. They were attached to Colonel Somerset's division, and served therewith until the end of December, when peace was concluded, and the detachment returned to Fort Beaufort.

The following is a list of the officers of the reserve battalion who served during the whole or part of the wars of 1846-47 :—

Lieutenant-Colonel J. F. G. Campbell; Major D. Forbes; Captains W. G. Scott, C. Campbell, E. W. Wright, J. G. Rawstorne, J. C. Cahill, J. Brown; Lieutenants T. M. Pennington, E. Dickson, R. H. Howard, J. Owgan, H. C. Metcalfe, G. W. Thom; Ensigns R. F. A. Lavers, A. Fitzgerald, J. F. Bethune, J. Macpherson; Ensign and Adjutant J. Gordon; Surgeon J. Power; and Assistant-Surgeon A. Barclay.

1848. In January, 1848, the reserve battalion of the 91st moved from Fort Beaufort to Grahamstown,

and nothing of note occurred till the month of 1815.
July.

In that month two companies, under command of Captain Rawstorne, marched to Colesberg to co-operate with a force under the immediate command of the governor, Lieutenant-General Sir Harry Smith, against the rebel Boers in the north-east district. This detachment was ordered to proceed as quickly as possible, but on arriving at Botha's Drift, it was found that the Great Fish River was in full flood, and there was no means of conveying the men across; so, after waiting two days, and finding it did not go down, Captain Rawstorne determined to try and ford the river. He first allowed a sergeant named Grant (promoted ensign in 1858), who volunteered to do it, to swim across and show that it was feasible; he then ordered the men to fall in and march down to the drift. The third man (Fraser) who entered the water was swept away, but Sergeant Grant immediately jumped in, and succeeded in bringing him to the bank a long way down the river. Another soldier, Private J. Hillyard, seeing that Grant was in difficulties, as Fraser was insensible, went to the rescue; but he no sooner reached them

1848. than he fainted, and Grant was left with two on his hands, and had to cling to a root in the bank, which was too high and perpendicular for him to get out alone. The three were, after a time, safely hauled out with a rope. The remainder of the detachment crossed in safety, and were eventually joined by other detachments under Lieutenant Owgan from Fort Beaufort, and Ensign Crampton from Fort England, the strength of the whole party being—1 captain, 5 subalterns, 7 sergeants, 2 drummers, and 153 rank and file. The entire force that Sir Harry Smith had with him was in light marching order, being composed of the two companies of the 91st above mentioned, two companies of the 45th, two companies of the Rifle Brigade, two squadrons of the Cape Mounted Rifles, and two 6-pounders. On arrival at the Orange River, it was found that it was also in flood and unfordable, and the means of crossing was limited to two indiarubber pontoons; however, a boat was discovered moored under the trees on the far side of the river, the only difficulty being how to get at it, as it was guarded by some of the Boers. Two men of the 91st—Hillyard, already mentioned in the account of crossing the Great Fish River, and Thomson—

volunteered to try and capture it. They swam the river at midnight, and managed to bring back the boat without disturbing the Boer sentinel. With the assistance of the boat the two pontoons were attached to ropes and made to work backwards and forwards, by which means the whole force and its baggage were carried over in four days.

After the troops had crossed, Captain Rawstorne remained on the Orange River, with a party of men of the 91st, to guard the drift, and keep open communication with the colony. On the 27th of July the troops started at daylight, and after a march of twenty miles encamped on the plains near Philippolis at Beulois Hoek. While marching at daybreak on the 28th, swarms of grey locusts were encountered, almost obscuring the sky. Passing Philippolis, a village of the Griqua Kaffirs, the force after a twenty-mile march encamped for the night, continuing the march at dawn on the 29th. After proceeding ten miles, a halt was made at some deserted farm-houses for breakfast. These houses were situated on the slope of a hill overlooking an extensive plain called the Boemplaats, which extending some miles, was terminated by a range of low

1848. rocky hills rising one above the other; through these hills the road wound, and on them the Boers had taken up their position, adding to its natural strength a breastwork of piled stones. While at breakfast, tidings reached the force that they were soon to meet the enemy, and resuming the advance at 11 o'clock, they arrived at the foot of the hills between 1 and 2 p.m. The Boers received them with a heavy fire. The Cape Corps attempted to turn the position, the riflemen and 45th Regiment in extended order then advanced, and on the third and highest crest the Boers rallied, and delivered a telling fire. The 91st remained with the guns till the rebel Boers advanced to turn their left, and attack the guns and waggons. The 91st were then ordered to fix bayonets and charge, which they did, causing the enemy to retreat in the greatest confusion. After two hours' hard fighting, the Boers fled, the guns coming to the front with their fire in the pursuit, which was continued for about eleven miles, until, from sheer inability to proceed further, the troops halted at Culverfontein for the night, the wounded being left at Boemplaats. At 10 o'clock the tents arrived and the troops encamped. Twenty-six miles had been marched, a smart action had been fought, and the enemy pursued; but the men had not long to rest. At 1 a.m. on the 30th they paraded, and at 2 o'clock, leaving all that could impede the rapidity of the march, they were again following the Boers. About daylight Welman Pass was reached, where it was thought the enemy might make a stand, but they never attempted to rally after their defeat. Lieutenant Pennington's name was mentioned by the commander-in-chief in his despatches, as commanding on that occasion the detachment of the reserve battalion which shared in the praise bestowed by his Excellency on the troops. The other officers of the reserve battalion who were present were: Lieutenants Owgan and Mainwaring, Ensigns Whittle and Crampton, and Surgeon Power. Lieutenant Owgan was hit with a spent ball, and Ensign Crampton sustained a fracture of the arm; five privates of the battalion being also wounded.

In the expedition thus concluded, the troops had marched between 1100 and 1200 miles, besides crossing rivers. On the 4th of September, before returning to Grahamstown, one burgher and one deserter were tried before a general court-martial, of which Lieutenant Owgan was a

1848. member, and were sentenced to be shot in the presence of the troops. The companies returned to Grahamstown on the 15th of October. After the events above named, the head-quarters of the battalion remained at Fort England and Drostdie Barracks, Grahamstown, for upwards of two years, sending out detachments to perform the ordinary outpost duties of the frontier.

CHAPTER XI.

Kaffir War, 1851–53—Reserve Battalion.

THE second Kaffir war broke out at the end of 1850, when every available man was required for active operations in the field. The reserve battalion of the 91st marched *en route* to Fort Hare on December 12th, and on the 26th a small detachment, under Lieutenant Mainwaring, marched from that fort to patrol the vicinity of the "military villages," about six miles distant. Among the arrangements for the protection of the colony, a force was organized in 1848, by placing soldiers discharged from various regiments, including the 91st, on certain grants of land in British Kaffraria, and thus forming military villages—the idea being that each man so located should be rationed at the public expense for the first year; seed, corn, and implements of husbandry to be found for the tillage of the land; each portion to consist of twelve acres with the

1850.

1850. right of common; to every ten men a span of oxen, and to every twenty a waggon. While actually serving they were to receive half a crown a day, with their other allowances; each village to be superintended by a retired military officer armed with magisterial authority. By this means it was expected that land would be cultivated and men provided for, who would invite their friends from England to join them, and at the same time a force would be ready at hand to check the inroads of hostile Kaffirs. The villages were named Woburn, Ely, Johannisberg, and Auckland. As Kaffirs were observed to be assembling in force in this district, a reinforcement from Fort Hare was sent for; on the arrival of which, under the command of Lieutenant Melvin, the patrol proceeded across the country to the Tyumie missionary station, where it halted for a short time, and offered to escort the missionary to Fort Hare, but he declined. On the patrol leaving the missionary station, a fire was opened on its rear, which was kept up until the party got in sight of Fort Hare, when a company was sent out to assist.

On the 29th of December a detachment of 150 men of the 91st, led by Colonel Yarborough, marched towards Fort Cox, under Colonel Somerset, for the purpose of opening a communication with the commander of the forces, who was surrounded by the enemy, and of throwing in a supply of cattle for the troops.

The officers of the regiment who went with this party were Captain Campbell, Lieutenants Melvin and Borthwick, and Adjutant Gordon.

When nearing the Yellow Woods River, the Kaffirs opened a heavy fire upon this force. Two companies were then thrown out in extended order, and advanced till they reached the base of the hill which surmounts the Umnassie, where a formidable force of the enemy had taken up a position behind the rocks which skirt the summit of the hill. It was then found necessary to retire, the Kaffirs endeavouring to outflank and cut off the retreat. A reinforcement of 100 men was sent from Fort Hare under Ensign Squirl of the 91st, to the assistance of the patrol, which enabled it to return to the fort after a severe struggle, in which Lieutenant Melvin, Lieutenant and Adjutant Gordon, and twenty men were killed, and Lieutenant Borthwick, two sergeants, and sixteen men were wounded, two of the latter dying of their wounds. The wounds in

1850. nearly every case were caused by the assegais. The loss of the enemy was over two hundred left dead on the field.

Lieutenant Gordon, who left a widow and five children, met his death in the following manner. It appears that when Lieutenant Borthwick was wounded in the cheek, and began to feel faint from loss of blood, so that he was unable to keep up with his men, the adjutant (Gordon) dismounted and put the wounded officer on his horse, and afterwards he himself from fatigue fell too much to the rear and was assegaied, several of the men who attempted to recover his body being killed. Six months afterwards a detachment of the 74th Highlanders passed the spot, and an officer of that regiment, in describing the place, says, "The ground, a thorny valley, still bore marks of the struggle of the 29th of December—rags of uniform and old forage caps, with bones of Kaffirs scattered about, while from the graves of the soldiers bones were protruding, scratched up by jackals and hyenas, which we carefully buried again in the best way we could."

1851. On the 5th of January the following order was issued from head-quarters, King William's Town:—"The Commander-in-Chief desires to express his admiration of the gallant conduct of the detachment of 150 men of the 91st Regiment, under Lieutenant-Colonel Yarborough, on the 29th ultimo, led by the gallant veteran Major-General Somerset, in action with a very superior force of the enemy. The steadiness of the troops under the disadvantages of the ground, the heat of the weather, and the vast numerical superiority of the enemy, shows well the effect of discipline combined with bravery; and his Excellency assures Lieutenant-Colonel Yarborough and the officers and soldiers respectively, that he will not fail to submit to his Grace the Duke of Wellington, to be laid before her Majesty, the gallant and meritorious conduct displayed by them on the 29th. Major Forbes, 91st Regiment, moving the detachment to meet Major-General Somerset, was a soldier-like and judicious act."

On the 7th of January Fort Beaufort, in which was a small detachment of the 91st under Captain Pennington, was attacked by a numerous force of Kaffirs under the chief, Hermanus. On the 10th the following order was issued from head-quarters, King William's Town: "The Commander-in-Chief congratulates the whole colony on the signal victory obtained over the numerous rebels

1851. under the traitor Hermanus, by the efforts of the united burghers and regular forces. The detachment of the 91st Regiment was, however, very judiciously kept in reserve. Hermanus was killed in the square of Fort Beaufort. The importance of the victory at a moment when the rebels and the coloured classes had gained some ascendency is incalculable, and demands our gratitude to Almighty God." Signed, W. G. Maydwell, military secretary.

On the 24th of February Lieutenant-Colonel Yarborough, Brevet-Major Forbes, Captain Campbell, Lieutenant Mainwaring, Ensigns Borthwick, Squirl, and Bruce, Surgeon Hand, Quarter-Master Paterson, sixteen sergeants, nine drummers, and 345 rank and file, were present at Fort Hare when the enemy in force, from 5000 to 7000, endeavoured to capture the Fingoes' cattle. Ensign Squirl and 100 men were sent to repel the enemy's advance, a duty which was successfully performed.

For the next few months the regiment furnished frequent detachments for the performance of patrol duty, which required considerable tact, and was attended with great danger. It was on one of these occasions, June the 27th, when a detachment of the 91st, commanded by Captain Middlemore, was with Colonel Eyre's division, that Ensign Pickwick and one private were wounded.

A detachment under command of Major Forbes, accompanied by Lieutenants Mainwaring and Crampton, Ensign Bruce, and Assistant-Surgeon Barclay, nineteen sergeants, three drummers, and 100 rank and file, went to the Amatola Mountains on the 24th of June, under command of Major-General Somerset, and was engaged with the enemy on the 26th, 27th, and 28th, and on the 2nd of July. A general order was issued on the 3rd of July, in which the commander-in-chief spoke in high terms of the conduct of the troops on this occasion, when the operations were crowned with signal success, and the complete discomfiture of the enemy; 2200 head of cattle and fifty horses fell into the hands of the troops, while the enemy were driven with considerable loss from every one of the strong and insurmountable passes they attempted to defend. "The accuracy and energy with which Major-General Somerset carried into effect with the 1st division (to which the 91st belonged) the part assigned to him in the complicated and combined movements, deserved the Commander-in-Chief's highest praise. His column sustained the chief opposition of the enemy, principally composed of rebel Hottentots, who resisted our troops with great determination." Previous to this, on the 6th of June, Captain Cahill, of the 91st Regiment, with Lieutenant Rae and a small detachment, joined a patrol under Lieutenant-Colonel Mitchell, which was attacked by a body of the enemy at Fort Wiltshire. It joined Colonel M'Kinnon's division on the Debe, captured a number of cattle and horses, and patrolled Seyolo's country, returning to Fort Peddie on the 12th.

The enemy, taking advantage of Major-General Somerset's absence from Fort Hare, on the 14th of June, assembled their bands in the neighbourhood, with the intention of carrying off the Fingoes' cattle. Lieutenant-Colonel Yarborough promptly despatched all the Fingoes, supported by 160 men of the 91st under Lieutenant Mainwaring, for the protection of the herds. The Fingoes gallantly attacked the Kaffirs, completely routing them, killing fifteen of their number, and recapturing the whole of the cattle.

On the 8th of August a detachment of the 91st, under Lieutenant Rae, proceeded from Fort

Peddie to escort cattle and waggons to Gentleman's Bush, and, after handing them over, returned and joined a patrol under Lieutenant-Colonel Mitchell. The patrol on the following morning marched to Kamnegana heights, and on arriving there lay concealed till 9 a.m., and, afterwards descending to reconnoitre, were nearly surrounded by the enemy. On this occasion the life of Major Wilmot, R.A., was saved by Sergeant Evan Ferguson of the 91st. The patrol retired, and attacked the enemy again on the following morning, returning to Fort Peddie on the 11th. On the retiring of the patrol, Lieutenant Rae had a narrow escape, a musket-ball having struck a stone on which he was standing.

From October the 13th to the 23rd a detachment of the 91st, consisting of 318 of all ranks, under Lieutenant-Colonel Yarborough, accompanied by Captain Middlemore, Lieutenants Mainwaring, Pickwick, and Squirl, Ensign Ricketts, and Adjutant W. Gordon and Assistant-Surgeon Barclay, was engaged with the enemy in a series of combined movements at the Waterkloof, and also on the 6th and 7th of November. On the night of the 13th, the force had encamped on one of the sprints of the Kaal Hoek River,

1851. and General Somerset, who had commanded the expedition, writes, "Marched out at 1 a.m.; very thick fog; gained the ascent above Bush Nek by 5 a.m. At 7 a.m. moved to the bush at the head of the Waterkloof; observed the enemy in force along the whole face of the ridge. At 7.30 I observed Lieutenant-Colonel Fordyce's brigade on the opposite ridge; moved up Lieutenant Field's guns, and opened on the enemy, who showed at the Blinkwater. Ordered Lieutenant-Colonel Mitchell's brigade forward, and sent a squadron of the Cape Mounted Rifles and two battalions forward, directing a strong body of skirmishers to be thrown into and line the forest. These were immediately received by a great fire from the enemy at several points. This sharp attack drove the enemy from their position, which they evacuated, and retired into Blinkwater and Waterkloof. The enemy continued to show themselves; I reinforced the skirmishers with two companions of the 91st, dismounted a troop of the Cape Mounted Rifles, and ordered the whole to push through the ravine and communicate with Colonel Fordyce's brigade, and to order them through. This movement was well effected. In the mean time the enemy continued their efforts to annoy us. Having brought the brigade through, and the enemy being beaten, and all the troops being under arms from 1 a.m., I retired to form camp at Mandell's farm, leaving one squadron, one battalion, and two guns of the Royal Artillery to cover the movement. On commencing our move, the enemy came out in great force, and opened a great fire, following the rear guard. The enemy were driven off. The troops encamped at Mandell's farm at 5 o'clock, after being under arms for eighteen hours."

The fighting continued almost without intermission up to the 7th of November, the loss to the regiment being one private killed, and Ensign Ricketts, who was dangerously wounded on the 14th of October by a ball in his chest; he managed to keep alive at Port Retief, where he was carried from Waterkloof, until the 8th of November, when he succumbed, and was buried at that place by the side of Colonel Fordyce of the 74th Regiment.

In all the operations of the succeeding days in and around the almost inaccessible Waterkloof, the 91st Highlanders continued to render the most important services. On the 31st of October a general order was issued, signed by Quarter-

1851. master-General A. J. Cloete, in which the commander-in-chief recorded his high opinion of the conspicuous gallantry and enterprise displayed on the part of the officers and soldiers. The fatigue of the operations, which continued from day to day with little intermission, was endured with that spirit that animates the soldier and leads him on to victory. Every Kaffir in Kaffirland and upon its borders believing the positions held by them to be impregnable, the enemy fought each day with the most determined bravery, yielding the ground he fought on to physical force alone. Such an enemy, the order continued, could not be fought day after day without loss on our side, while that of the enemy, from the superiority and rapidity of the firing of the troops, was known to be very great. The country recently held by Macomo's force, and comprising a mountain range of twenty square miles—a mountainous country intersected by almost impassable forests and ravines—afforded shelter for an innumerable force, protected by immense ridges and rocks, every one of which afforded a strong position. In this order his Excellency specially noticed the gallant conduct of Colonel Yarborough amongst other officers of the force.

On the 30th of December, Lieutenant Mackenzie and one sergeant and seventy rank and file joined a patrol under Major Wilmot, R.A., which proceeded from Fort Peddie to the Goga, where it arrived at daylight on the following morning. The patrol lay concealed in the bush until the morning of the 1st January, and then proceeded to the Kamnegana, scouring the bush and destroying a number of huts. On entering a path lined on both sides with huts, the patrol commenced to destroy them, and was vigorously opposed by the Kaffirs, who commenced a heavy fire on its advance. Here Major Wilmot was killed by a musket-ball fired from one of the huts. Lieutenant Mackenzie immediately assumed command of the patrol, which was between three camps occupied by the enemy, when he found it necessary to retreat to Fort Peddie, carrying Major Wilmot's body with him. On the 26th of January, 1852, a detachment of 416 of all ranks of the 91st, under Lieutenant-Colonel Yarborough—who had the following officers of the regiment with him: Captain Middlemore, Lieutenants Mainwaring, Borthwick, Pickwick, Ensigns Bond and Hibbert, Lieutenant and Adjutant W. Gordon, Assistant-Surgeon Barclay, and Quarter-Master

1852. Paterson—marched from Fort Hare, and was employed in destroying the enemy's crops on the Amatola Mountains and Tyumie until the end of February, when it proceeded to Haddon. On the 4th of March the force proceeded to the Waterkloof, and was engaged in a combined movement against the Kaffirs from daylight on that morning until evening, the casualties to the regiment being one sergeant and three privates killed, and Lieutenant-Colonel Yarborough, Ensign Hibbert, three sergeants, and twelve privates wounded; one of the sergeants and one private ultimately dying of their wounds.

When the force was returning in the direction of the camp, each regiment covered by a company in skirmishing order, that of the 91st was under Lieutenant Bond. This officer was very shortsighted, and by some means or other was separated from his men and was nearer the enemy than his skirmishers. Suddenly he was attacked by two Kaffirs armed, one of whom seized him by the coat. At that time men wearing only sidearms were always told off to carry stretchers for the wounded; one of these men—John Sharkie by name—suddenly saw Lieutenant Bond in the clutches of the savages: he rushed up, struck one of them on the head with his stretcher, killing him, and, drawing a butcher's knife which he carried in a sheath, plunged it in the throat of the other. Lieutenant Bond, who then realized the extent of his escape, coolly adjusted his eyeglass, which he always carried, looked steadily at Sharkie, then at the Kaffirs, and said, "By God, Sharkie, you're a devilish plucky fellow! I will see you are properly rewarded for this bravery" —and he kept his word.

Sir Harry Smith, in writing to Earl Grey, said, "Lieutenant-Colonel Yarborough, of the 91st, is a steady officer, and greatly distinguished himself on the day he was wounded;" and in reference to this occasion a division order, dated March the 5th, was issued by Major-General Somerset, from which the following is an extract: "A very superior force of the enemy was attacked in his strong position, his horses and cattle captured, and five large kraals and 150 huts of the rebel Hottentots and Kaffirs fired and destroyed. The movement was most ably and gallantly conducted by Lieutenant-Colonel Yarborough. The attacking of so strong a position as that held by the enemy, who, as the alarm was sounded, became greatly reinforced, could not be effected without loss; but while the Major-General deeply regrets the loss of the valiant soldiers, and the wounds of his gallant officers and men, he attributes the comparatively small loss to the manner in which the enemy was charged, checked, and driven back when pressing on in great force, although with every advantage of ground. The Major-General will bring the gallant conduct of the troops on this occasion under the notice of the Commander-in-Chief."

At this point in the history of the 91st, it is necessary to pass for a short time from the incidents of the Kaffir War, and narrate an action which furnishes one of the most glorious examples on record of the triumph of military discipline over the love of dear life itself.

On the 7th of January, 1852, the iron paddle troopship *Birkenhead*, of 1400 tons and 556 horsepower, commanded by Master Commander Robert Salmond, sailed from the coast of Cork, bound for the Cape of Good Hope, with detachments from the depôts of ten regiments, all under command of Lieutenant-Colonel Seton, of the 74th Highlanders. Altogether there were on board about 631 persons, including a crew of 132, the rest being soldiers with their wives and children. Of the soldiers, a detachment under Captain Wright belonged to the 91st. The *Birkenhead* made a fair passage out, and reached Simon's Bay, Cape of Good Hope, on the 23rd of February, when Captain Salmond was ordered to proceed eastward immediately, and land the troops at Algoa Bay and Buffalo River. The *Birkenhead* accordingly sailed again about 6 o'clock on the evening of the 25th, the night being almost perfectly calm, the sea smooth, and the stars out. Men as usual were told off to keep a look-out, and a leadsman was stationed on the paddle-box next the land, which was at a distance of about three miles on the port side. Shortly before 2 o'clock on the morning of the 26th, when all who were not on duty were sleeping peacefully below, the leadsman got soundings in twelve or thirteen fathoms. Ere he had time to get another cast of the lead, the *Birkenhead* was suddenly and rudely arrested in her course : she had struck on a sunken rock surrounded by deep water, and was firmly fixed upon its jagged points. The water immediately rushed into the fore part of the ship, and drowned many soldiers who were sleeping on the lower deck.

It is easy to imagine the consternation and wild emotion with which the hundreds of men, women,

1852. and children would be seized on realizing their dangerous situation. Captain Salmond, who had been in his cabin since 10 o'clock of the previous night, at once appeared on deck with the other naval and military officers. The captain ordered the engine to be stopped, the small bower anchor to be let go, the paddle-box boats to be got out, and the quarter-boats to be lowered and to lie alongside the ship. On coming on deck, Lieutenant-Colonel Seton, of the 74th Highlanders, at once comprehended the situation, and without hesitation made up his mind what it was the duty of brave men and British soldiers to do under the circumstances. He impressed upon the other officers the necessity of preserving silence and discipline among the men. He then ordered the soldiers to draw up on both sides the quarter-deck, the men obeying as if about to undergo an inspection. A party was told off to work the pumps, another to assist the sailors in lowering the boats, and another to throw the poor horses overboard. "Every one did as he was directed," says Captain Wright, of the 91st; "all received their orders, and had them carried out as if the men were embarking instead of going to the bottom; there was only this difference—that I never saw any embarkation conducted with so little noise and confusion."

Meanwhile Captain Salmond, thinking no doubt to get the ship safely afloat again and to steam her nearer to the shore, ordered the engineer to give the paddles a few backward turns. This only hastened the destruction of the ship, which again struck upon the rocks so that a great hole was torn in the bottom, letting the water rush in volumes into the engine-room and putting out the fires.

The situation was now more critical than ever; but the soldiers remained quietly in their places, while Colonel Seton stood in the gangway with his sword drawn, seeing the women and children safely passed down into the cutter which the captain had provided for them. This duty was speedily effected, and the cutter was ordered to lie off about 150 yards from the rapidly sinking ship. In about ten minutes after she first struck, she broke in two at the fore-mast, the mast and the funnel falling over to the starboard side, crushing many, and throwing into the water those who were endeavouring to clear the paddle-box boat; but the men kept their places, though many of them were mere lads who had been in

1852.

1852. the service only a few months. Besides the cutter into which the women and children had been put, only two small boats were got off, all the others having been stove in by the falling timbers, or otherwise rendered useless. When the ship had broken in two, she began rapidly to sink forward, and those who remained on board clustered on to the poop at the stern, all, however, without the least disorder. At last Captain Salmond, seeing that nothing more could be done, advised all who could swim to jump overboard and make for the boats. But Colonel Seton told the men that if they did so, they would be sure to swamp the boats and send the women and children to the bottom; he therefore asked them to keep their places, and they obeyed. The *Birkenhead* was now rapidly sinking. The officers shook hands and bade each other farewell, immediately after which the ship again broke in two abaft the mainmast, when the hundreds who had bravely stuck to their posts were plunged with the sinking wreck into the sea.

"Until the vessel disappeared," says an eye-witness, "there was not a cry or murmur from the soldiers or sailors. Those who could swim struck out for the shore, but few ever reached it;

most of them either sank from exhaustion, or were devoured by the sharks, or were dashed to death on the rugged shore near Point Danger, or entangled in the death-grip of the long arms of seaweed that floated thickly near the coast."

About twenty minutes after the *Birkenhead* first struck on the rock, all that remained visible were a few fragments of timber and the main-topmast standing above the water. Of the 631 souls on board, 438 were drowned, only 193 being saved; not a woman or child was lost. Those who did manage to land at Point Danger were Captain Wright and seven men, and, exhausted as they were, they had to make their way over a rugged and barren coast for fifteen miles before they reached the residence of Captain Small, by whom they were treated with the greatest kindness until taken away by H.M.S. *Radamanthus*.

Eight men of the 91st were saved in the three boats, which picked up as many men as they safely could, and made for the shore, but found it impossible to land. They therefore pulled away in the direction of Simon's Town. After a time they were descried by the coasting schooner *Lioness*, the master of which, Thomas E. Ramsden, took the wretched survivors on board, his wife

1852. doing all in her power to comfort them, distributing what spare clothes were on board amongst the many men, who were almost naked. The *Lioness* made for the scene of the wreck, which she reached about half-past two in the afternoon, and picked up about forty-five men who had managed to cling to the still standing mast of the *Birkenhead*. The *Lioness*, as well as the *Radamanthus*, took the rescued remnant to Simon's Town.

The appalling circumstances of the wreck were mentioned in a general order, dated Blinkwater, March 11th, in which it was stated that Captain Wright himself merited every encomium; that true valour was never better exemplified on similar awful occasions; and the bravery and gallant and soldier-like conduct with which the men had met their fate would be reported to his Grace the commander-in-chief. In the monument erected at Chelsea Hospital, by command of her Majesty, Queen Victoria, recording the heroic constancy and unbroken discipline shown on board the *Birkenhead*, and to preserve the memory of the officers, non-commissioned officers, and men who perished on that occasion, are the names of Sergeant Butler, Corporals Webber and

Smith, of the 91st Regiment; the names of forty-one privates of the 91st, as follows:—

Private	J. Birt.	Private	G. Kemp.
,,	J. Brian.	,,	F. Hackenley.
,,	J. Buckingham.	,,	J. Evans.
,,	W. Weybrow.	,,	A. Montgomery.
,,	T. Cavanagh.	,,	W. Matheson.
,,	D. Daily.	,,	J. Smith.
,,	J. Drury.	,,	W. S. Smith.
,,	H. Ford.	,,	P. Smith.
,,	P. Gaffey.	,,	W. Clark.
,,	J. Grant.	,,	J. Jarney.
,,	J. Moore.	,,	C. Wyer.
,,	W. Woodman.	,,	A. Winnington.
,,	G. Justier.	,,	P. Kelly.
,,	J. Moon.	,,	J. Delaney.
,,	W. Foster.	,,	A. M'Fadden.
,,	W. Measures.	,,	H. Hayward.
,,	W. Ledgwood.	,,	P. Hussey.
,,	J. Harpey.	,,	J. Sweeny.
,,	S. Haggan.	,,	D. Pratt.
,,	P. Haggan.	,,	T. Walsh.
,,	T. Jays.		

being inscribed on brass plates adjoining.

Captain Wright attributes his escape to having had in his possession a swimming belt and a clasp-knife. When the vessel sank he was carried down by the falling of the rigging, and although his jaw was broken thereby, he succeeded in cutting himself free with the knife, when the buoyancy of the life-belt brought him to the surface.*

On January the 26th Lieutenants Rae and Mackenzie, three sergeants, and seventy men joined a patrol under Major Kyle, 45th Regiment, at Tamacha, and destroyed the whole of the crops in Seyola's country, had several skirmishes with the enemy, proceeded from thence to King William's Town, where they arrived on the 24th of February, and from thence returned to Fort Peddie.

On the 10th of March a force consisting of two guns, four companies of the 74th Highlanders, 375 of all ranks of the 91st Highlanders, under Major Forbes, with the following officers: Captain Middlemore, Lieutenants Mainwaring, Borthwick, Pickwick, and Crampton, Ensign Bond, Lieutenant and Adjutant W. Gordon, and Quarter-Master Paterson; 150 Cape Mounted Rifles, and 200 Fingoes and burghers, was again engaged in the Waterkloof in a combined movement, in which ten men of the 91st were wounded, two of whom died of their wounds.

* In the "History of the Scottish Regiments, 1862," there is a picture of the wreck of the *Birkenhead*, illustrating the transferring of the women and children from the ship to the small boats.

In reporting these operations, the commander-in-chief said, "Lieutenant-Colonel Napier moved on the 10th up the Waterkloof Valley, and on entering the narrow and difficult ground near its head, it was evident that the enemy meditated an attack upon the rear, and Colonel Napier accordingly placed the 91st Regiment, under Major Forbes, in a position to resist it. This was most effectually done after a short fight, and Colonel Napier gained and maintained his position."

On the 17th of March the battalion, under Major Forbes, proceeded from Blinkwater, *en route* to Thomas River, with Colonel Napier's division, patrolling the country, capturing the enemy's cattle, and destroying the crops. The following extracts from a report of Colonel Napier, dated "Bivouac on Quantie River, 8th April, 1852," give some details of the work done by the force of which the 91st formed part :—

"I marched from the camp at Thomas River at 9 a.m. on the 5th inst., and encamped at the Quantie River at 4 p.m. Next morning I sent Captain Tylden's force, the whole of the mounted burghers and Fingoes, before daylight, to scour the country between the Thomas River and the

Kei, while I followed in support with the Cape Mounted Rifles, sixty of the 74th Regiment, 200 of the 91st Regiment, and the Kat River levy, leaving Captain Robinson, R.A., with a gun and 100 of the line, to take charge of the camp. At noon I perceived Captain Tylden on a hill to my front, and the burghers on another to my left, who made a signal (previously agreed upon) that they saw cattle and wanted support."

The cattle, however, were too far off to attempt to capture them that afternoon, and the infantry remained on the heights. The attack was resumed next day, when the Kaffirs were made to retreat, and a great quantity of cattle, horses, and goats were captured.

"The infantry under Major Forbes," the report says, "were not engaged with the enemy, but, from the judicious position the major took up, were of great use in preventing the cattle escaping from Captain Tylden."

The battalion returned to Blinkwater on the 16th of May, where it remained until the 30th of July. During the greater part of July operations were carried on against the enemy in the Waterkloof region, in which a detachment of the 91st formed a part of the force engaged. It was during these operations that an attack by a body of the rebels upon Elands Post was gallantly repulsed by a small detachment of the 91st under Captain Wright (the survivor of the *Birkenhead*).

1852.

The enemy appeared in considerable force, and manœuvred with all the skill of disciplined soldiers, extending, advancing, and retiring by sound of bugle. After endeavouring almost successfully to draw the little garrison into an ambuscade, they sounded the "close" and the "advance," and moved on to the fort. Captain Wright, with only twenty-three men of the 91st, then marched out to meet them, and, being joined by a party of the Kat River levy, drove them off with loss. The strength of the enemy was computed at 130 mounted and 200 on foot.

On the 30th of July the battalion marched from Blinkwater under Major Forbes, on an expedition, which lasted during the greater part of August, across the Kei to capture cattle from the chief, Kreli. The expedition was very successful, having captured many thousand head of cattle. The battalion returned to Blinkwater on the 30th of August.

On the 14th of September the battalion, under

1852. Major Forbes, marched from Blinkwater to unite with a force under his Excellency General Cathcart, to expel the Kaffirs and rebel Hottentots from the Waterkloof.

The 91st, under Major Forbes' command, was composed of Captains Cahill and Middlemore; Lieutenants Mainwaring, Crampton, Squirl, Borthwick, and Bruce; Ensigns Bond, Hibbert, Lane, and Thomas; Lieutenant and Adjutant Gordon; Assistant-Surgeon O'Neal, and Quarter-Master Paterson, with 406 rank and file.

The force, consisting of four guns and 3000 troops, having been concentrated in the neighbourhood of the Waterkloof, was so posted as to command every accessible outlet from the scene of the intended operations, which consisted of an irregular hollow of several miles in extent, nearly surrounded by precipitous mountains, the bases of which, as well as the greater part of the interior basin, were densely wooded. The arduous nature of the duty imposed upon the troops in dislodging such an enemy from such a position may thus be fairly imagined. Four companies of the 91st and Cape Mounted Rifles were posted on the northern heights of the Waterkloof, while another detachment of the regiment and some irregulars from Blinkwater were to move up the Fuller's Hoek Ridge; other troops were judiciously posted all round the central positions of the enemy. The dispositions having been completed, the several columns moved upon the fastnesses they were to clear, at daylight on the 15th.

An order, issued by General Cathcart, says: "The operations of that and the following day were conducted with unabated ardour and great judgment by the officers in command. The troops bivouacked each night on the ground of their operations, and pursued on the following day, with an alacrity which cannot be too highly commended, the arduous task of searching for and clearing the forests and krantzes of the enemy. These appeared to be panic-stricken, offering little resistance, but endeavouring to conceal themselves in the caverns and crevices of the wooded hills, where many of them were killed. The result of the three days' operations have been the evacuation of the Waterkloof and other fastnesses by the Tambookie chief, Quashe, and the Gaika chief, Macomo and his adherents, and the expulsion and destruction of the Hottentot marauders."

Among those especially mentioned by the

commander-in-chief was Major Forbes of the 91st.

The battalion returned to Blinkwater on the 20th of September, where it stayed until the 27th, when it proceeded to Fort Fordyce, sending out detachments to the Waterkloof, Post Retief, and other posts. The head-quarters remained at Fort Fordyce till the 10th of November, 1853, when it marched to garrison Fort Beaufort, where it remained till June, 1855, sending out detachments regularly to occupy various frontier posts. During the month of June orders were received to hold the battalion in readiness for embarkation to England; accordingly all the detachments were recalled to head-quarters. On the 5th of the following month a general order was issued by the commander of the forces, dated from Grahamstown, and was as follows:—

"The reserve battalion of the Argyll Highlanders is ordered to return home with every prospect of being speedily employed in the Crimea. The Commander of the Forces cannot permit the regiment to depart from South Africa, where it has so highly distinguished itself during a period of nearly twenty years, including the Kaffir wars of 1846, 1847, 1850, 1851, 1852, and

1853, without expressing his reluctance at losing a corps from under his command, which has served in this colony with so much credit and gallantry, and which has rendered such essential benefit to the frontier districts by the numerous roads which have been made by it. The Commander of the Forces, although not having had the honour of serving with the 91st Regiment during the late war, parts with these veteran soldiers with regret, and he wishes Major Wright (whom he has found a valuable officer), and the officers, non-commissioned officers, and soldiers, all happiness and success in whatever part of the world they may be called upon to serve their Queen and country.

  (Signed)   " E. S. SMYTH,
        " Deputy-Adjutant-General."

The inhabitants of Fort Beaufort also took leave of the battalion with expressions of the most sincere friendship, and presented the following address:—" To Major Wright, the officers, non-commissioned officers, and men of the 91st Regiment. We, the undersigned inhabitants of Fort Beaufort, impressed with a sense of the efficient services you have rendered to this frontier, during your protracted residence among us, cannot

1855.   allow you to leave this place without expressing our regret at your being removed. The harassing and extremely arduous duties imposed upon you during the last two most obstinate wars which have vexed this country, and the intrepid and inflexible manner in which those duties have invariably been performed by your brave regiment, have been such as will ever lead us to refer to them with feelings of extreme gratitude. We would also specially refer with thankfulness to the very great kindness and consideration evinced by your regiment in providing for the safety of our wives and families, by voluntarily relinquishing all your quarters to be appropriated as a place of refuge for them at a period when this town was threatened with a combined attack by our traitorous enemies. These and many other benevolent acts to which it would be needless for us to more especially allude, and which are too numerous to be embodied in this brief address, induce us to tender you our warmest acknowledgments, and trust that Divine Providence may protect you and your gallant regiment wherever duty may call you. We beg to subscribe ourselves, etc., etc." (Signed by nearly all the inhabitants of Fort Beaufort.)

In replying to this address, Major Wright "returned sincere thanks for the honour done to the regiment." He stated "that it was about fifteen years since the 91st Regiment first made its appearance in Fort Beaufort, and it was no slight gratification to find that all their exertions had been appreciated and acknowledged in so grateful a manner. He trusted the day was far distant when their peaceful occupations would be again interrupted by their border neighbours; and the 91st Regiment, which was now leaving, would always be glad to hear of the welfare and prosperity of the inhabitants of Fort Beaufort, amongst whom they had passed so many pleasant years of their lives."

1855.

In marching through Grahamstown, the battalion received a perfect ovation from the inhabitants, and from the other regiments stationed there. About the middle of the pass, which leads out of the town, a sumptuous luncheon had been prepared for officers and men by the residents, before partaking of which, however, the regiment was presented with an address in the name of the inhabitants. This was presented by Mr. G. Wood and Mr. R. Godlonton, members of the Legislative Council, and it expressed the high sense enter-

1855. tained of the services of the regiment, and stated that the protracted detention of the regiment in the colony and the eventful occurrences of that period had enabled the inhabitants to observe its high character, both in times of peace and of war; also that they felt a lively interest in the future of the regiment. Knowing, as they did, that the regiment was officered by gentlemen of the highest military qualifications, and that the men whom they commanded were conspicuous for their orderly and soldierly conduct, they felt assured that in whatever portion of the globe their services might be required, their deeds would add lustre to her Majesty's crown, and the country over which she reigned. In conclusion, they wished the regiment a prosperous voyage.

Loud cheers having been given, Major Wright, in reply, acknowledged the high compliment, which he knew was both deserved and appreciated by the regiment. This reply was received with another outburst of hearty cheers by the assembled civilians. From their long and arduous service the regiment had become so identified with the frontier, that, in parting with men with whom they were so familiar, the people among whom they had so long dwelt felt that they were bidding farewell to friends as well as defenders. That this feeling was reciprocated may be inferred from the fact that a number of the men who had obtained their discharge remained to cast in their lot amongst the colonists there. Those who returned did not number more than 294 men, and more would have remained had it not been for that gallant spirit which led so many to return in expectation of confronting the enemy in the Crimea.

1855.

The 91st embarked at Port Elizabeth, on board the *Penelope*, on the 30th of July, and sailed the same evening. The vessel touched at Simon's Bay to coal, arrived at Ascension to coal on the 23rd of August, at Madeira on the 15th of September, and reached Portsmouth on the 28th of that month. There orders were received for the battalion to proceed to Sheerness, and it finally disembarked at Chatham on the 29th of September.

On the 10th of November a letter was received from the Horse Guards directing a redistribution of the regiment into six service and six depôt companies, the term "reserve battalion" being thenceforth discontinued.

CHAPTER XII.

Redistribution of the Regiment—The name Reserve Battalion discontinued—Depôt companies' history to their absorption in 1857.

1855. THE order for the redistribution of the service and depôt companies on the name "reserve battalion" being discontinued was as follows:—The six service companies to consist of two field officers, six captains, eight lieutenants, four ensigns, five staff, and 650 rank and file. The depôt companies to have one field officer, six captains, six lieutenants, six ensigns, one staff, and 642 rank and file. The command of the
1856. latter was assumed in January by Lieutenant Colonel Bertie Gordon, who had been sent home from Greece from the old 1st battalion for this purpose.

At the end of March, medals were presented to ninety-one of the men who had served in the Kaffir wars of 1846–47 and 1851-52-53, the officers having received theirs for these services in the previous November.

On the 4th of April the depôt companies were moved to Aldershot, being placed in the " M lines, North Camp." The following are the names of the officers present on that date :—Lieutenant-Colonel Gordon ; Majors Rawstorne and Savage; Captains Conway, Gordon, Sweny, and Lane; Lieutenants Boehmer, Bond, Hall, and Pike ; Ensigns Burke, Allen, Tingcombe, and Brock ; and Assistant-Surgeon Franks.

On the 19th and 20th of the month her Majesty the Queen reviewed the troops at Aldershot, and on the 2nd of June the battalion assisted at the ceremony of laying the foundation-stone of the Staff College at Sandhurst, erected in honour of the late Duke of Wellington.

After inspecting the troops at Aldershot on the 16th of June, her Majesty visited the lines of the 91st, and stopping in the centre opposite the hut of No. 2 Company (Captain Lane's), she alighted and went inside, and asked the commanding officer many questions about the men, and on leaving the hut expressed her gracious satisfaction at what she had seen. Her Majesty was then shown the cook-house, which she entered and

1856. praised for its cleanliness and order, and noticed the excellence of the soup that was being prepared. Re-entering her carriage, she drove through the rest of lines at a footpace, while Colonel Gordon walked by the side, pointing out the various arrangements for the comfort and amusement of the men. In the afternoon the review was held from 4 to 8 o'clock, her Majesty and the Princess Royal being on horseback. The Queen wore a scarlet tunic with the riband of the Garter. Prince Frederick of Prussia was in attendance, and the German legion was on the ground for the first time. The following day Prince Albert manœuvred the division, at the termination of which the Queen drove down the line.

The following superscriptions were placed on the doors of the hut visited by her Majesty on the 16th:—

Front door—

"Her Most Gracious Majesty, the Princess Royal, and the Princess Alice visited the lines of Her Majesty's faithful soldiers of the XCI Argyll Highlanders, and deigned to enter this Hut, 16th June, 1856."

On the back door—

"Henceforth this hut shall be a sacred place,
And its rude floor an altar, for 'twas trod
By footsteps which her soldiers fain would trace,
Pressed as if the rude planking were a sod,

By England's monarch; none these marks efface,
 They tell of Queenly trust, and loyalty approved of God."

Orders were afterwards issued to the troops in camp, by direction of the Duke of Cambridge, calling attention to the manner in which the lines of the 91st camp were kept, and desiring that the same order and the same efforts to procure occupations and amusements for the soldiers might be made in other regiments. A strict order was at the same time issued to the Barrack department to maintain the inscriptions on the "Queen's Hut," as it was called.

On the 7th of July the lieutenant-general commanding at Aldershot (General Knollys) unexpectedly visited the lines of the 91st, and on leaving expressed himself highly satisfied; on the same day orders were received for the depôt companies to move at a moment's notice to Berwick-on-Tweed—and the same evening, her Majesty again visited the lines of the regiment, and stopped to read the superscriptions on the hut she had previously visited.

The next day the companies of the 91st left Aldershot, and arrived at Berwick on the 10th, having stopped *en route* at Peterborough and York.

1856.   In October the establishment of the regiment was altered to 1000 rank and file, of which the service companies had 800. This was again changed in December, when the service companies were reduced to 600 rank and file, while the depôt had 400.

1857.   The companies remained at Berwick until the 3rd of March, when they received orders to go to Preston to be incorporated with the depôt battalion commanded by Lieutenant-Colonel Smith, C.B. On leaving Berwick, the mayor and the sheriff expressed to Lieutenant-Colonel Rawstorne, who was in command, the general respect which the conduct of all ranks had inspired among the citizens, and the public regret which was felt at the removal of the 91st.

On arrival at Preston, two companies were ordered to embark in the *Minna* transport to join the service companies at Corfu; at the same time nearly 100 rank and file received their discharge, while the remainder, consisting of twenty-one sergeants and 206 men, were on the 30th of March incorporated with the depôt battalion at Preston. This closes the history of the old "reserve battalion;" for although they were not called by that name after 1855, the depôt companies were really the same battalion.

CHAPTER XIII.

First Battalion—England—Ireland—Malta—Greece—
Ionian Islands.

WE must now return to follow up the history of the 1st battalion, which was left at Gosport in May, 1848.

1848.

In October, 1848, Lieutenant-Colonel Lindsay retired from the service, having commanded this battalion for six years, including the Kaffir wars of 1846-47.

On the 1st of January Lieutenant-Colonel Campbell joined from the reserve battalion and took command. The regiment was moved during this month from Gosport into the Cambridge Barracks at Portsmouth. Nothing of special importance occurred for the next few months.

1849.

In September the battalion was engaged with the rest of the garrison in celebrating the fast-day, which was appointed to be kept in Portsmouth and the neighbourhood by the bishop of

1849. the diocese, on account of the cholera, from which the 91st were mercifully preserved. The rest of the garrison were, however, not so fortunate, and several succumbed to the dreaded epidemic. The men of the regiment came forward liberally with money on this occasion to assist the bereaved wives and families of their less fortunate comrades. The colonel and the medical officers were very watchful over the sanitary condition of the barracks during the continuance of cholera, and regimental games and amusements were established for the men; the officers were also mindful of their own health, and, by way of example to the men, bought an eight-oared gig, which, pulled by a strong crew dressed in regular rowing trim, made a good appearance amongst other boats. The crew was generally composed of the following officers:—Colonel Campbell, Major Gordon, Captains Wright and Patterson, Lieutenant the Hon. E. Sinclair, Ensigns Mackenzie and Pickwick, and Surgeon Munro, with Horsburgh (the lightest weight in the regiment) as coxswain.

1850. The next station the regiment was ordered to was Dover, where they went in April. The headquarters, under Lieutenant-Colonel Campbell, occupied the Heights Barracks, the following officers being also quartered there :—Captains Ward, Bayley, Patterson, and Cochrane; Lieutenants Bethune, Ussher, and Sinclair; Ensigns Stanton and Mackenzie; Adjutant Boehmer, Paymaster Dalrymple, Surgeon Forrest, and Quarter-Master Blackburne. In the Castle were Major Gordon (in command), Captain Savage, Lieutenants Owgan and White, Ensign Pickwick, and Assistant-Surgeon Munro.

1850.

While at Dover the battalion was inspected by Major-General G. Brown, C.B., K.H., adjutant-general to the forces, who ordered the immediate abolition of the bagpipes, which had been clung to as the last relic that remained of the origin, history, and nationality of the corps. At the end of the year the regiment received orders to move to the northern district. Accordingly the grenadier company, under Captain Bayly and Lieutenant Bethune, left for the Isle of Man on the 27th of December. Three days later, two companies under Captain Wright, with Lieutenant Cole, and Ensigns Pickwick and Battiscombe, and Assistant-Surgeon Peile, moved to Manchester *en route* for Liverpool. The day following, the head-quarters, under command of Lieutenant-Colonel Campbell, and the following

1850. officers—Captains Savage and Cochrane, Lieutenants Owgan, Ussher, Stanton, and Mackenzie, Ensign Spraight, Paymaster Dalrymple, Lieutenant and Adjutant Boehmer, Quarter-Master Blackburne, and Surgeon Armstrong—proceeded to Liverpool.

1851. In March a draft consisting of Captain Middlemore, Ensign Pickwick, two sergeants, and 100 rank and file, left for the Cape of Good Hope, to join the reserve battalion. Lieutenant Mackenzie left for the same place with a small draft in June. The regiment was moved to Manchester for a short time, previous to the embarking at Fleetwood for Ireland, in July. On arrival it was quartered at Belfast; and the draft of one sergeant and sixty men, under command of Captain Wright, was despatched from here in December to the Cape of Good Hope, in the ill-fated *Birkenhead*. The account of the wreck of this ship has already been given in another chapter.

The 91st did not remain long at Belfast, but during that time the officers and men won the respect and attachment of the inhabitants by their excellent behaviour, which was exemplified by the flattering address presented to them on leaving, which was signed by the mayor, the Earl of

Belfast, and about 200 of the magistrates, principal merchants, and professional men residing there. 1851.

Enniskillen was the next quarter of the regiment, which was reached in April. Here there were out-stations, namely, at Cavan, Ballyshannon, and Charlemont, and the regiment was continually being employed in the aid of the civil power. In September the army went into mourning for the Duke of Wellington; and on the occasion of reading the general order announcing his death, on a full-dress parade, the regimental colour was covered with black crape. 1852.

On the 11th a party of officers and men was sent to London to represent the regiment at the funeral. The names of those selected for this special duty were as follows:—Major Bertie Gordon, Captain Cochrane, Lieutenant Bruce, Colour-Sergeant McKay, Corporal Smith, Private James Murphy, and Private James Hunter. On the 17th the representative detachments of corps assembled at Chelsea Hospital, and marched past the body lying in state. The following day the detachments paraded at the Horse Guards, and marched in the procession to St. Paul's Cathedral.

In December 100 stands of the new Minié

1853. rifle were received by the battalion; at this time the men were armed with percussion muskets.

In March the regiment marched to Dublin by detachments, and was quartered in the Richmond Barracks. During its stay there, the Queen visited Ireland and held a review in the Phœnix Park, which was witnessed by an enormous crowd. Nothing else of special interest is to be recorded of the remainder of the stay of the 91st in Dublin, 1854. which was left in April for Cork.

Although the regiment did not take part in the Crimean War, it furnished a great number of men to the Highland regiments who took such a distinguished part in the contest, and also to the 50th Regiment, by which means it parted with some 250 of its best men.

In December the 91st received orders to hold themselves in readiness to go to Malta, and on the 15th they were embarked on H.M.S. *Saint George*, Captain Henry Eyres. The regiment on this occasion was composed of the following officers:—Colonel Campbell (in command); Majors Gordon and Scott; Captains Patterson, Howard, Mackenzie, and Battiscombe; Lieutenants Sweny, Macqueen, Dewell, Bruce, Wood, and Dobie; Ensigns D'Eye, Blackall, Gurney, Wade, Glass, Burton, and

Green; Lieutenant and Adjutant Boehmer; Paymaster Dalrymple, Quarter-Master Blackburne, Surgeon Murphy, and Assistant-Surgeon Watson; together with 649 non-commissioned officers and men, 30 women, and 51 children. The regiment was distributed on this old three-decker as follows:—The troops on the third deck, the women and children on the after-part of the middle deck, and the officers on the poop. The ship sailed the next day, and passed Gibraltar on the 23rd, after which she was becalmed for six days, and it was found that she was drifting on to the dangerous coast of Northern Africa. On the 1st of January it was found the ship was within ten miles of the shore. For nine days hardly any progress was made, and it was found the *Saint George* was then off the island of Pentelarie, when fortunately H.M.S. *Malacca* was sighted, and was signalled to come and tow the transport, which was done, and the ship arrived at Valetta on the 11th, the regiment being landed that afternoon, and sent to occupy the St. Elmo Barracks, the officers being placed at the Bavière. Here the 91st remained for more than a month, when they were embarked on board the s.s. *Emen* to be conveyed to the Piræus, in Greece, arriving there

1855. on the 23rd of March. The battalion landed in the afternoon in the boats of H.M.S. *Fury*, and those of the French squadron, the horses being swum ashore. The men were encamped that night on the racecourse, about a mile from the town of Piræus, where next day they took up their quarters in the miserable warehouses used as barracks, vacated by the 3rd Buffs in the morning. The command of the British force in Greece was handed over from Colonel Straubenzee to Colonel Campbell, which gave the command of the 91st to Major Gordon. The commandant of the French land forces was Colonel de Vassoigne. The whole allied forces were under the command of the French admiral, Le Barbier-de-Tinan, whose flag was hoisted on H.I.M. steam frigate *Gomez*, the French land troops consisting of two battalions of marine infantry and a few gens d'armes.

The accommodation allotted to the regiment consisted principally of buildings facing the harbour, which had been used as corn stores. They were very defective in every detail which is deemed necessary for barracks for British troops, and, owing to the difficulty of getting money from home at this period, and to the fact that it was not expected the regiment would remain long in permanent quarters, very little was done to improve them, besides the few things that the regiment did out of its own funds.

On the 14th of September the allied troops were paraded on the quay to celebrate the fall of Sebastopol, which had taken place on the 8th of the month. The 91st, with its colours, was on the right of the line. The ships in harbour, consisting of H.M.S. *Fury*, H.I.M. ships *Gomez* and *Salamander*, were dressed, and fired at noon a salute of twenty-one guns; the French half battery on shore then fired a salute of 101 guns. The troops presented arms and gave three cheers, after which the parade terminated by the French battalions, headed by the commandant, marching past the 91st, who stood at the shoulder, the Frenchmen, as they passed the front of the line in column of half companies, cheering their English comrades lustily.

On the 26th of September the French "Sous officiers" of the frigate *Gomez* invited the sergeants of the 91st to dinner, which was attended by Sergeant-Major Stewart and thirty-one sergeants, the guests being conveyed on board in the ship's pinnace. This invitation was given in return to a similar compliment paid to the " Sous officiers "

1855. on the 11th of the month, at which entertainment the sergeants of the 91st were honoured by the presence of his Excellency, M. Mercier (the French minister), and Vice-Admiral Jacquinot (who had replaced Admiral Le Barbier-de-Tinan), commanding the French naval division in the Levant, who both addressed the sergeants and their assembled guests. The chief of the staff wrote next day to Major Gordon, referring to the hospitality shown by his non-commissioned officers, as follows:—
"Dans la fête toute fraternelle qui les réunissait hier, L'Amiral Jacquinot s'en estimé heureux de se trouver auprès de braves gens qu'il honore, et de donner un témoignage de la haute considération qu'il professe pour la nation Anglaise, et en particulier pour les sergens du 91me régiment."

On the evening of the 5th of October it was reported that a French officer, Captain Bertrand, had been carried off to the mountains by brigands. Detachments of the French troops were immediately despatched in the direction of Phalerum Bay and towards the Hymettus range of hills, and Major Gordon, who was still in command of the 91st, ordered two companies of the regiment to start off at once under his personal command, to assist in the recovery of this officer. After a laborious pursuit over the rocks of Munycheum and through the sands of Phalerum Bay, searching every place, and finding no trace of the missing officer, the 91st party returned to their quarters. The French officer was given up on the 7th by the brigands, on payment of 1000 sovereigns in English gold, which amount was paid by the Greek Treasury. Captain Bertrand was an old and much-respected officer, and the result of his capture by these well-known lawless brigands was awaited with the greatest anxiety by his friends in the garrison.

Owing to the apprehension of future acts of brigandage, two picquets were established about a mile from the entrance of the town of Piræus, on the old and new roads to Athens. They were composed of one officer and fifty rank and file at each post, which were relieved monthly by the French and English troops alternately.

In December the regiment paraded with the French troops for the purpose of joint manœuvres on the plain under the Acropolis of Athens. The brigade thus formed was commanded by the French commandant, who for two hours executed brigade movements with complete success. After the parade, the 91st, having piled arms and packs,

1855. were marched up to the Acropolis, where the men were allowed to break off to visit the remains of the old citadel. Many wandered over the Parthenon, that beautiful relic of the art of ancient Greece, built nearly 2300 years ago. Great interest was shown when Mar's Hill was pointed out, and the spot where St. Paul addressed the court of the Areopagus.

In November the order was received from home directing that the division of the regiment into 1st and reserve battalions should cease, and that the companies of the 1st battalion should be called the service companies; the strength and detail of these companies has already been given in the beginning of Chapter XII.

During the stay of the regiment in Greece, the men were engaged in many useful occupations which were of great benefit to the district in which they were performed. Soon after their arrival at the Piræus, a detachment which had been sent to Salamis Bay, a place about three miles from head-quarters, constructed a road to it, built a small landing-place, and made other improvements which soon turned the camp into a cheerful and accessible spot. The great difficulty which had to be encountered was the want of proper tools, which were supplied from headquarters in a most stinted way, and consisted of only three spades and pickaxes; but by dint of persistant application, the officer in command (Major Gordon) obtained an additional supply from the Greek authorities. Amongst other useful works done by the regiment should be mentioned the re-construction and elevation of the whole parade ground on the quay, used by the battalion for drill purposes; also the raising, draining, and levelling of the streets in which the barracks of the men were situated.

Detachments were formed from time to time, to give the men a change from the defective accommodation supplied at the head-quarters.

In June the regiment was brigaded for a second time with the two battalions of French marine infantry, and took part in a field-day representing the battle of Islay, in Algeria, for which purpose a plan was furnished by the French rear-admiral (Count E. Bouet Willaumez, K.C.B.), commanding the expeditionary force in Greece.

The following February, it being known that the force of occupation was likely to be withdrawn soon, it was agreed for the French and English commands to hold a general parade of the allied

Marginal years: 1855, 1856, 1857.

1857. troops, on which occasion the rear-admiral addressed the regiments as follows:—" Officers and soldiers of the 91st, the time is near when we must part, and I now offer you my sincere thanks for your admirable discipline, and for your hearty support. In Greece, just as in the Black Sea, or before Sebastopol, English and French troops have proved the firmness of their alliance in the midst of circumstances of the gravest nature. A cheer, then, for the united flags of France and old England!"

On the 26th of the same month her Majesty's minister at Athens reviewed the regiment, and after the march past addressed them as follows:— " Officers and men of the 91st, I have witnessed your evolutions to-day with the satisfaction which every one must feel in seeing the exercises of British troops, amongst whom, I need not say, your regiment holds a distinguished place for efficiency and discipline. But you have other claims to praise of a special character. A British force has now occupied, in conjunction with French allies, this country for nearly three years, not invited, and yet not in the territory of an enemy—a difficult and often a very delicate position, requiring much firmness and circumspection. Both these qualities you have equally exhibited. You, and the regiments which have preceded you, have successfully accomplished the task for which you were sent here, and you have accomplished it in a manner in which brave men would naturally have accomplished it. Whatever may have been the misapprehensions with which you were received, you have vanquished them, and have won by pure force of good conduct and respect for others, the esteem and regard of the most reluctant. You have met from the inhabitants many acts of kindness and good-will, and in return, I am proud as yourselves to say, that not a single complaint of wrong done to person or property has reached me, or of any act which between you and the inhabitants would produce dissensions or disturbance. To this praise, high and deserved as it is, I have to add another. You were landed here not alone, you came with your French allies by your side; with them I need not say you have lived, as well as those before you, as brothers. Your remembrance of the time you have passed together must be one of continual harmony and mutual good feeling, without a word or deed for a single day to interrupt it. In a word, the occupation of Greece stands, I believe, unexampled in the history of occupations. It is an instructive example and lesson to all within its influence.

"But, as we are now soon about to part, I cannot take leave of you without pain as well as pleasure. I have only to add my sincere wishes that you may continue to add to the honours you have already acquired, and maintain everywhere, as here, the highest boast of the British soldier, respect for law and consideration for others. May you ever be united as you now are" (Admiral Willaumez, M. Mercier, and others of the French military and naval service and the French Legation were present), "and as you have been all this time, but one camp, as we of the civil service have been one legation. May you keep for years to come the union, so fortunate for all, indissoluble. You came here arm-in-arm, and arm-in-arm I am glad to see both officers and men, men and officers, now departing. Expressing anew my own personal acknowledgments, and, I may venture to add, those of our Governments, I wish each and all, with all my heart, a happy journey to your new destination, and all manner of prosperity."

Orders were received to embark in February.

During its stay in Greece, the regiment had to deplore the loss of one officer, Paymaster Dalrymple, who was killed by the fall of his house. His remains were buried in the plain just outside the town of Piræus, to the right of the road to Athens, in the same place as nineteen non-commissioned officers and men, who had died since the regiment landed. The graves were marked by marble slabs and monuments; and, on leaving, the place was committed to the care of the local authorities.

On the 18th of the month head-quarters and the right wing embarked on board H.M.S. *Majestic*, the left wing on H.M.S. *Cressy*. The French troops had left the previous evening on French war-steamers, so that the evacuation of Greece was completed on that date.

On arrival in the Ionian Islands, the head-quarters and part of the battalion were stationed at Corfu, while the remainder were detached to Vido, and other detachments were formed in April at Zante and Ithaca.

The following is a list of the officers who landed in the Ionian Islands with the regiment:— Colonel Campbell (in command); Major Patterson; Captains John Bruce, Battiscombe, Hibbert, and

1857. Rae; Lieutenants Dewell, Crampton, A. C. Bruce (adjutant), Wood, Dobie, Gurney, Barton, and Pike; Ensigns Blackall, Perkins, and Armstrong; Surgeons Murphy, O'Neal, and Watson; Quarter-Master Paterson.

Shortly after, Majors Gordon and Savage, Captain W. C. Gordon, and Lieutenant D'Eye, joined from England.

In September the head-quarters and four companies were ordered to Cephalonia, where they arrived on the 6th, and disembarked at Argostoli, and encamped on the esplanade. Small detachments were furnished to Lixuri and Fort St. George, the former being the second town of the island, with a population of above 5000. It is on the northern side of Argostoli Bay, about twenty miles distant by road. Fort St. George is about five miles inland; it was an ancient Venetian fortress, and crowns a lofty and isolated hill. There is a small town close to its walls, in which many large old houses attest the former importance of the place.

While the 91st were quartered in the Ionian Islands, they were employed in the construction of many useful works. Among these was an approach to the esplanade at Argostoli, in the shape of steps upon a large scale, formed from the materials of a useless five-gun battery, which work was described by a resident of Cephalonia as a "great public improvement;" it was named the "Argyll Steps."

During the twelve months that the regiment furnished a detachment at Zante, they executed the following works:—Two rifle ranges, one on the shore near the city of Zante, and the other about three miles off, on the shore of a bay facing Cephalonia. They renovated the burial-ground used by the garrison, and repaired all the roads within the castle, and constructed two skittle alleys.

Nothing of much interest is recorded of the regiment during the remainder of its stay in the islands. Orders to proceed to India were received on the 26th of June.

CHAPTER XIV.

India.

1858. The regiment having received orders to proceed to India by the overland route, embarked at Corfu on H.M.S. *Perseverance*, sailing on the 5th of September, 1858, to Alexandria, where they arrived on the 8th of the same month. The strength of the regiment on board was twenty-nine officers and 785 non-commissioned officers and men.

On the 18th the head-quarters with the right wing, composed of five and a half companies, were disembarked, and were at once entrained to be conveyed to the station nearest Suez, which was at that time about seventeen miles distant from it.

Arriving at daybreak on the 19th, they found a hot meal provided, consisting principally of Irish stew, which having been disposed of, the men were paraded to start on their ride to Suez on donkeys.

The animals were drawn up in sections of thirty rank entire, and the mode of mounting was: the men were paraded in rear of their donkeys, and when ordered to mount, scrambled up over their tails. Each section then advanced to thirty yards interval, with 100 yards between companies, the pace being at the rate of about four miles an hour, and there being two halts during the march at the post stations.

Before the regiment had disembarked at Alexandria, the arms and accoutrements had been packed in boxes, on account of the arrangement which had been made by the British Government and the Khedive, that troops taken through his country should proceed only as private individuals.

The colours were in charge of Ensigns Hamilton and Grant, and were conveyed across the seventeen miles of desert in a van drawn by horses; the sick being carried in the same manner.

The men were dressed in white duck frocks and trousers, with covers to the forage caps; the chacos had been left at Corfu by special authority. The knapsacks were placed in sacks and conveyed on camels, all the impedimenta had been sent on a day previous to the march of the men, so that they found everything ready to embark on arrival.

1858.   The left wing crossed Egypt in a similar way, and were embarked, under command of Major Patterson, on board the East India Company's ship *Zenobia*, commanded by Captain Manners (whose brother, Douglas Ernest Manners, had previously served in the regiment). The right wing embarked on board the East India Company's ship *Feroze*, together with the head-quarters, under Colonel Campbell.

In a typical song describing the voyage, journey, etc., from Corfu to India, the following lines appeared :—

> "Number seven was the troop of all others made the show,
> With gallant Baillie at their head, how they make their donkeys go!"

This novel mode of conveyance, by means of donkeys, across the Suez desert, had been used by the 46th Regiment a few days previous to the 91st trip.

The vessels conveying the regiment coaled at Aden, where the great heat necessitated the landing of the left wing during the detention of three days, and the regiment arrived at Bombay on the 7th and 9th of October, being reunited at Poona on the 11th.

The names of the officers who had embarked

at Suez with the regiment were as follows:— 1858.
Colonel Campbell, C.B.; Majors Patterson and
Savage; Captains Battiscombe, Rae, Lane, Squirl,
Bond, and Thomas; Lieutenants Hall, Gurney,
Wade (adjutant), Pike, Blagg, Perkins, Armstrong, Burke, Tingcombe, Obbard, and Jones;
Ensigns Hollway, Buller, Baillie, Hamilton,
Spearman, and Grant; Paymaster Kysh;
Assistant-Surgeons O'Neal and Watson; and
Quarter-Master Paterson.

On the 21st Major Patterson assumed command of the regiment in place of Colonel Campbell, C.B., who was appointed to the command of a brigade at Tonghoo, in Burmah.

On the 3rd of November the 91st commenced its march to Kamptee, where it did not arrive till the 11th of the following month. They were clothed in a suit of cotton twill (loose tunics and trousers) of a light drab colour, which had been received from England before quitting Corfu.

During its march, while at Jefferabad, on the 20th of November, an order was received by telegraph from the commander-in-chief of the Madras army to leave a wing at Jaulna. The left wing, under command of Major Savage, accordingly returned to that place, where he was

1858. ordered to proceed with 200 men against the Rohillas; on their march they came across a field force under Brigadier-General Hill, from Hyderabad, that had been engaged two days previously with the insurgents, whom they had found shut up in a mud fort, where they were attacked by the native infantry, who, however, were not successful in driving them out. The insurgents had escaped during the night, being pursued by the Hyderabad Irregular Cavalry under Captain Nightingale (whose brother was serving in the 93rd) and Lieutenant Clogstown; the latter out-distanced the rest of the cavalry, and catching up the insurgents, rode straight in among them, killed several, and dispersed the remainder, for which gallant deed he received the Victoria Cross.

The remainder of the wing, under Captain Bond, were attached for a time to a force under Sir Hugh Rose, and were mounted on ponies. Major Savage did not rejoin the regiment with the
1859. left wing until the 25th of February, 1859.

On the 7th of March Lieutenant-Colonel Bertie Gordon arrived from England and assumed command; and on the 9th a small detachment, under Lieutenant Gurney, consisting of Lieutenant Armstrong and forty-three rank and file, proceeded to Chindwarrah, a village about eighty-four miles north of Kamptee. On the same day Captain Battiscombe marched a part of a field force directed on Mooltye and Baitool. On the 27th Major Patterson joined and took command of this force, having Lieutenant Hollway as his staff-officer, which remained out until the 18th of April. A similar field force was sent out on the 22nd of April, for a short time to the same districts, under command of Major Savage, with Lieutenant Perkins as staff-officer.

On the 7th of November, 1859, No. 1 company joined the irregular forces, the services of which were required to disperse a band of marauders which had for some time held defined positions in the hills between Chindwarrah and the Nerbudda River. These marauders were dispersed and their strongholds taken.

The first officer of the regiment who died in India was Lieutenant Obbard, who was attacked by cholera, and expired on the 24th of April, 1860, at Oomerapore. Some strong drafts arrived for the regiment in January and October of this year; the former commanded by Captain Gregg with two ensigns, Kemm and Roberts.

1859.

1860.

1861. In March, 1861, the wives and families of the non-commissioned officers and men arrived at head-quarters. On the 28th of August Ensign Roberts met an awful death through falling into a well at night, he having in the darkness mistaken his way. We should not omit mentioning that in the regimental orders of February, 1861, great praise was given by the commanding officer to two young soldiers of the draft—Privates J. Yorke and Robert Carson—for their devoted attention to the cholera patients of the draft that had joined the regiment. They were at their posts night and day. The gallant conduct of Private Griffin was also mentioned in orders for his plucky attempt to save the life of a comrade, who was drowned whilst bathing in a large tank. In August of this year Lieutenant-Colonel Gordon was promoted to be colonel by brevet. He had succeeded to the command of the regiment in November, 1860, on the promotion of Lieutenant-Colonel Campbell to the rank of major-general.

There had been for some time, in accordance with the regulations for the augmentation of the Indian establishment, two lieutenant-colonels to the 91st, Major W. T. L. Patterson having been raised to that rank on the retirement of Colonel Campbell.

On the 11th of November, 1860, Quarter-Master Paterson took his final leave of the regiment, which as a private he had joined in 1832, and from which he had never been absent from that date. He was with it in St. Helena, Africa, Greece, the Ionian Islands, and India, from which latter place he left as an invalid.

In February, 1863, the 91st left Kamptee for Jubbulpore, which it reached on the 19th, after a march of fifteen days. The regiment was now in the Bengal Presidency, and under the immediate command of General Sir Hugh Rose, G.C.B., then commander-in chief in India.

On the 6th of August Ensign Henry Robert Rolf died from remittent fever after an illness of eleven days, and was buried in the cemetery at Jubbulpore.

One of the chief events of the year 1864 was the restoration to the regiment of its original Highland designation, along with the Highland dress; the tartan trews, however, taking the place of their original kilt.

As far back as 1833 an ineffectual effort had been made to have nationality restored to the

1864. regiment. Colonel Gordon resumed the attempt shortly after he obtained command in 1854, and found a willing and powerful supporter in the Duke of Argyll, who was naturally anxious to have the regiment raised by his ancestors once more recognized by its original name of "The Argyllshire Highlanders." A copy of some of the letters on the subject are to be seen in the regimental records.

In 1859 he directed a letter to the Horse Guards, pointing out the Scotch origin of the regiment and the history of its losing the kilt and tartan, and asking that the corps of pipers might be re-formed; to which he received reply that his request could not be complied with.

In 1861 he again wrote, preferring like requests, and again giving a history of the dress of the regiment, and received in reply H.R.H. the Commander-in-Chief's regret that at present he was unable to entertain his requests. After this followed a correspondence with the Duke of Argyll, the end of which was, the authorities agreed to the regiment wearing part of the Highland dress.

In the same year the regimental dinner was first started, and was presided over by General

Hay, the colonel of the 91st. A Benevolent Club Fund was started in connection with it, having as its object, besides the annual social meeting of those who may have been long separated, the starting of a charitable fund, which could disburse small contributions in aid of any one who had been in the regiment, and whom misfortunes may have overtaken. *1864.*

In January, 1865, Colonel Gordon arrived at Jubbulpoor, and assumed command of the regiment. In December of the same year, the 91st left that station, and proceeded partly on foot and partly by train to Dumdum, which it reached on the 11th. While at this place Colonel Gordon's health broke down, and on recommendation of a medical board, he left India for Europe in October, 1866, handing over the command of the regiment to Major Battiscombe. *1865. 1866.*

After staying a year at Dumdum, the 91st were removed in January to Hazaareebagh. In November, Colonel W. T. L. Patterson rejoined and took command of the regiment. On the 1st of December the regiment set out again for Kamptee, which it reached after a long and tedious journey, partly on foot and partly by train, on the 26th of January, 1868. On the 2nd of April *1867. 1868.*

1868. Colonel Patterson assumed command of the Nagpore force, the command of the regiment devolving on Captain Squirl, who handed it over to Major Battiscombe on the 24th of April.

After eight months of Kamptee, the 91st got the welcome route for home, setting out in two detachments on the 7th and 8th of October for Bombay, where it embarked, under the command of Colonel Patterson, for Suez on the 12th, arriving at Alexandria by rail from the latter place on the 30th of October, on which date it sailed for Portsmouth in H.M. troopship *Crocodile*, and disembarked at that port on the 15th of November, proceeding by rail to Dover, where Colonel Bertie Gordon resumed command.

Fourteen years had elapsed since the regiment went on foreign service, and it is worthy of note, that during this long period in many different quarters, only ten desertions are recorded.

In August of this year the name of Colonel Bertie Gordon was placed on the list of officers receiving the reward of £100 a year for distinguished service.

CHAPTER XV.

Dover—Aldershot—Princess Louise's Wedding—Scotland—Ireland.

ON the 24th of August, 1869, new colours were presented to the regiment on the glacis of the western heights at Dover, by Mrs. Bertie Gordon, who represented the Duchess of Argyll, who was unable to be present, as she and the duke were at Inverary at the time.

Before the ceremony of consecration, Colonel Bertie Gordon addressed the regiment, informing them that their old colours were to find a home at Inverary Castle. The Archbishop of Canterbury, who was assisted by five other clergymen, then performed the service of consecration, concluding with a benediction composed for the occasion by the Rev. John Puckle, Canon of Canterbury Cathedral and Vicar of St. Mary's, Dover. The new colours were then handed to Mrs. Bertie Gordon by Majors Penton and Sprot, and by her

1869. given to Ensigns Lloyd and Gurney; Mrs. Gordon addressed a few appropriate words to the regiment, which were replied to by Colonel Gordon, after which the Archbishop gave an address beginning with a graceful allusion to his having been at school with Colonel Gordon, and to the fact that he claimed connection with the clan that wore their tartan. After a march past before General Brownrigg, C.B., the proceedings terminated, the old colours being carried by Ensigns Provost and Fallowfield, and the escort commanded by Lieutenant Grant.

The old colours remained in charge of the regiment until the 12th of October, when they were forwarded to their final destination at Inverary with suitable honours. Captain Burton's company, with band and colour-escort, took them to the station, where they were handed over to Lieutenant Grant and Ensign Craufurd, who were deputed to deliver them over to the Duke of Argyll. Ensign Gurney and four colour-sergeants were appointed as colour-escort as far as King's Cross Terminus, London; and guards of honour were given at Edinburgh and Glasgow, to meet and escort the colours on arrival and departure, by the 42nd Highlanders and 5th Fusiliers; and the two Argyllshire corps of the reserve forces were drawn up on the quay at Inverary to escort the colours from the steamer to the castle, where they arrived on the 15th of October.

1869.

It may be as well to record here the end of these colours, which were destroyed in a fire at Inverary Castle, on the 12th of October, 1877. The Marquis of Lorne wrote on the occasion to the colonel of the regiment, Lieutenant-Colonel Kirk, "Alas! for the old Flags, all we can hope to recover are the metal leaf-shaped heads of the staff, and they are perhaps melted. Besides the colours, all the arms used by our people in 1745 are gone."

On the 11th of November Colonel Gordon retired from the regiment, handing over the command to Major Sprot. His farewell order is dated, "Ellon Castle, Ellon, 29th January, 1870," and is as follows:—

1870.

"H.R.H. having been pleased to grant compliance with the request preferred by Colonel Bertie Gordon, to be permitted to retire on the half-pay of the army, Colonel Gordon bids farewell to the noble regiment in which he has served for more than seven and thirty years, and in which he has held command ever since April, 1855.

"Colonel Gordon's services in the 91st High-

1870. landers comprise exactly one half the period of its existence as a corps, and he has held command during a fifth part of its history.

"Years have gone by since every officer, non-commissioned officer, and private soldier, with whom he stood in the noble ranks, when he commenced his career in the army, have passed away. For twelve years Colonel Gordon has been the very last of the 800 who formed the Argyllshire Regiment of 1832, and in its ranks of the present day he leaves behind him but one soldier (Lieutenant Grant) who shared with him those hours of impending death, when he commanded the reserve battalion of the regiment in 1842, cast away on the shores of Africa, in that dark night of tempest, when its discipline and devotion came forth from the shattered wreck unbroken and undiminished by that sorest trial. Colonel Gordon calls to mind, that he has served under three stands of colours presented to the regiment, and that at the recommendation of H.R.H., he was permitted, by the favour of her Majesty, to announce to his old regiment, seven years ago, the restoration of that nationality in its designation and uniform, under which it was embodied by its ducal chieftain in the last century.

"Colonel Gordon believes that the time has come to retire from the regiment he has loved, and to leave its fortunes in younger and stronger hands. But although severed from its noble ranks, Colonel Gordon will still feel that the words of his regimental order of 1863 must ever prove true: 'The Argyllshire Regiment has ever served their sovereign and their country steadily;' while he calls upon all ranks to remember those that the late Lieutenant-General Sir George Napier addressed to the reserve battalion in 1842: 'Ninety-first, I have known you in camp and quarters, and I have seen you in action, and I have never known or seen a better.'"

1870.

Colonel Gordon did not long survive his severance from the regiment; he died on the 27th of July, 1870.

Before proceeding with the history of the regiment, a few personal details of Colonel Gordon's life will not be out of place. He was born at Auchlurries, Aberdeenshire, on the 17th of December, 1813, being a son of Alexander Gordon, of Auchlurries, afterwards of Ellon Castle, Aberdeenshire, and Albinia, daughter of Lady Albinia Cumberland. He was educated at Rainham, Kent, the Edinburgh Academy,

1870. and the Edinburgh Military Academy. At school he showed abilities above the average. He obtained his first commission in the 91st in 1832. The chief incidents in his military career have been related. He was a strict disciplinarian, and yet no officer could take more care than he of the personal comfort and welfare of his men. While in command he founded many institutions for their benefit; among others a gymnasium, reading-rooms, refreshment-rooms, dancing-rooms, and children's homes. He loved his regiment above everything, and was very proud of the high state of efficiency it attained.

Major Sprot succeeded to the lieutenant-colonelcy of the regiment on the 29th of January. In the following June, orders were received to proceed to Aldershot by road; the march commencing on the 18th, and Aldershot was reached on the 25th, after a most arduous march, owing to the excessive heat. On arrival the regiment went under canvas at Rushmoor Green, where they remained quartered until September, when they were removed into huts in G. H. and D. lines, North Camp.

In October, when it was first notified to the public that a matrimonial alliance would shortly take place between H.R.H. Princess Louise, fourth daughter of her Majesty, and the Marquis of Lorne, eldest son of the Duke of Argyll, whose ancestor had raised the regiment in 1794, Lieutenant-Colonel Sprot wrote the following letter to the Duke of Argyll:—

1870.

"It was with great gratification that we observed in the newspapers the announcement of the intended marriage of H.R.H. the Princess Louise with your eldest son, and I write in the names of the officers and soldiers of the 91st Highlanders, as well as my own, to congratulate your Grace on the auspicious event. We understand that the ceremony is likely to take place at Windsor early in the spring, and we venture to hope that the Argyllshire Regiment of Highlanders, which was raised by your Grace's grandfather, may be permitted to form a guard of honour at the wedding, where we shall be prepared to send 100 picked men with band, pipers, and full complement of officers from Aldershot.

"Trusting that your Grace will obtain for us this privilege, I remain," etc.

The duke replied that he would inquire her Majesty's pleasure as to the proposal.

1871.   It was not, however, till some ten days before the date fixed for the wedding that an order was received for a guard to be furnished.

On Saturday morning, the 18th of March, 1871, the guard of 100 picked men paraded under command of Captain Gregg, accompanied by Lieutenant H. Gordon Fallowfield, who carried the colour, the third officer being Lieutenant Grant, who had served twenty-eight years in the regiment. After being inspected, they marched off for Windsor, to the tune of "Haste to the Wedding," amidst the encouraging cheers of their comrades, reaching their destination at 4 p.m., having performed the distance of twenty miles in seven hours. The men were in full marching order, and carried their valises, and on arrival found that the Grenadier Guards had everything prepared for them; not only had they drawn rations and filled beds, but they had also cooked their dinners.

On Monday, the 20th, Colonel Sprot proceeded to Windsor, and was commanded by her Majesty to go to the Castle in order to present the wedding present which the officers of the regiment intended to give the Princess Louise.

The gift of the officers consisted of a brooch,

the facsimile of that worn by them to fasten their plaids, but in pure gold, with a handsome Cairngorm stone set transparently, together with a copy in miniature of the regimental dirk, suited for a shawl-pin. On the back of the brooch were engraved the names of all the officers then serving in the regiment.

1871.

The gift of the men, to which they unanimously subscribed, was a silver biscuit box, in shape of a drum, with the honours of the regiment engraved on the side, and an appropriate inscription on the head. It was mounted on a stand of Scotch bog oak, with silver corners and feet.

Colonel Sprot was accompanied at his audiences with the Queen by Lieutenant Grant, Sergeant-Major Fasinidge, and Pipe-major McDougal. After presenting the officers present to Princess Louise, Colonel Sprot explained to her Majesty that on the previous day it had been notified to him that the men of the 91st had unanimously subscribed towards a present, which had been got up entirely at their own suggestion, and he therefore requested her Majesty's permission to present it. Her Majesty, in reply, expressed herself greatly pleased and much touched with this mark of affection on the part of the non-commissioned officers and men.

1871.   At the ceremony, which took place on the 21st of March, the guard of the 91st was drawn up at the entrance to St. George's Chapel, Colonel Sprot being in command of the troops. The following day the guard returned to Aldershot, where, during the drill season, the usual routine of field-days and other duties were gone through. In July the Queen reviewed the troops, and sent a complimentary message to the general commanding on the smart appearance of the regiment at the march past.

In August the wedding present which the men were to give the Princess Louise was completed and forwarded to Inverary, where festivities in connection with the marriage were going on. The Pipe-major with three pipers were sent, at the request of the Duke of Argyll, to assist at the rejoicings.

In September the regiment received orders to proceed to Scotland. They accordingly left Aldershot on the 27th and 30th of September, in two detachments, and on arrival were quartered at Fort George and Aberdeen, having the headquarters, consisting of eighteen officers and 382 men, at the former station, while ten officers and 211 men were quartered at the latter.

Shortly after the wedding of H.R.H. the Princess Louise, her Majesty expressed a wish to confer some distinguishing mark on the regiment to commemorate the event, and desired that Colonel Sprot should be communicated with on the subject as to what the regiment should like. Colonel Sprot, after consulting with the officers, suggested the kilt, which proposal her Majesty readily accepted. The Commander-in-Chief was duly communicated with, as also the Secretary of State for War; but objections being raised by the former on the ground of the difficulty of recruiting for kilted corps, and by the latter on the increased expense of dress, the idea was for the time abandoned. This being made known to Colonel Sprot, he intimated that the corps would like to be designated the "Princess Louise's Argyllshire Highlanders," and bear on its colour the boar's head (crest of the Argyll family), with the motto, "Nil obliviscaris."

1872.

Accordingly, on the 2nd of April, the following notice appeared in the *London Gazette*:—

"War Office, April 2nd, 1872.

" Memorandum.

"Her Majesty has been graciously pleased to approve of the 91st Regiment (Argyllshire High-

1872. landers) being in future styled the 'Princess Louise's Argyllshire Highlanders,' and of its being permitted to bear on its Regimental Colour the Boar's head (the Campbell Crest), as a device, surmounted with the motto 'Ne obliviscaris,' with the Princess Louise's coronet and cypher in the three corners."

In June the regiment furnished the guard of honour at Ballater, during her Majesty's stay at Balmoral, Captain Stevenson being in command, with Lieutenants Fallowfield and Schank as subalterns; they returned to head-quarters at the end of the month, a second guard being sent in August, having Captain Alison in command, with Lieutenants Fallowfield and Craufurd as subalterns.

1873. In May the 91st were removed to Edinburgh, relieving the 93rd Highlanders (now its second battalion). In July the 58th Brigade Depôt was formed at Stirling, consisting of the 72nd Highlanders and the 91st. Major Kirk, Captains Barton and Robley, Lieutenants Fallowfield and Gurney, with thirty-three non-commissioned officers and men, formed the 91st portion, which left for Stirling on the 27th of the month.

In the course of this year a tablet was, by

permission of the Commissioners, erected in Chelsea Hospital, to the memory of Colonel Edward W. C. Wright, C.B., late of the 91st Highlanders. This tablet was put up with the joint subscriptions of officers who had served and were serving in the corps. It is a handsome mural brass, and bears the following inscription:—"To the memory of Colonel Edward W. C. Wright, C.B., late 91st Highlanders, and Deputy Inspector of Reserve Forces, who died 26th August, 1871, aged 57. Captain Wright was the senior surviving officer of her Majesty's ship *Birkenhead*, wrecked off the Cape of Good Hope on 26th February, 1852. For his distinguished service on this occasion he was promoted to the rank of Major, and awarded a good service pension. He was engaged in the Kaffir War of 1846-47 and 1852-53, for which he was granted the medal and promoted for service in the field to the rank of Lieut.-Colonel. This tablet is erected by his brother officers, MDCCCLXXIII."

1873.

In February, at the request of the Royal Scottish Academy of Arts, the regiment furnished a sentry at the entrance of their exhibition, for which service the academy presented the regiment with £10, which sum was expended in a hand-

1874.

1874. somely engraved bell, which has been since used to strike the hours throughout the day, and is kept under the charge of the sentry of the main-guard.

During the winter of 1873–74, the officers of the regiment hired the Assembly Music Hall once a week, and the band played there when too cold to play in the gardens. To defray the cost, a small charge was made at the doors for admission; this accumulated during the season to £42, with which sum a drinking-fountain, close to the cabstand at the castle gate, was erected.

In June the regiment left Edinburgh, and embarked on board H.M.S. *Tamar*, for conveyance to Belfast, which was reached on the 1st of July.

The head-quarters proceeded to Newry, sending three companies to Armagh and one company to Monaghan, one company being also sent to Newtownards for musketry. At the end of this year the Henry-Martini rifle was issued to the regiment.

1875. On the 31st of March the 91st proceeded to the Curragh.

1876. Colonel Sprot presented to the officers' mess, on the 1st of January, as a new year's gift, an old Masonic Charter, which had been granted to the corps, signed by "Athol, Worshipful Grand Master." The charter, which is dated London, 4th of March, 1801, gives permission to the 91st Regiment of foot, to form and hold a Lodge of Free and Accepted Masons at the Cape of Good Hope, or elsewhere, upon the second and fourth Wednesdays in every month.

On the 19th of January Colonel Sprot was appointed assistant-adjutant and quarter-master-general for the northern district, and the command of the battalion devolved on Lieutenant-Colonel Kirk.

In April the head-quarters moved to Enniskillen, leaving a detachment at Londonderry, where they remained until the following May, when the regiment was brought together again at Belfast, sending one company to Carrickfergus, under command of Lieutenant Tottenham. While quartered here, they were on several occasions called out to aid civil power.

After nearly a year the battalion moved to Dublin, to be quartered in the Royal Barracks. While stationed here, the strength of the regiment was augmented to over 1000 men, which was done by calling up the army and militia reserves, in consequence of the threatening aspect of affairs

1878. in the East. Four hundred and sixty-five men joined the colours in April and May; of these ninety were from the Highland Borderers, 175 from the Royal Renfrew Militia, and 200 from other parts of Scotland. The men called up were kept on until July, when they were allowed to return to their homes. Nothing of unusual interest occurred during the remainder of the stay of the 91st in Dublin, which they left on
1879. the 1st of January to go to Aldershot, proceeding from Kingstown in H.M.S. *Assistance* to Portsmouth, reaching their new quarters on the 6th, when they were placed in the permanent barracks.

CHAPTER XVI.

England—Natal—Causes of Zulu War.

On the 11th of February news was received in England of the great disaster in Zululand at Isandlhwana, where the camp of part of the troops under command of Lord Chelmsford was surprised by the Zulus, and the force nearly annihilated. This intelligence caused the Government to decide on sending out reinforcements at once, and among the battalions of infantry selected was the 91st, who were ordered to prepare for embarkation in the s.s. *Pretoria*, one of the steamers belonging to the Union Company, on the 19th of the month.

In order to bring the 91st up to the required strength, volunteers were received from the following regiments—viz. 2/5th, 1/8th, 1/10th, 2/19th, 2/20th, 32nd, 36th, 41st, 55th, 84th, and 108th, the total number required being 374 men. The last party of volunteers to arrive only joined on

1879.

the 17th. On the morning of the 18th, H.R.H. the Duke of Cambridge inspected the regiment in field-service order, after which they marched past in fours—the volunteers from other regiments, being dressed in their own uniform, gave the battalion a mixed appearance. After the men were dismissed, the Commander-in-Chief addressed the officers, congratulating them on the compliment which had been paid to the regiment, in its having been selected for this service, and expressing confidence that they and all ranks would sustain the reputation the regiment had always borne.

The battalion was on this occasion under command of Major A. C. Bruce, Lieutenant-Colonel Kirk having been compelled to put himself on the sick list, from a cancerous tumour in the right foot, from which he had been suffering for some months previously, and which resulted shortly afterwards in amputation of the leg above the knee. He was thus obliged with deep reluctance to relinquish, when almost within his grasp, this opportunity to proceed in command of his regiment on active service. In this heavy blow to his prospects as a soldier, Colonel Kirk met with the deepest and most sincere sympathy from all his brother officers and comrades in the 91st.

EMBARKATION OF REGIMENT AT SOUTHAMPTON.

On the morning of the 19th, the 91st, consisting   1879.
of thirty officers and 906 men, left Aldershot by
special trains for Southampton, being played
down to the station from the Permanent Barracks
by the 41st Regiment. The trains arrived at the
docks at about 11.30 a.m. and the men were
paraded on the quay facing the transport.

The s.s. *Pretoria*, Captain George Larmer,
which was the newest of the Union Company's
Cape fleet, had only arrived home eight days
previously, and in that short space of time had
discharged her homeward-bound cargo, been
docked and fitted with a new propeller, and had
all the necessary alterations made to convert her
into a transport ship. The main deck aft, with
the sleeping berths, remained in its usual state
for the use of the officers and transport officials.
The fore main deck, usually occupied with cabin
and state room for second-class passengers, was
entirely stripped of its fittings, and with the
orlop deck, fore and aft, ordinarily used for
goods, was appropriated and fitted up for troops.

The embarkation commenced at twenty minutes
to twelve, and was completed by twenty-five
minutes to one, the whole regiment having been
safely housed on board in five minutes less than

an hour. At five minutes past one, the last gangway was hauled ashore, and the *Pretoria* steamed slowly off, amid the cheers of an enormous crowd who had forced their way into the docks to bid the regiment God-speed. The transport anchored in Southampton Water, off Netley, and, after a final inspection, sailed in the evening about seven o'clock for her destination.

The names of the officers who sailed with the regiment were as follows:—Major A. C. Bruce (in command), Major W. P. Gurney; Captains G. Stevenson, J. Rogers, W. S. Mills, G. O'Sullivan, J. Boulderson, W. Prevost; Lieutenants H. Fallowfield, W. R. Craufurd, D. MacDonald, A. Tottenham, F. Cookson, G. Robbins, D. Fowler, G. Goff, G. Collings, H. Johnston; Second-Lieutenants T. Fraser, C. Richardson; Lieutenant and Adjutant J. St. Clair; Quarter-Master J. Gillies, and Paymaster W. Caudwell.

The voyage to the Cape was uneventful. Madeira was reached on the 24th, where the ship remained about six hours to coal; from there on, there was a fair-weather passage to Cape Town, which was sighted mid-day on the 12th of March. The *Pretoria* only stopped for twenty-four hours to coal and provision, and arrived outside Durban

on Sunday the 16th. The officer commanding, with the adjutant, went ashore to report arrival and receive orders, which latter were, that the regiment should disembark the next day. The disembarkation began early the next morning, but owing to the heavy swell, and the consequent difficulty in getting the tugs which were to convey the men over the bar alongside, there were still two companies left on board in the evening. However, the next day everybody had arrived in the camp, which was situated close to the centre of the town, on some waste ground. During the voyage the men who had joined from other regiments as volunteers had been dressed in 91st clothes, and the kits of the whole battalion had been thoroughly inspected and weeded in order that each man should go into the field with a kit in thoroughly serviceable condition, consisting of one serge coat, two pairs of trews, two pairs of boots, three pairs of socks, two towels, and one hold-all. The remaining articles were packed in waterproof bags to be left at Durban.

With the exception of the 57th Regiment, which had arrived from Ceylon two days previously to the 91st, the regiment was the first of the reinforcements to reach Natal.

1879.   The day after arrival, the Scotchmen of Durban formed a deputation to present an address to the regiment, which was presented by Mr. Jameson, a merchant of that town, and was as follows:—

"To Major Bruce, commanding 91st Highlanders.

"Sir,—The undersigned Scotchmen, residents of Durban, beg to tender you and your officers, non-commissioned officers, and men, a very hearty welcome to the colony. It affords us the utmost gratification to see among us, for the first time in our history as a colony, the tartans of our Highland soldiers, and to hear the familiar accents of our countrymen once more, reviving as they do associations of our native land, which we cherish as our most precious heritage. Our little colony yields to none of her Majesty's dependencies in loyalty to our Queen, and we welcome therefore at all times her uniform; but on this auspicious occasion we feel justified in doing more in extending to our countrymen of your regiment a particularly hearty greeting, which we beg you will convey in our name to all ranks. We are confident that if your services are brought into requisition in the field, the traditions of the 91st will be gallantly sustained by the officers and men under your command, and that in Zululand, another laurel will be added to your colours."

1879.

Attached were the signatures of over seventy of the leading Scotchmen of Durban.

Major Bruce, in a few words, thanked the deputation for their address and the compliment they had paid to the regiment.

Before commencing the account of the movements of the 91st during the Zulu War, it will be interesting to give a short history of the nation and the state of affairs which brought about the war.

About 1820 a Zulu king called Chaka conquered all the surrounding tribes, and converted their chiefs into his own vassals. Chaka was the grandson of Dingiswayo, who was the first Zulu to raise regiments and make a standing army. He is supposed to have copied his system from the white troops which he had seen; he had also noticed there were no women with the white troops, so he came to the conclusion they were not allowed to marry, and framed his military laws accordingly. The reigning Zulu chieftains, for their subsequent safety, always made it their custom to slay their male children, but the mother of Chaka, just before giving him birth, went into hiding with another tribe, where she left her child, and so preserved its life. Neither Chaka nor the Zulus forgot this act of motherly solicitude, and when his mother died, general mourning was ordered, and numbers of people, to show their grief at the loss of such a good mother, slew their cows which had young calves, so that the latter might suffer, and thus, in company with the nation, feel how terrible it was to be bereaved of a mother.

When Chaka became king, he greatly developed the military system of his grandfather, and, as already stated, subjugated the neighbouring tribes. Although Chaka ruled his people with unmitigated severity, every Zulu speaks of him with pride, especially with reference to his military prowess. Among his other military reforms, he introduced the short or stabbing assegai instead of the long-handled ones that had been used formerly as missiles. This was to make his men come to close quarters with their enemy. Chaka was assassinated by his brother Dingaan about the year 1830, who became king in his place.

The new monarch was a most cruel man, as he murdered all his brothers except Panda. His treacherous slaughter of the Boers under Retief

CETYWAYO.

is a matter of history. On that occasion he received the party, who had come with the object of entering into a treaty, most hospitably, and then invited them into his kraal, making them leave their arms outside, as it was explained to them that that was the etiquette; directly he got them inside, he butchered the lot. The result of this dastardly deed was that the Boers invaded Zululand, but without success. Shortly after this, Panda, who was the brother he had thought not worth while to murder while he was getting rid of the rest, revolted and joined the Boers, and succeeded in driving Dingaan out of the country. He fled to Swaziland, where the inhabitants put him to death.

Panda now became king. This was in the year 1840. His reign was not marked with so much bloodshed as his predecessor's, but nevertheless the country was continually fighting over who was to be his successor. The Natal Government eventually induced Panda to name Cetywayo his successor, so on Panda's death, in 1872, the Government sent Mr. Shepstone with an escort of Natal volunteers to install Cetywayo as king.

At this ceremony, which was conducted without the usual scenes of bloodshed, the following

1879. articles were agreed to:—" That the amicable relations existing in the time of Panda between the Zulus and the Natal Government should continue, and should be strengthened if possible; that the indiscriminate shedding of blood should cease; that for minor offences fines should be instituted; that no Zulu should be condemned to death without a fair trial; that he should have the right of appeal to the king."

Mr. Shepstone also tried to bring about the abolition of witch doctors, but this he was unable to add to the agreement, as the people believed in them too strongly.

Cetywayo worked hard at developing the military system of Chaka. Every male from the age of sixteen to that of seventy was a soldier. No one was allowed to marry without permission, and this was generally granted to a whole regiment at a time, when they reached the age of forty. Consequently there were married and unmarried regiments. The former wore a ring of black resin round their heads, which distinguished them from the unmarried, who wore no ring.

Before the war of 1879 broke out there were about thirty-three regiments, nineteen of whom were married. They differed greatly in numerical strength. As a corps got old, its numbers diminished, for the vacancies were not filled up.

The men were armed with assegais and knobkerries, while a certain number had guns; but opinions as to how many there were who had them are so diverse that it is impossible to do more than guess. There were probably some 8000 or 9000 guns in the country. Each man carried a shield made of bullock's hide, slashed down the centre, with a long stick run through.

There is no doubt that, a long time previous to the outbreak of the war, the attitude of the Zulus had become very threatening. It is said that the young regiments were clamouring to "wash their spears," one of the traditional qualifications for matrimony, and Cetywayo was looking about to give them an opportunity.

In 1878 a Zulu impi (army), composed of some 3000 men, made a demonstration on the Natal border, along the left bank of the Lower Tugela. This was done under the pretence of hunting. It nevertheless alarmed the white inhabitants of Natal, who felt that there was nothing to prevent the Zulu king from marching 30,000 men over the border and sacking Durban in twenty-four

1879. hours. Under these circumstances, it was decided to station troops along the border.

In December a meeting was held between the commissioners of the Natal Government and Indunas respecting the Zulu king. The former consisted of Colonel Forester Walker, C.B., Scots Guards, and Messrs. J. Shepstone, Brownlie, and Fynn. The Natal Government representatives presented an ultimatum, which demanded fines for raids and outrages committed by Zulus, also insisted that promises made by Cetywayo at his coronation should be carried out, and further demanded that the Zulu army should be disbanded; that a British resident should be appointed, and should live in the Zulu country, and be a medium of communication between the two governments; and also that the missionaries should be respected and allowed to return to their places, from which they had been driven out by the Zulus. No notice being taken of this ultimatum, a force advanced into Zululand, under command of Lord Chelmsford, in five columns, during the second week of January, 1879. The columns were stationed as follows :—

No 1, commanded by Colonel Pearson, was encamped at Lower Tugela Drift, and numbered nearly 4000 men; its base was Durban and its advanced depôt was at Stanger.

No 2 column, under command of Lieutenant-Colonel Durnford, R.E., was stationed at Middle Drift, with Pietermaritzburg as its base and Grey Town for its advanced depôt; it was composed of about 3500 men.

No. 3 column, commanded by Colonel Glynn, C.B., was at Rorke's Drift, with Pietermaritzburg as its base and Ladysmith as its advanced depôt; it numbered about 4500 men.

No. 4 column, under command of Colonel Wood, V.C., C.B., was stationed at Conference Hill, on the Blood River, with Utrecht as its base, and numbered about 3000 men.

No. 5 column was commanded by Colonel Rowlands, V.C., C.B., and was ordered to watch Secocoeni, and for that purpose was left at Luneberg. This column numbered about 1500 men.

Lord Chelmsford, therefore, had a force of about 16,000 men under his command. More than half, however, were natives.

Immediately after entering the Zulu country, skirmishes with the enemy occurred; but it was on the 22nd of January that the small camp at

1879. Isandhlwana, composed of some 900 men, exclusive of natives, who ran away after the first shot, were cut to pieces by a large army of Zulus.

The details of this terrible disaster, the cutting to pieces of the 24th Regiment, and the gallant defence of Rorke's Drift, are well known and need not be retold here. It was this disaster, as before mentioned, that caused the 91st and many other regiments to find themselves so quickly brought to South Africa.

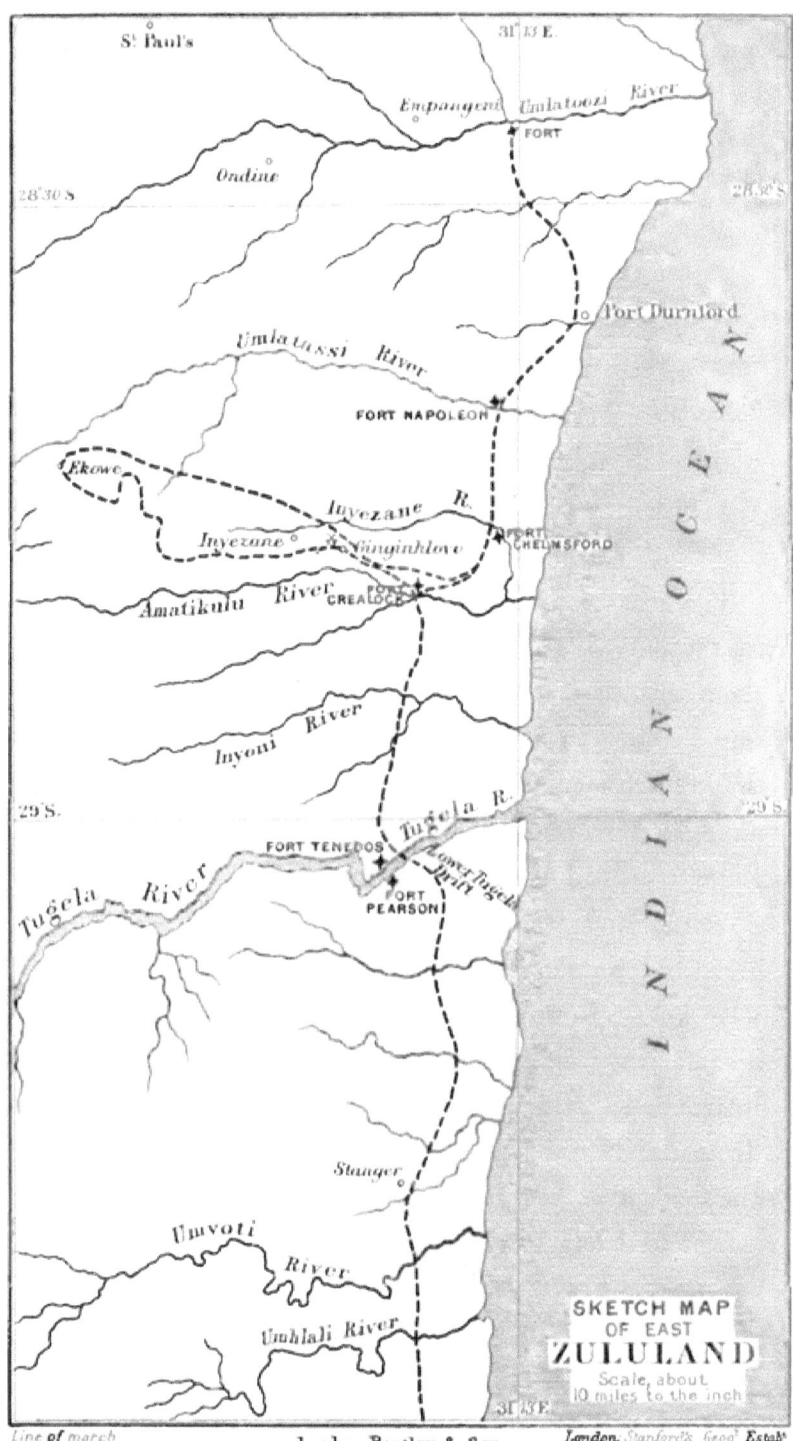

CHAPTER XVII.

Zulu War—April to September, 1879—Cape Town—Mauritius—St. Helena—Loss of Regiment's Number.

WE will now proceed with the history of the regiment's march up country.   1879.

The weather during the two days which the 91st spent at Durban was wretched, and gave them an idea of how it could pour in Natal. Before leaving for the front, the band was broken up and the men told off to act as hospital-bearers and orderlies, under the orders of Surgeon-Major Edge, who had accompanied the regiment in the *Pretoria*, and was placed in medical charge on arrival in Natal. The boys, seventeen in number, were left in camp under Bandmaster Kelly, with a sufficiency of musical instruments for their instruction. Nine pipers and a small corps of drums and fifes accompanied the regiment into the field.

The 91st left Durban on the 19th for the front,

1879. to form part of a column with which Lord Chelmsford determined to start as soon as possible, for the purpose of relieving the force under Colonel Pearson, then shut up in Ekowe, whose provisions were nearly exhausted, and who was surrounded by a body of Zulus variously estimated at from 12,000 to 20,000 strong. The departure of the regiment, which mustered twenty-three officers and 832 non-commissioned officers and men, was witnessed by a large number of townspeople at the railway station at Durban, where three special trains were provided, to convey them to Saccharine, which at that time was as far as the railway was laid. The last detachment arrived at Saccharine by 2 o'clock in the afternoon, and a little after 4 o'clock the 91st started to march to the front. A halt for the night was made on the north bank of the Verulam River.

The Naval Brigade of H.M.S. *Boadicea*, numbering about 250 men, under command of Lieutenant Carr, R.N., accompanied the regiment on its march to the Tugela from this place. The following night a place called Victoria was reached, and owing to the heat an early start was made the next morning. The night of the 21st

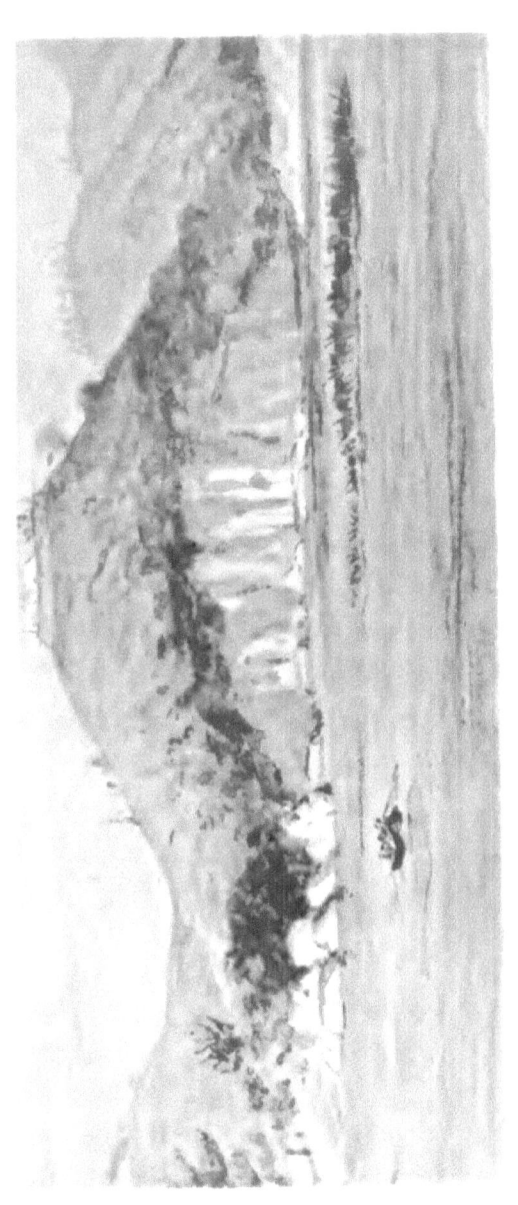

FORT PEARSON, LOWER TUGELA DRIFT (FROM ZULULAND BANK OF RIVER).

was spent on the banks of the Umtati River, when heavy rains fell, causing a halt next day to get things cleaned up. The march was resumed on Sunday, the 23rd, and the Tugela River was reached on the 25th, and was crossed in a pont, the regiment encamping near the 57th Regiment, which had arrived the previous day. Two companies of the 3rd Buffs and five companies of the 99th Regiment, formed into one battalion, were also encamped on the enemy's side of the river. On the 26th Lord Chelmsford inspected the regiment, and made a speech to the men.

1879.

The force collected at this place to move up to the relief of Ekowe was divided into two divisions. The first division, under Colonel Law, R.A., was composed of the 91st, and of the battalion made up of the Buffs and 99th, the Naval Brigades of the *Shah* and *Tenedos*, who had with them two 9-pounders, two 24-pounder rocket-tubes, and a gatling gun, the mounted infantry under Major Barrow, and one battalion of Natal native contingent.

The second division, under Colonel Pemberton of the 3/60th Rifles, was composed of the 57th Regiment, 3/60th Rifles, Naval Brigade of the *Boadicea*, and a portion of the marines of the

1879. *Shah* and *Boadicea*, with one gatling gun and two 24-pounder rocket-tubes, and one battalion Natal native contingent; the whole force being under the immediate command of Lord Chelmsford. The orders were to proceed without tents, and in the lightest possible marching order, men to carry seventy rounds of ammunition, and thirty rounds per man to be carried on pack-mules, two of which mules followed in rear of each company, with 1500 rounds in canvas waterproof bags.

Camp was struck on the 28th, and spare baggage and camp equipment were stacked in some tents protected by Forts Pearson and Tenedos, while twenty weakly men were ordered to be left behind to form a guard.

The troops had a very bad time of it during the following night, as it rained like it knows how to do in Zululand, and having no tents, and in fact nothing but a waterproof sheet per man to cover them, the ingenuity of each man was exercised as to how he should keep himself comparatively dry; as a matter of fact, it was impossible to manage this last detail, and in consequence a most miserable night was spent.

The following morning, at 6 a.m., the 91st started as advanced-guard to the force. Progress

RELIEF FORCE CROSSING A RIVER.

was very slow, continued halts having to be made to allow the great number of waggons to keep together, which was no easy matter to arrange, in consequence of the heavy state of the track after the recent rains. The waggons numbered 122, and occupied nearly two miles in length when on the move.

In the afternoon an entrenched laager was formed on the banks of the Inyoni River.

A South African laager consists of an enclosure formed by waggons placed closely together; at some distance outside them the shelter trench is dug; the defenders occupy the space between the trench and the waggons, and the area enclosed by the waggons contains the cattle.

The next morning the troops stood to their arms an hour before daybreak. This plan was adopted throughout the campaign, as the idea was that the hour just before daybreak was the one at which the Zulus generally attacked. The march was resumed in the same order as the previous day, and by the afternoon the banks of the Amatikulu River were reached, and another entrenched laager was formed. On Monday, the 31st, the river was crossed; this was a very long and wet operation, as the river was high, reaching over the men's waists, necessitating their carrying their ammunition on their shoulders. It took all day to get the waggons over, so that the laager formed in the evening was only a mile and a half from the one used the previous night. Major Bruce here received a telegram addressed to Captain Chater, from H.R.H. the Princess Louise, which ran as follows :—" Convey to the 91st my regrets at not seeing them before their departure, also the interest I take in their welfare, wishing them every success, with God-speed and a safe return."

The following day the 91st formed the rearguard, and the enemy was seen for the first time. The laager in the evening was formed at Ginginhlovo. The day had been oppressively hot, and after the trenches had been dug, a heavy thunderstorm came on, which nearly filled them. A most miserable night was passed by every one, as there was not a dry spot to lie down on, and all the ground had got into such a fearfully dirty state, that even walking was difficult.

When morning broke it was found that the country was too heavy to move the waggons; the Zulus also were observed to be advancing in considerable numbers from the direction of a hill beyond the Inyezane. The camp, which was square in shape, having sides about 130 yards long, had its waggons in the centre; the 60th were in line on the front face, the 57th on the right, and the 91st on rear face, except two companies of the latter, which together with the Buffs and 99th detachment held the left face; two gatlings and two nine-pounders were distributed at the corners, in charge of the Naval Brigade. Behind the 91st was a battalion of the Natal native contingent.

A little before six o'clock native scouts, which had as usual gone out to scour the country at daybreak, were seen to be falling back, firing while doing so, and directly after, large columns of the enemy were observed coming down the Inyezane hills, and also from the Amatikulu bush. When they had come within range, the gatling and nine-pounders opened fire, as also did the rockets, the first attack being made on the front of the laager, which was met by a heavy fire from the 60th. The Zulus then continued their usual mode of attack, which is to advance in the shape of a pair of horns, so as to envelope their opponents, and then finally rush them in rear. The shining of bayonets in the rear face appears to have led them to believe that the native contingent was there, and that the weakest point in the camp would probably be found in that direction; and a most determined attack was accordingly made there on the 91st, which lasted about twenty minutes, when the Zulus wavered and then fled, leaving many of their number within a few spaces of the trenches. When it was noticed that they were breaking, the mounted troops, under Major Barrow, together with the native contingent, were sent in pursuit, and terrible execution they did. By half-past seven the engagement was over.

The 91st's loss was one man killed, Private Marshall; while eight were wounded, namely, Sergeant D. McIntyre, dangerously, in the left eye (he died at Stanger, on the 15th); Private Stantidge, flesh wound in the thigh; Private Richards, penetrating wound in the leg; Privates O'Brien and Mallie, wound in their heads; Private Hanlon, wound in abdomen; Private Sutton, wound in left arm; Private Gillespie, slight wound on side of head. The adjutant, Lieutenant St. Clair, had a narrow escape, a bullet having gone through his helmet, within an inch of his head. The total casualty of the force was, one officer and four men killed, while five officers and thirty-nine men were wounded. The strength of the regiment present at this action was twenty-two officers and 801 non-commissioned officers and men. The colours were in charge of Second-Lieutenants Fraser and C. F. Richardson.

The enemy's loss on this occasion has been variously estimated, but it must have been considerable, as nearly 500 bodies were counted within a radius of 400 yards of the laager, and the route taken by the flying enemy was strewn with corpses cut down by the mounted infantry and native contingent.

The remainder of the day was employed in burying the dead and altering the laager to suit the reduced garrison which was to be left while a flying column made for Ekowe. The evening passed off quietly without any signs of an enemy.

The morning after the action, a flying column, composed of six companies of the 57th, 60th, and 91st, with about 100 of the Naval Brigade, John Dunn's scouts, and some mounted men, started early, with the object of reaching Ekowe in one day's march, the 91st forming the rear-guard.

Colonel Pearson, who was in command at

1879. Ekowe, and had been regularly communicated with by means of the heliograph, received orders to hold his force in readiness to evacuate his fort the day after the arrival of the relieving force. The garrison at Ekowe had been a witness of the action of the 2nd of April, as the fort stands on hills which overlook the plain over which Lord Chelmsford's column had marched, and the battlefield was at the foot of the hill. The march of the relieving column commenced at daybreak, and at half-past six the rear-guard had moved off. When the sun had got up, the day became excessively hot, and the march, especially for the rear-guard, was most tedious, numerous halts having to be made to allow the waggons to be got through the marshy places on the road. To show how the column straggled, the advance-guard, which was formed by the 60th, arrived at Ekowe at half-past six, while the rear-guard did not arrive until midnight. The 91st only got their dinners at 1 o'clock in the morning. The men on this occasion marched splendidly, when it is taken into consideration that they had been seventeen hours and a half on the move, yet when they passed the fort, headed by their pipers, there was not one man out of the ranks.

Ekowe had before the war been a Norwegian mission station, under charge of the Rev. Oftebro, and consisted of a church; a long building containing several rooms, one of which was used as a school; and a third building, which was the residence of the missionary. The two latter were thatched with reeds, while the church was roofed with corrugated iron. The station stood on an extensive plateau, about 2000 feet above the sea, and was commanded on every side except the south by low hills distant about a quarter of a mile. The surrounding hills were destitute of trees, but were covered by long rank grass and overgrown vegetation.

If it had not been for the hurry in which the fort was made, owing to the disastrous news of Isandhlwana, a better position would have been taken up, but there was no time to do anything, and as the buildings, etc., were on the spot, the best was made of the position. A big parapet was made with various traverses, the ditch outside being ten feet deep and fifteen feet wide at the top, with stakes running along the bottom. The garrison was composed of nearly 1400 white and 450 native men.

The next day, the 4th of April, it was decided

to rest the relieving force, while those relieved marched out on their way to the Tugela, which they reached eventually without seeing any signs of the enemy.

The flying column left Ekowe on the 5th, and only marched about six miles, the road taken being different to that which they had come up by. The following morning an unfortunate accident happened, which was caused by a picquet of the 91st, under command of Captain Prevost, who, thinking they saw Zulus creeping in the bushes in front of them, fired, which raised an alarm in the camp and made the scouts and picquets run in. They were fired on by the 60th trench party, who mistook them for the enemy in the darkness. Fifteen were wounded in this unfortunate business. The march was resumed at 9 o'clock, and the laager at Ginginhlovo was reached in the afternoon; but it was found to have become very unpleasant, owing to the frightful smell from the number of dead buried in its vicinity. So a new laager was formed about two miles from the old camp, on a piece of rising ground. The camp was again moved the following day, to a place which was considered to answer the purpose better. The Buffs and the 99th detachments proceeded to the Tugela to join their regiments, and the force in the new camp consisted of the 57th, 60th, 91st, and a portion of the Naval Brigade, with a regiment of native contingent and some mounted men, the whole under command of Lieutenant-Colonel Clarke of the 57th Regiment, who received the local rank of brigadier-general.

1879.

The entrenchments round the new camp were made of larger dimensions than those of the laagers on the march up country, the position being further strengthened with abattis. The daily routine was as follows:—Trenches manned at 4 a.m. until daylight, men standing with fixed bayonets in perfect silence. At daylight, leave trenches; wood and water parties sent out; after breakfast, company inspections; during the forenoon one or two companies marched to adjacent stream to bathe; after dinner brigade or regimental drill, or bivouac outside the camp, in order that the ground should be thoroughly cleaned; at 7.30 p.m. man trenches, first post sounded; lie down at 7.45, each company in rear of its own alarm post; lights out at 8. One company of each regiment was on trench duty every night, and stood in the trenches all night, one company on picquet covering the front.

1879. On the 18th a convoy arrived from Tugela, bringing up men's kits and officers' light baggage. The kit of the latter, since they had left the Tugela, had been limited to ten pounds weight. Tents, however, were not provided, and owing to the heavy rains and general unhealthiness of the plains on the coast, sickness became prevalent. On the 23rd Second-Lieutenants Dickson, Wyllie, and Lane-Fox joined the regiment on appointment, bringing with them two sergeants, one corporal, and four privates from the hospital on the Lower Tugela.

After being seventeen days in the Ginginhlovo camp, it was decided to evacuate it and advance to a new position about four miles off on the Inyezane River, where a fort was commenced (afterwards called Fort Chelmsford). The construction of another fort was also commenced in the beginning of May, on the Amatikulu River, on the line of communication about half-way to Tugela. This was named Fort Crealock.

The troops at this time were employed on convoy duty, each convoy being escorted by one British regiment, a battalion of natives, two guns R.A., and a few mounted scouts. The three regiments, under command of Brigadier-General

Clarke, took it in turns to furnish the escort. Sickness was now rapidly increasing. On the 5th of May the empty convoy on its return to the Lower Tugela took 150 sick from various corps, including Captain Mills and Lieutenants Tottenham and Goff of the 91st. The nature of the sickness was generally fever and dysentery.

1879.

On the 10th of May the regiment was moved to Fort Crealock to garrison it, and also complete the earthworks. The troops then, which were under command of Major Bruce, were composed of the regiment, half a company of Royal Engineers, two guns R.A., sixteen mounted men, and a battalion of native contingent. The regiment remained here a month, during which the officers in their spare time made expeditions in the vicinity to shoot what game they could find. There was, however, very little to shoot, except an occasional bustard or duck. This was probably owing to the number of Kaffir dogs which were to be found prowling about the deserted kraals, which must have found it very hard to get a living now that their owners had left their habitations.

In June, Lieutenant Cookson was attached to the Mounted Infantry under Major Barrow, and

1879. served with them during the rest of the war. On the 15th of June the 91st moved forward with the force under command of General Crealock. No enemy was met with, but every precaution was taken against surprise. On the 27th the Umlatazi River was crossed, and the next day Port Durnford was reached. Here it had been arranged a fresh landing-place should be opened, as the naval authorities had ascertained that it could be effected, and accordingly the general in command proposed to make the place a fresh base of operations where a depôt would be formed for supplies.

During this month Major Bruce was promoted to the rank of lieutenant-colonel, *vice* Lieutenant-Colonel Kirk, who was placed on half-pay, and appointed to the Intelligence Department.

During the first week in June the Prince Imperial Louis Napoleon lost his life, which sad event cast a gloom over the whole of the troops in Zululand. His remains were at once sent down to Durban to be embarked on board H.M.S. *Boadicea*, for conveyance to England. The band used at Durban on this occasion was one which had been collected and trained by Mr. Kelly, bandmaster of the 91st, and was principally com-

PORT DURNFORD (FROM THE ANCHORAGE).

posed of boys of the regiment left behind at Durban.

On the 2nd of July Sir Garnet Wolseley arrived in H.M.S. *Shah*, at Port Durnford, but owing to the bad weather he could hold no communication with the shore. The next day, accompanied by his staff, he tried to land in a lighter; the surf was running rapidly, and although a good effort was made, the tow-line breaking, he failed to make the land, and had to return to the *Shah*, which immediately started on its return to Durban, where Sir Garnet landed, and proceeded by road to the front, arriving at Port Durnford on the 7th.

On the 24th the 91st changed its quarters to a post on the Umhlatoosi River, which was established to assist in maintaining the line of communication between Port Durnford, St. Paul's, and Ulundi; 200 of Nettleton's native contingent, and some mounted volunteers, forming part of the garrison.

On the 27th Captain Mills's company proceeded to Fort Napoleon, which lay between Fort Chelmsford and Port Durnford, with the object of holding a post to maintain communication.

Shortly after Captain Craufurd's company made a small fort with the same object, afterwards

1879. known as Fort Inverary, as a half-way post to St. Paul's. At the same time Captain Stevenson's and O'Sullivan's companies were sent down to garrison the fort at Port Durnford, which was the head-quarters of Lieutenant-Colonel Hale, R.E., who had been appointed assistant-adjutant and quarter-master-general on the lines of communication and base, Lieutenant Goff being appointed his staff officer.

On the 17th of August a party of mounted men was ordered to proceed, under command of Captain Yeatman Biggs, R.A., in the direction of St. Lucia Bay, in pursuit of Cetywayo, the Zulu king, who was supposed to be in hiding in that part of the country. Captain O'Sullivan and Lieutenants MacDonald and Goff accompanied this party, which was composed of some ten officers and fifty mounted men, together with about 100 native contingent, under Commandant Nettleton. This party were out about a fortnight, traversing a large extent of wild country seldom before visited by white men. The road taken was along the coast to St. Lucia Bay. Nothing being heard of the fugitive, Captain Yeatman Biggs decided to make for the junction of the Black and the White Umvoloosi River, and if

EMBARKATION OF CETYWAYO AT PORT DURNFORD.

no news was heard on the way, to go direct to Ulundi, which was eventually done. During the ride it was noticed that there was no game to be seen except a few guinea-fowl, and one or two antelope; this was accounted for by the fact that the Zulus had shot or driven away all the larger sorts of animals since they had got guns. At Ulundi news arrived at the same time as the expedition that Cetywayo had been captured by Major Marter, of the King's Dragoon Guards, and he was brought in the following day.

1879.

Captain O'Sullivan and the officers of the 91st only remained at Ulundi a few hours, when they proceeded to Port Durnford. Another officer of the 91st (Lieutenant Cookson), who was attached to the Mounted Infantry, was also out for several days in pursuit of the king. Cetywayo and the women who were with him were sent, directly after their arrival at Ulundi, to Port Durnford, at which place they arrived under a strong escort on the 5th of September, and were at once taken down to the sea-shore to be embarked on the s.s. *Natal* for Cape Town. The guard on the beach was composed of Captain Stevenson's company of the 91st, and an escort was sent with Cetywayo

1879. on board, of a sergeant (Keene) and six men of the regiment, who afterwards gave a graphic account of the abject state of the deposed monarch when he first felt the effects of the very choppy sea which he encountered in the surf boat taking him out to the steamer. He was accompanied by three female attendants, who seemed to feel more comfortable than he did, and who were apparently vastly amused at the discomfiture of their royal master. The story is that his escort, who were all men picked on account of their being good sailors, were themselves nearly as unhappy as their prisoners.

The capture of the king was the termination of the war, and on the 13th of September orders were received for the regiment to proceed to Durban; the head-quarters left the next day, followed by the other detached companies. Nothing of importance happened on the return march, and Verulam, the terminus of the railway from Durban, was reached on the 22nd of the month. There they remained until the 28th. Orders had in the meantime arrived that a detachment of three companies should go to Mauritius and one to St. Helena, while head-quarters were to proceed to Cape Town. The

Mauritius detachment was composed of F, G, and H companies, under command of Major Gurney, and the company selected for St. Helena was that of Captain Mills.

The head-quarters and remaining companies, on arrival at Durban, were embarked on the 30th on the s.s. *City of Venice*, and were composed of sixteen officers and 588 non-commissioned officers and men. The transport sailed the next day, and anchored in Table Bay, after a rough passage, on Sunday, the 5th of October. The following day the regiment was disembarked, and went into the main barracks at Cape Town, with the exception of the B and D companies, who were sent on to Wynberg to be encamped, there being no room for them in Cape Town, as part of the barracks was occupied by a detachment of the 88th Regiment.

In November, 1879, Lieutenant-Colonel Bruce was appointed a " Companion of the Bath."

The detachment of three companies who were detailed for Mauritius, embarked at Durban on board H.M.S. *Crocodile*, on the 8th of October, and arrived at Port Louis on the 15th. The transport also had on board the 88th Regiment, and 17th Lancers for India. The names of the

1879. officers who landed with the detachment at Mauritius were as follows:—Major W. Gurney (in command), Lieutenants MacDonald, Robbins, Fraser, and Wilson; and with them were 250 non-
1880. commissioned officers and men. On the 27th of January Major W. P. Gurney died of fever, contracted in the field during the Zulu campaign. He was buried with full military honours at Bease Bassin. A tablet to his memory was erected in Stirling Church by his brother officers, as a token of their esteem and respect.

The population of Mauritius, in 1880, numbered about 370,000, composed principally of coloured people of mixed race, of which the imported Indian coolies brought over to work the sugar plantations were the most numerous. The influx of these people, who imported their diseases, spread fever over the island, and in 1867, when the great outbreak of fever occurred, the number of deaths was enormous, the troops themselves losing a great number. This fever, which is called "Mauritius fever," attacks every one living on the low land, and as the barracks are situated in the unhealthy part, the 91st suffered considerably, which necessitated frequent drafts being sent up to the Cureppe in the hills for change of air.

On the 22nd of April, 1881, the Zulu War medals were presented to those of this detachment who had served in Zululand.

Nothing of any public interest happened to these companies during the remainder of their stay on the island; they simply spent their time in passing through hospital and sanatorium, so that when they arrived at Cape Town, under command of Major Robley, to rejoin head-quarters, on the 26th of May, 1881, they presented a most sickly appearance, and the non-commissioned officers and men had to be kept off duty for a month after their arrival.

The detachment which had gone to St. Helena under command of Captain Mills in January, 1880, remained at that out-of-the-way spot twenty-two months, when they were relieved by another company from the regiment. During their stay there the island was visited by the ex-Empress Eugéne, who landed to pay a visit to the place where Napoleon I.'s body had so long lain. She was then on her way out to visit the spot where the Prince Imperial had met his death. On landing she was received by a guard of honour, composed of the detachment of the 91st.

1881. In March, 1881, Sir Frederick Roberts, G.C.B., touched at St. Helena on his way out to the Transvaal, to take command of the troops in succession to General Colley, so the opportunity was taken to get him to present the officers and men with the South African war medal, which had just arrived to be distributed to those who had taken part in the Zulu War.

1880. At the end of 1880 the Transvaal War broke out. The regiment itself was not engaged in it, but Captain Cameron, who had joined the 91st from the 71st Light Infantry, was employed at Maritzburg on the staff until the termination of the war. On the 29th of December Captain Craufurd and Lieutenant Goff were ordered to proceed to Natal with 100 picked men of the 91st, in H.M.S. *Boadicea*, as convoy to the guns she was to land to proceed to the front. This move, however, was countermanded the day they were to embark. Lieutenant Goff was ordered, in
1881. February, to Natal, in charge of 300 horses and mules, which were sent to the front. He was employed at Durban and Maritzburg for some time, returning to Cape Town in April.

The medals for the Zulu War were presented to the head-quarters of the battalion in March, by Lieutenant-General the Hon. Leicester Smyth, C.B., on which occasion the lieutenant-general addressed the battalion as follows:—

1881.

"I am grateful to Colonel Bruce for the pleasure he has given me in asking me to present these medals—honourable emblems of hardships undergone, valour displayed, and victory won; and I wish the recipients one and all many happy years to wear them. I am the more pleased at being here to-day, for a long time ago, how long I hardly like to say, I had the honour of campaigning in this country with the 91st Regiment, and then had many opportunities of witnessing and appreciating their gallant deeds; and as the 91st fought in those days of old, and as those to whom I have now given their medals fought in more recent times, so, I feel sure, will the 91st Highlanders of the present day, should they be called upon, in stubbornly upholding the great tradition of their regiment, and do their duty to their Queen and country."

Soon after the regiment got settled down in its new quarters in Cape Town, it was decided to start a pack of fox-hounds, to hunt jackals in the country near the town. There had been hounds before this, during the stay of the 24th

1881. Regiment, but all remnants of the pack had disappeared, so drafts were sent for from England, and after a short time, mainly owing to the energy of Captain Cookson, a very fair lot of hounds were got together, and hunting commenced in the spring months. The jackal was to be found within a short distance of Rondebosch and Wynberg, and the flats, as the waste ground is called there, were at this time left quite undisturbed, and only had a few very thin sheep grazing on them; sport therefore was fairly good.

Expeditions were also made by officers to shoot antelopes, but the sport within easy distance of Cape Town was indifferent.

On the 1st of June a general order of that date directed that "South Africa" should henceforth be borne on the regimental colours.

The 1st of July brought in the new scheme, in which the regiment lost its number, and, being incorporated with the gallant 93rd, became known as the "Princess Louise's Argyll and Sutherland Highlanders," becoming the 1st battalion of this new amalgamation.

APPENDICES.

A.

COLOURS.

The following brief account is all that can be found relating to the history of the colours which the regiment has possessed :—

The first colours, of which there is no record as to when they were presented, were carried throughout the Peninsular War, and about the year 1826 came into the possession of Lieutenant-Colonel John Macdonald (afterwards Sir John Macdonald, K.C.B.), who was then in command of the regiment.

In 1883 Major-General Alastair Macdonald, the son of the above, presented these colours to St. Giles, Edinburgh, on the occasion when all the Highland regiments collected their old colours to be placed in the cathedral. The escort to the colours at the function was composed of Captain MacDonald and Lieutenant Goff, Colour-Sergeants Keene and Nowell. Of the royal colour only a fragment remains, while the regimental colour is almost complete, and bears on it "Pyrenees," "Nivelle," "Nive," "Orthes," "Toulouse," and "Peninsula," on a circular scroll, the names being nearly illegible. The colours are painted.

The colours presented about 1826 were carried until the year 1845, when they came into the possession of Lieutenant-Colonel Lindsay, who was then in command of the regiment.

After his death they were sent to Colonel Bertie Gordon in 1848, who had them placed in Ellon Castle, Aberdeenshire.

The next colours—those presented in 1845, of which an account is given of the ceremony of presentation in Chapter IX.—were carried until the year 1869, when they found a resting-place at Inverary Castle, only to be destroyed by fire (as related in Chapter XV.) eight years later. In this chapter is also given an account of the new colours being presented, which are the present colours carried by the regiment.

Of the colours carried by the second battalion raised in 1804 there appears to be no record except of their existence, as it is related in Chapter I. that Sergeant-Major Cahil received a commission " for saving one of the colours."

There is no record of the reserve battalion having any colours.

C.

SUCCESSION LIST OF COLONELS.

Duncan Campbell, May 3, 1796. Died April 18, 1837.
Gabriel Gordon, April 19, 1837. Died August 7, 1855.
Hon. Charles Gore, August 8, 1855, to March 8, 1861.
Charles Murray Hay, March 9, 1861. Died July 3, 1864.
Charles George James Arbuthnot, July 4, 1864, to August 26, 1870.
James Robertson Craufurd, August 27, 1870.

D.

SUCCESSION LIST OF LIEUTENANT-COLONELS.

Duncan Campbell, from the raising of the regiment to May 3, 1796.

Fielder King, May 4, 1796, to June 24, 1801.

Alexander Loraine, June 25, 1801, to November 24, 1808.

William Douglas, November 25, 1808. Died August 23, 1818.

Donald Macneil, August 24, 1818, to September 22, 1824.

John Macdonald, September 23, 1824, to August 15, 1827.

James Milford Sutherland, August 16, 1827, to December 1, 1831.

Robert Anderson, December 2, 1831, to July 1, 1841.

Cornwall Burne, July 2, 1841, to July 15, 1841.

Roderick Macneil, P. W., July 16, 1841, to April 14, 1842 (never joined).

Martin George Thomas Lindsay, April 15, 1842, to October 13, 1848.

Charles Cooke Yarborough (reserve battalion), October 14, 1848, to January 29, 1856.

John Francis Glencairn Campbell (April 14, 1846, to October 14, 1848, in reserve battalion), October 14, 1848, to October 21, 1858.

Bertie Edward Murray Gordon, October 22, 1858, to January 28, 1870.

John Sprot, January 29, 1870, to January 18, 1876.

James Buchanan Kirk, January 19, 1876, to June 20, 1879.

Alexander Cunningham Bruce, June 21, 1879.

E.

LIST OF CAMPAIGNS AND BATTLES THE REGIMENT HAS TAKEN PART IN.

Wynberg, September 14, 1795.
Roleia, August 17, 1808.
Vimiero, August 21, 1808.
Reserves (under Paget)—actions during retreat to Corunna, January, 1809.
Corunna, January 16, 1809.
Talavera (a strong company of regiment took part), July 27 and 28, 1809.
Walcheren Expedition, 1809.
Vittoria, pursuit after the battle of June 21, 1813.
Sauroren, July 28 and 30, 1813.
Affair at Urdax, October 7, 1813.
Nivelle, November 10, 1813.
Nive, December 9, 1813.
Orthes, February 27, 1814.
Affair at Aire, March 2, 1814.
Bergen-op-Zoom, March 8, 1814.
Toulouse, April 10, 1814.
Waterloo (in reserve), June 18, 1815.
Cambray, June 24, 1815.
Expedition against Tola, 1843.
Block Drift, January, 1846.
Amatola Mountains, April 16, 17, and 18, 1846.
Block Drift, April, 1846; May 12, 1846.

Fort Peddie, May 27 and 28, 1846.
Boemplaats, 1848.
Numerous outpost engagements in Kaffir War, 1846–47.
Kaffir War, 1851–52.
Ginginhlovo, April 2, 1879.

F.

LIST OF BATTLES INSCRIBED ON THE REGIMENTAL COLOUR.

Roleia.
Vimiero.
Corunna.
Pyrenees.
Nivelle.
Nive.
Orthes.
Toulouse.
Peninsula.
South Africa.

G.

THE WATERLOO ROLL.

ANOTHER interesting relic of this regiment is the Waterloo roll, now handsomely bound. This document lay hidden among a mass of office papers until the year 1848, when it was saved from destruction by a sergeant of the name of Hirst, who was employed in turning out a quantity of old books and papers which had been ordered to be destroyed as useless. This sergeant laid the roll aside, and it was not until the 27th of August, 1871, that it was again discovered, and this time it was carefully sent to be bound. It is dated, "Camp before Paris, 1815" (at which date it appears to have been rendered to the War Office). The roll of the officers is as follows:—

Lieutenant-Colonel Sir W. Douglas, K.C.B.
Captain James Walsh (Major).
,, T. H. Blair, Major of the 3rd British Brigade (wounded).
Captain William Steuart.
,, Archibald Campbell (1).
,, Dugald Campbell.
,, James C. Murdoch.
,, Alexander J. Callender (Major).
,, Archibald Campbell (2).
,, Robert Anderson.
Lieutenant John Campbell.
,, John Russell.
,, Alexander Campbell (1).
,, Robert Stewart.

APPENDICES. 313

Lieutenant Andrew McLachlan.
- ,, Carberry Egan.
- ,, Andrew Cathcart (wounded on 24th).
- ,, John McDougall.
- ,, James Hood.
- ,, Alexander Smith.
- ,, T. L. Fenwick.
- ,, Thomas Murray.
- ,, R. S. Knox.
- ,, Charles Stuart.
- ,, John McDonald.
- ,, Eugene Brown.
- ,, Alexander Campbell (2).
- ,, George Scott (Adjutant).
- ,, William Smith.
- ,, James Black (wounded on 24th).
- ,, Alexander Sword.

Ensign N. Lamont.
- ,, W. Trimmer.
- ,, James Paton.
- ,, Dugald Ducat.
- ,, Andrew Smith.
- ,, Lawrence Lind.

Paymaster Dugald Campbell.
Quarter-Master James Stewart.
Surgeon Robert Douglas.
Assistant-Surgeon G. M. McLachlan.
- ,, ,, W. H. Young.

H.

REGIMENTAL RECORD BOOK.

THE present handsome book was presented to the regiment by Colonel Bertie Gordon, at Kamptee, on the 20th of November, 1861. In his preface he relates his object for so doing, and states that before that time the records had been kept in an irregular and shameful manner, the entries being left in most cases to the Orderly Room clerks to enter, and finally the volume had been lost. He therefore determined to have them re-written from documents in possession of the regiment, and adds to the preface the following words: "A very special duty devolves on the officer who commands the regiment, in preparing and recording in the volume, which contains the history of the regiment, every event illustrative of its state during each year of its existence; of the scenes and places of its service; of its composition, and the changes in its different ranks, its uniform and establishment; of the marches and voyages which it performs; of the deeds of valour, of benevolence, of endurance, and of whatever else may be worthy of remembrance for after times, in which its individual members or itself as a body may have borne a part."

These records, up to the time the book was presented, were beautifully written out by Private Frederick Harlington, of the 91st, the remainder being in the handwriting of the successive commanding officers.

I.

REGIMENTAL RELIC.

SERGEANT-MAJOR'S WALKING-STICK.

AMONGST the relics in possession of the regiment is a celebrated stick, only used on certain anniversaries. Its history is as follows:—When the transport left the Cape of Good Hope in 1802, to convey home the regiment, it was attacked by a sword-fish, which left sticking in its timbers a portion of its ivory weapon, $33\frac{1}{2}$ inches in length. This became the property of Andrew McLean, afterwards regimental sergeant-major, who made it into a walking-stick, and by him it was carried during the whole of his services in the Peninsular War. Fighting in the South of France, at Waterloo and at Cambray, and with the army of occupation at Paris, Sergeant-Major McLean was promoted to a lieutenancy, and, having been specially recommended by the late General Sir Charles Rowan, he was appointed superintendent of the Metropolitan Police in London, in which post he served for many years, and ultimately retired to Boulogne on a pension of £120 a year. Here Colonel Browne found him residing, when that officer retired from the command of the Dublin Metropolitan Police. Lieutenant McLean died in August, 1869, and Colonel Browne, deeming that this relic of its war services would be acceptable to Colonel Gordon and his regiment, transmitted the staff to Dover, to be the property of the regiment in all times coming, and to be handed over to its successive sergeant-majors. The names of the battles it was carried in are inscribed on eight plates of solid gold, and it is now used on parades with all honour by the sergeant-major, on the anniversaries of the following battles :—

    Roleia, August 17, 1808.
    Vimiero, August 21, 1808.
    Corunna, January 16, 1809.
    Pyrenees, August 8.
    Nivelle, November 10, 1813.
    Nive, December 9, 1813.
    Orthes, February 27, 1814.
    Toulouse, April 10, 1814.

K.

TABLE SHOWING DURATION OF STAY OF REGIMENT IN DIFFERENT QUARTERS.

	Years.	Months.
Scotland	3	0
England	13	1
Ireland	15	6
Channel Islands	0	7
Continent of Europe	7	9
Mediterranean	3	9
Cape and St. Helena	21	9
India	11	0
Jamaica	9	1
Travelling	1	11
Total	87	5

SERVICES OF OFFICERS.

COMPILED FROM ANNUAL ARMY LISTS AND OTHER AUTHENTIC SOURCES.

[NOTE.—The year given in brackets at the close of the record of an officer's service, refers to the date of the last annual Army List in which his name appears.]

Aitcheson, William. Ensign, 21st March, 1845. Served with the regiment in the Kaffir War of 1846; had his horse shot under him, 21st May, 1846, while proceeding from Grahamstown to Fort Peddie (medal). To 3rd Guards (Scots Guards), 2nd October, 1846.

Alison, Charles German. Ensign, 18th December, 1863; lieutenant, 9th March, 1867. Served in India with the regiment. Captain, 29th January, 1870. Retired, 23rd July, 1875.

Allen, John Michael. Ensign, 2nd October, 1855; lieutenant, 23rd March, 1858. Served in the Ionian Islands with the regiment. Died, 1st July, 1859.

Anderson, Robert, P. W. and K. H. From 14th battalion of reserve. Lieutenant, 12th October, 1804; captain, 30th April, 1812; major, 23rd September, 1824; lieutenant-colonel, 2nd December, 1831. Served in the expedition to Hanover, 1805–1806. In battles of Roleia, Vimiero, and Corunna; in the expedition to Walcheren, 1809; to Swedish Pomerania, 1813; Holland in 1814, including the attack of Bergen-op-Zoom. Was present at Waterloo, storming of Cambray, and capture of Paris. Commanded the 91st from 2nd December, 1837, to 1st July, 1841. Retired, 1841.

Anderson, ——. Ensign, 13th August, 1805; lieutenant, 25th August, 1807. Died, 1814.

Anderson, Matthew. Ensign, 11th May, 1808; lieutenant, 12th October, 1809. To 52nd Foot, 19th July, 1810, with which he served at Waterloo (wounded). Retired, 1821.

Anderson, Robert. Ensign, 11th August, 1808 (1810).

Anderson, William. Ensign, 27th August, 1829; lieutenant,

14th September, 1832. To 11th Light Dragoons, 4th October, 1833. Retired, 1838.

Antrobus, Philip. From 9th Light Dragoons. Lieutenant, 2nd February, 1844. To 2nd Dragoons as paymaster, 1st January, 1849. Retired, 1854.

Arbuthnot, Honourable Francis. Ensign, 29th August, 1801; lieutenant, 1802. To 9th Foot, 10th February, 1803.

Arbuthnot, Charles George James. Served in the 11th Light Dragoons. Colonel of the 91st, 4th July, 1864, to 26th August, 1870.

Arden, William. Surgeon, 1851. To Military Train, 1856.

Armstrong, Daniel. Surgeon, 1850 to 1851.

Armstrong, Elliot. Ensign, 8th June, 1855; lieutenant, 11th December, 1857. Served in Greece, Ionian Islands, and India with the regiment. Retired, 19th July, 1864.

Arthur, George. Ensign, 26th August, 1804. To 35th Foot, 24th June, 1805.

Ayton, Robinson. Surgeon, 1821 to 1827.

Baillie, William Hunter. Ensign, 11th December, 1857; lieutenant, 2nd July, 1859. Served with the regiment in the Ionian Islands and India. To 8th Foot, 30th November, 1860.

Bankes, Thomas Holme. Ensign, 8th June, 1867; lieutenant, 28th May, 1870. Retired, 1st September, 1875.

Barfoot, William. Quarter-master, 1836. Retired, 1841.

Barker, William Henry. Ensign, 9th July, 1813; lieutenant, 8th January, 1818. To half-pay, 1st July, 1819.

Barnes, George Adam. Ensign, 12th December, 1822; lieutenant, 23rd September, 1824. Joined the St. Helena Regiment, 6th November, 1835, on the staff as town-major. Captain, 30th October, 1840 (1842).

Barney, John Edward. From 58th Foot. Lieutenant, 29th September, 1825; captain, 7th January, 1842. Served through the Kaffir War of 1846-47. Retired, 8th January, 1847.

Barrington, Henry. From 87th Foot. Major, 1st April, 1819. To half-pay, 100th Foot, 4th October, 1822.

Barton, Henry Charles Benyon. Ensign, 12th July, 1839. Retired, 1842.

Battiscombe, William Benjamin. Ensign, 15th March, 1850; lieutenant, 21st May, 1852; captain, 10th November, 1854. Served in Malta, Greece, Ionian Islands, and India with the regiment. Major, 12th November, 1860. To half-pay, 27th July, 1869.

Baumgardt, John. Ensign, 1st August, 1798; lieutenant, 20th March, 1801. To 8th Light Dragoons, 9th September, 1801.

Bayley, Frederick. Ensign, 30th October, 1838; lieutenant,

23rd April, 1841; captain, 13th October, 1848. Served at the Cape (Kaffir War). Retired, 1854. Subsequently commanded one of the Yorkshire Militia regiments.

Baylis, Robert. Ensign, 21st April, 1846. To 99th Foot, 2nd November, 1847.

Baynes, Charles Dyneley. From 8th Foot, 1860. Lieutenant, 1st October, 1858. To Madras Staff Corps, 1865.

Beatty, James McNeill. Surgeon, 1868. Served in India with the regiment. To 11th Hussars, 1874.

Berkeley, Charles. From 2nd Foot. Lieutenant, 22nd July, 1819. To half-pay, 71st Foot, 20th May, 1824.

Bethune, John Trotter. Ensign, 13th October, 1843; lieutenant, 19th February, 1847. Served at the Cape (Kaffir War) with the regiment. Retired, 1851. Became Earl of Lindsay and Lord of the Byres, 1878.

Black, James. Ensign, 16th May, 1811; lieutenant, 22nd July, 1813. Served with the regiment during their second visit to the Peninsula. Was present at Waterloo and Cambray (wounded). To half-pay, 25th March, 1817. Subsequently appointed in July, 1841, as lieutenant to the Royal Canadian Regiment (1848).

Blackall, Gardner B. Ensign, 10th February, 1854. Retired, 7th July, 1857.

Blackburne, William. Quarter-master, 1st August, 1848. To half-pay, 27th July, 1855.

Blackwell, Thomas Eden. From 13th Foot, with which he had served throughout the whole of the Burmese War, including the capture of Rangoon (wounded, 1st December, 1824), and also at the storming of the stockade of Kokaign, 15th December, 1825. Joined the 91st, 12th August, 1834. Commanded the three companies left at St. Helena in 1839, when the rest of the regiment proceeded to the Cape of Good Hope, until 1842, when they rejoined head-quarters Retired, 1843. Died at Bath, 22nd December, 1845.

Blagg, James. Ensign, 10th November, 1854; lieutenant, 27th November, 1857. Served with the regiment in Greece and Ionian Islands. Died at sea, 14th December, 1858.

Blair, Thomas Hunter. Lieutenant, 14th September, 1804; captain, 28th March, 1805; major, 8th January, 1818. Served with the regiment at Roleia, Vimiero, Corunna, and was left behind in Portugal in 1808 when the regiment returned to England; present at the battle of Talavera as major of brigade, when he was severely wounded and made prisoner; was not released until 1814. Present at Waterloo as major of brigade, when he was again wounded, and received a brevet of lieutenant-colonel for his "meritorious conduct." To the 87th Foot, 1st April, 1819.

.**Blaney, John.** Ensign, 23rd December, 1795; lieutenant, 9th September, 1796; captain, 4th August, 1804; major, 25th November, 1808. To half-pay, Royal Regiment of Malta, 1812.

Bloomfield, Benjamin. Surgeon, 1810 (1811).

Boehmer, Frederick. From sergeant-major, 60th Foot. Ensign, 1st August, 1848; adjutant, 1st August, 1848, to 12th July, 1855. To 4th Foot, 6th November, 1857.

Bond, Henry Auburey. Ensign, 4th April, 1851. Served in the Kaffir War and was nearly captured by the Kaffirs, 4th March, 1852, owing to his being short-sighted, his life being saved by Private Starkie. Lieutenant, 24th August, 1853. Served with the regiment in the Ionian Islands and India. Captain, 23rd March, 1858. Retired, 10th April, 1866.

Borthwick, Robert. Ensign, 13th April, 1849; lieutenant, 31st December, 1850. Served in the Kaffir War of 1851-52; wounded at Fort Hare. Retired, 1854.

Boulderson, John. From 71st Foot, with which he served in the Indian Campaign of 1858; was present at the battle of Kotakeserai, recapture of Gwalior (medal with clasp), also against the hill tribes of the north-west frontier of India in 1863 (medal with clasp). To the 91st, 18th December, 1875, with which he served in the Zulu campaign of 1879; present at the battle of Ginginhlovo, relief of Ekowe, and subsequent operations (medal with clasp).

Bowman, David. Ensign, 27th September, 1804; lieutenant, 19th June, 1806; captain, 16th December, 1813. To half-pay, 25th February, 1816.

Boyd, John. From 82nd Foot. Captain, 23rd September, 1836; major, 10th January, 1837. Retired, 1839.

Bozon, Mark Anthony. Ensign, 8th October, 1794; lieutenant, 1795. To 55th Foot, 20th August, 1802.

Brady, Hugh. From 21st Light Dragoons. Captain, 5th September, 1805. Retired, 1810.

Briggs, James. Ensign, 10th September, 1812; lieutenant, 28th July, 1814. Served in Holland, wounded severely through the shoulder, and taken prisoner at Bergen-op-Zoom. To half-pay, 25th February, 1816.

Brock, Nicholas M. Ensign, 21st December, 1855. To 82nd Foot, 1856.

Brown, Eugene. Ensign, 14th September, 1809; lieutenant, 9th July, 1812. Present at Waterloo. To half-pay, 25th April, 1817.

Brown, John. From 2nd West India Regiment, 1835. Adjutant, 14th November, 1835, to 26th January, 1843; lieutenant, 31st December, 1839; captain, 14th April, 1846. Served in the reserve battalion, and on the staff at the Cape. Retired, 1852. Died at Longford, Ireland.

Bruce, John. Ensign, 15th February, 1850; lieutenant, 14th October, 1851; captain, 1st September, 1854. Served at the Cape (Kaffir War) and in Greece with the regiment. Retired, 17th November, 1857. Died in Edinburgh, 1858.

Bruce, Alexander Cunningham (p. s. c.). Ensign, 18th June, 1852; lieutenant, March, 1854. Served in Malta, Greece, Ionian Islands, and India, with the regiment. Adjutant, 1855 to 1857; captain, 31st August, 1858. Served on the staff in India as deputy-adjutant and quarter-master-general, Bengal, 1863 to 1868. Brigade-major at Shorncliffe, 1869 to 1871. Major, 1st January, 1873. Commanded the regiment during the Zulu War of 1879; was present at the battle of Ginginhlovo, relief of Ekowe, and subsequent operations; was mentioned in the despatches. Lieutenant-colonel, 21st June, 1879. Medal with clasp and C.B.

Bruce, Stewart Hervey. From 63rd Foot, with which he had served in the Crimea from the 6th September, 1855, including the siege and fall of Sebastopol; also the bombardment and capture of Kinbourne (medal with clasp and Turkish medal). Captain, 19th December, 1861. To 91st, 6th November, 1863. Served with the regiment in India. To half-pay, 4th February, 1871.

Brunker, James Robert. Ensign, 9th April, 1825; lieutenant, 9th September, 1828; adjutant, 8th January, 1829, to 4th October, 1832. Served in Jamaica with the regiment. Captain, 14th September, 1832. To 15th Foot, 1833.

Bryant, John Valentine. From 44th Foot. Captain, 16th January, 1812. Died, 1814.

Buchan, Alexander. From half-pay, 25th Foot. Lieutenant, 1st July, 1819; adjutant, 24th October, 1821, to 23rd April, 1823. To 77th Foot, 10th November, 1825.

Bulkeley, Thomas. Ensign, 1796. Retired, 1797.

Buller, John Edward. Ensign, 4th December, 1857; lieutenant, 15th December, 1858. Served in the Ionian Islands and India with the regiment, and as aide-de-camp to Sir William Mansfield, Commander-in-Chief in India. Died, 1870.

Bunbury, Thomas. From 3rd Foot. Lieutenant, 17th August, 1809. Served in the Peninsula, at Nive (severely wounded), Nivelle, and Toulouse, attached to Portuguese service. To half-pay, 25th October, 1814. Subsequently served in 80th Foot.

Burcham, John. Ensign, 2nd September, 1812. Retired, 1813.

Burke, Hubert P. Ensign, 10th July, 1855; lieutenant, 5th March, 1858. Served in the Ionian Islands and India with the regiment. To 8th Hussars, 15th November, 1864.

Burne, Cornwall. From 64th Foot. Lieutenant, 4th January, 1821; captain, 3rd February, 1825; major, 8th February, 1831. Commanded the regiment at St. Helena for a short time after Colonel Anderson left. Lieutenant-colonel, 2nd July, 1841. To half-pay, 16th July, 1841. Died in Ireland.

Burton, Samuel Judge. From 76th Foot. Lieutenant, 4th November, 1836. Retired, 1839.

Burton, John Edward. Ensign, 19th May, 1854; lieutenant, 14th December, 1855; captain, 22nd October, 1861. Served in Malta, Greece, Ionian Islands, and India, with the regiment. Adjutant, 1st Adm. Batt. Banffshire Rifle Volunteers, 1874 to 1879. Brevet-major, 23rd February, 1875. Retired, 1879.

Burtsal, Henry. From 22nd Foot. Lieutenant, 6th September, 1802. Retired, 1804.

Butler, Richard. Ensign, 16th July, 1812; lieutenant, 9th June, 1814. To half-pay, 25th February, 1816.

Cahil, Patrick. Promoted from the rank of sergeant-major to ensign, 31st March, 1814, for conspicuous conduct while serving with the 2nd battalion at Bergen-op-Zoom. Was present at Waterloo. Promoted lieutenant, 11th August, 1822; adjutant, 24th April, 1823, to 1827. Died in Jamaica, 9th December, 1827.

Cahil, David. Ensign, 10th November, 1825 (lieutenant in the 2nd Foot, 21st December, 1832).

Cahill, John Campbell. Ensign, 28th February, 1828; lieutenant, 8th May, 1835. Was on board the *Abercrombie Robinson* when wrecked in Table Bay in 1842. Captain, 14th October, 1842. Served in the reserve battalion at the Cape. Drowned at Fort Beaufort in 1855.

Calder, William. Ensign, 28th April, 1825; lieutenant, 8th January, 1829. Died in Jamaica, 1st August, 1829.

Calder, John Mitchelson. From Royal African Colonial Corps. Lieutenant, 19th July, 1827. To 9th Foot, 1836.

Caldwell, Hugh. Assistant-surgeon, 1815. To half-pay, 1816.

Caldwell, Charles Benjamin. From 8th Foot. Lieutenant, 7th October, 1829; captain, 4th October, 1833. To half-pay unattached, 23rd April, 1841.

Callender, Alexander James. From 25th Foot. Captain, 10th October, 1811; major, 4th June, 1814. Served with the regiment during their second visit to the Peninsula, at Toulouse (wounded). Was present at Waterloo. To half-pay, 1821.

Callender, Alexander. Assistant-surgeon, 1829. To 69th Foot, 1831.

Campbell, Archibald. From 69th, 71st, and 74th Regiments. Major, 10th February, 1794. To brigadier-general in the West Indies, 7th September, 1795.

Campbell, **Archibald**. From half-pay. Captain, 14th February, 1794. To Cape Regiment, 27th June, 1801.

Campbell, **Archibald**. Lieutenant, 14th February, 1794. To paymaster 92nd Foot, 23rd January, 1800.

Campbell, **Archibald**. From half-pay. Captain, 13th August, 1794. To Scotch Brigade, 16th June, 1801. Subsequently assisted at the storming of Fort Gawilghur in India, 14th December, 1803.

Campbell, **Archibald**. Lieutenant, 6th November, 1801; captain, 1st October, 1807. Served with the regiment in the Peninsular War. Was present at Waterloo. To half-pay, 1816.

Campbell, **Archibald**. Ensign, 30th August, 1801; lieutenant, 25th February, 1804; captain, 12th October, 1809 (1810).

Campbell, **Archibald**. Ensign, 5th November, 1803; lieutenant, 19th September, 1804; captain, 15th January, 1812. Served with the regiment in the Peninsular War. Was present at Waterloo. Died, 1822.

Campbell, Angus. Lieutenant, 26th September, 1794. To 78th Foot, 30th September, 1796.

Campbell, Alexander. From half-pay. Lieutenant, 4th February, 1795 (1799).

Campbell, **Alexander**. Ensign, 28th April, 1802; lieutenant, 12th August, 1803 (1808).

Campbell, **Alexander**. Ensign, 15th August, 1805; lieutenant, 12th May, 1808; captain, 3rd September, 1818. Served with the regiment during the Peninsular War, at Orthes (wounded). Was present at Waterloo. To half-pay, 16th December, 1821. Died, 1835.

Campbell, **Alexander**. Ensign, 14th December, 1809; lieutenant, 20th July, 1813. Was present at Waterloo. To half-pay, 25th March, 1817. Subsequently served in 38th Foot.

Campbell, **Archibald**. Ensign, 13th January, 1831; adjutant, 5th October, 1832, to 13th November, 1835; lieutenant, 29th November, 1833. Retired, 1838.

Campbell, **Breadalbane**. Ensign, 8th January, 1829; lieutenant, 18th January, 1831. Retired, 1835.

Campbell, **Colin**. Captain, 17th February, 1794. To 60th Foot, 3rd June, 1796.

Campbell, **Colin**. Lieutenant, 12th October, 1794; captain, 3rd January, 1801. To 70th Foot, 1808.

Campbell, **Colin**. Ensign, 10th April, 1835; lieutenant, 2nd February, 1838; captain, 12th October, 1841. Served in the Kaffir War of 1846-47 in reserve battalion. To half-pay, 25th August, 1852. Died, 15th June, 1872.

Campbell, **Colin**. Sub-lieutenant, 11th December, 1872; lieutenant, 29th November, 1876. Retired, 1878.

Campbell, Colin. Lieutenant, 29th November, 1876. Retired, 1878.

Campbell, Donald. Captain, 16th February, 1794. To Cape Regiment, 1801. Subsequently served in the 40th Foot.

Campbell, Dugald. Ensign, 22nd October, 1801; lieutenant, 9th August, 1804; adjutant, 14th April, 1808, to 25th April, 1810; captain, 23rd November, 1809. Served with the regiment in the Peninsular War. Was present at Waterloo. Died, 1825.

Campbell, Dugald. Lieutenant, 12th August, 1805; captain, 1st July, 1813. Served in the Peninsular War with the regiment, and was killed at Nive, December, 1813.

Campbell, Dugald. Paymaster, 1808. Was present at Waterloo (1817).

Campbell, David. Ensign, 5th October, 1815. To half-pay, 25th February, 1816. Returned to the 91st as captain, 30th July, 1829. Retired, 13th November, 1835.

Campbell, Duncan (of Lochnell). From 1st Foot Guards. Appointed first commanding officer of the regiment, 10th February, 1794; colonel, 3rd May, 1796; major-general, 29th April, 1802; lieutenant-general, 25th April, 1808; general, 12th August, 1819. Was colonel of the regiment from 3rd of May, 1796, to the date of his death at Edinburgh, 18th April, 1837.

Campbell, Duncan. Lieutenant, 21st April, 1794. To 42nd Foot, 1803.

Campbell, Duncan. Quarter-master, 1794 to 1797.

Campbell, Duncan. Ensign, 12th of October, 1804; lieutenant, 25th December, 1806; captain, 3rd March, 1814. To half-pay, 25th February, 1816. Died, 25th September, 1833.

Campbell, Hugh. Lieutenant, 12th February, 1794. To 83rd Foot, 2nd December, 1795.

Campbell, James. Captain-lieutenant and captain, 3rd July, 1794 (1800).

Campbell, James. From 86th Foot. Major, 19th July, 1798; lieutenant-colonel, 25th September, 1803 (1807).

Campbell, James. Ensign, 17th September, 1803; lieutenant, 25th August, 1804; captain, 31st March, 1808. Retired, 1812.

Campbell, James. Surgeon, 10th February, 1794 (1805). Succeeded his brother to the Jura Estate, and died 2nd December, 1838.

Campbell, John. Captain, 23rd February, 1794 (1798).

Campbell, John. Lieutenant, 19th April, 1794; captain, 25th June, 1803. To 10th Foot, 1807.

Campbell, John M. Ensign, 27th November, 1794; lieutenant, 27th July, 1795. Served with the regiment at the Cape of Good Hope. Retired, 1802.

Campbell, John. Ensign, 18th March, 1795; lieutenant, 3rd October, 1798 (1800).

Campbell, John. Lieutenant, 9th September, 1796 (1802).

Campbell, John. Lieutenant, 25th August, 1804 (1806).

Campbell, John. Ensign, 6th June, 1805; lieutenant, 23rd August, 1807; captain, 19th May, **1814.** Served in Holland, wounded and taken prisoner at Bergen-op-Zoom in 1814. To half-pay, 25th February, 1816.

Campbell, John. Ensign, 11th August, 1805; lieutenant, 24th August, 1807. Served with the regiment in the Peninsular War. Was present at Waterloo. Captain, 7th September, 1815. To half-pay, 25th February, 1816.

Campbell, John. Ensign, 19th June, 1806. To 56th Foot, 1807.

Campbell, John. Ensign, 10th August, 1808; lieutenant, 23rd January, 1812. To half-pay, 25th March, 1817.

Campbell, John. Ensign, 21st January, 1819. To 46th Foot, 1821.

Campbell, John Alexander. Ensign, 8th April, 1825. To half-pay, 2nd July, 1829.

Campbell, John Francis Glencairn, C.B. Ensign, 25th October, 1827; lieutenant, 27th August, 1829; captain, 23rd November, 1832; major, 8th July, 1843. Commanded the infantry force against insurgent Boers, beyond the Orange River, South Africa, in April, 1845. Lieutenant-colonel, 14th April, 1846. Commanded the reserve battalion, 91st Regiment, throughout the Kaffir War of 1846–47. Commanded a party of 200 men of the regiment and 180 Hottentot burghers which forced the pass in the Amatola Mountains on the 16th April, 1846, inflicting a loss of 200 men on the enemy; on this occasion had his charger shot whilst assisting a wounded man to mount (mentioned in despatches). Commanded 175 men of the regiment on the 17th April, 1846, despatched to the assistance of Major Gibson, 7th Dragoon Guards, by which timely reinforcement the ammunition waggons were saved, the baggage of the division being in the hands of the enemy (mentioned in despatches). Commanded the regiment dispersed to meet the disposition of the enemy on the retreat to Block Drift on the 18th April, and held the Drift for two hours in the face of an overwhelming force of the enemy (mentioned in despatches). Commanded the advance post at Block Drift on the 12th May, when it was attacked by 2000 Kaffirs, who were beaten off with considerable loss. Appointed commandant of Fort Beaufort, and subsequently to command one of the three columns of the attack against the chief Sandilla, which terminated the war. Specially mentioned in Colonel Somerset's despatches of the 17th and

18th April, 1846, and also in Lieutenant-General Sir George Berkeley's general order of the 17th December, 1847 (medal and C.B.). Colonel, 20th June, 1854. Commanded the British contingent in Greece from April, 1855, to the conclusion of the Crimean War. Resigned command of the regiment on the 21st October, 1858, on appointment to command a brigade at Tonghoo in Burmah. Major-general, 12th November, 1860; colonel, 79th Foot, 12th July, 1868.

Campbell, John B. Ensign, 14th August, 1860. Retired, 9th October, 1863.

Campbell, Robert. Ensign, 17th August, 1804; lieutenant, 14th August, 1805 (1808).

Campbell, Robert. Ensign, 18th December, 1806; lieutenant, 16th May, 1808. To half-pay, 22nd July, 1819.

Capel, Christopher. Ensign, 23rd April, 1841; lieutenant, 14th October, 1842. To 75th Foot, 1842.

Carlisle, Andrew Pattison. From half-pay, 54th Foot. Lieutenant, 3rd March, 1825. Retired, 1829.

Cathcart, Andrew. Ensign, 26th August, 1807; lieutenant, 11th May, 1809. Served with the regiment in the Peninsular War. Was present at Waterloo and Cambray (wounded slightly, 24th June, 1815). To half-pay, 4th January, 1821.

Caudwell, William Darling. Ensign, 21st February, 1860; lieutenant, 25th February, 1864. Served in India with the regiment. Captain, 1st January, 1873. To Pay Department, 8th July, 1878. Served in the Zulu War, 1879 (medal with clasp). Died, 1883.

Cavendish, Alfred E. J. Second lieutenant, 14th January, 1880; lieutenant, 1st July, 1881.

Chambers, William. Assistant-surgeon, 1805. To 18th Light Dragoons, 1808.

Chater, Vernor. Ensign, 12th July, 1864. Served in India with the regiment. Lieutenant, 29th January, 1870; adjutant, 29th January, 1870, to 30th November, 1875; captain, 12th February, 1875. Aide-de-camp to the general officer commanding North Britain, 31st March, 1877, to 31st October, 1878. Aide-de-camp to the Governor-general of Canada, 25th November, 1878, to 14th November, 1881. Served during the latter part of the Zulu War of 1879, part of the time as provost-marshal and deputy assistant-adjutant-general to the first division (medal with clasp).

Chatfield, George Kemp. From 49th Foot, 1861, with which he had served in the Crimean campaign of 1854–55, including the siege of Sebastopol (wounded in the trenches on the 3rd September, 1855), storm and capture of the Quarries, and assault of the Redan, on the 18th June (medal and clasp, Sardinian and Turkish medals). Captain, 4th February, 1856. Served with the regiment in India. Died, 1862.

Christian, Ewan John. From 25th Foot. Lieutenant, 14th July, 1869. Retired, 1870.

Christie, James. Ensign, 24th July, 1835; lieutenant, 22nd February, 1839; captain, 13th October, 1843. Served through the earlier part of the Kaffir War of 1846–47 with the battalion, and the latter in the reserve, with which he served until he retired, in 1849.

Clavering, Henry M. From half-pay. Major, 30th July, 1794. To Argyllshire Fencibles, 1795. Was appointed brigadier-general in South America, 1807, where he remained until 1826.

Clinch, Charles. From 71st Foot. Lieutenant, 1st January, 1799; captain, 5th August, 1804 (1806).

Cloete, Peter Graham. Ensign, 17th September, 1839 (1840).

Cochrane, James Day. Ensign, 31st December, 1841; lieutenant, 13th October, 1843; captain, 4th May, 1849. Served in the Kaffir War of 1846–47, and was severely wounded by a shot through the body and left hand, with a contusion in the groin, during the retreat on the 18th April, 1846, of Colonel Somerset's division from the Amatola Mountains to Block Drift. Served with the regiment in Greece in 1855. To half-pay, unattached, 7th September. Died March, 1867.

Cole, Richard Sweet. From 6th Foot. Ensign, 12th August, 1836; lieutenant, 25th December, 1838. Served at the Cape (Kaffir War) with the regiment. Retired, 1851.

Collett, Thomas S. Assistant-surgeon, 1803. To 83rd Foot, 1804.

Collins, George. Ensign, 20th May, 1799; lieutenant, 8th October, 1801. To half-pay, 1803.

Collings, Godfrey Disney. Sub-lieutenant, 28th February, 1874; lieutenant, 28th February, 1876. Served during the Zulu War of 1879; was present at the battle of Ginginhlovo (medal with clasp). Was invalided home shortly afterwards. Served in Mauritius with a detachment of the regiment.

Colls, Edward Cooper. Paymaster, 1831. Died at Grahamstown, 30th January, 1840.

Cooke, Robert. Quarter-master, 1797 (1804).

Cookson, Freville. Sub-lieutenant and lieutenant, 26th February, 1873. Served during the Zulu War of 1879; was present at the battle of Ginginhlovo and relief of Ekowe with the regiment, and during the subsequent operations served in the Mounted Infantry (medal with clasp).

Cooper, John Cole. Ensign, 23rd December, 1795. To 22nd Light Dragoons, 21st September, 1799.

Cooper, Samuel. Ensign, 1797; lieutenant, 8th August, 1798. Retired, 1802.

Corbett, Patrick. Quarter-master, 1804 to 1807.

Crampton, Robert Henry. Ensign, 5th November, 1847. Served in the Kaffir War, 1847. Dangerously wounded in action with the Boers at Boemplaats, after which he never recovered the use of his right arm. Lieutenant, 15th August, 1850. Served in Greece with the regiment. To 2nd Foot, 17th November, 1857.

Craufurd, James Catlin. From the Independents. Major, 1796; lieutenant-colonel, 25th April, 1797; colonel, 30th October, 1805. Served with the regiment in the Peninsula, at Roleia, and at Corunna as brigadier. Died, 1810.

Craufurd, George Douglas. Ensign, 27th December, 1806; lieutenant, 18th May, 1808. Served in the Peninsular War with the regiment, and afterwards attached to the Portuguese service. Killed at Pyrenees, 28th July, 1813.

Craufurd, James Robertson. Colonel 91st, 27th August, 1870, to date. (Received his first commission in 1821. General, 25th October, 1871, and was placed on the retired list, 1st October, 1877.)

Craufurd, William Reginald Houison. Ensign, 6th March, 1869; lieutenant, 14th September, 1870; captain, 23rd March, 1879. Served during the Zulu War of 1879; was present at the battle of Ginginhlovo, relief of Ekowe, and subsequent operations (medal with clasp).

Crawford, W. H. Lieutenant, 11th October, 1794. To 98th Foot, 1795.

Creighton, Abraham. From 55th Foot. Captain, 21st July, 1823. Retired, 1826.

Crofton, William Edward. From 50th Foot. Captain, 13th April, 1826. Retired, 29th November, 1833.

Croker, Edward. From 16th Foot. Lieutenant, 24th August, 1826. Retired, 1829.

Cruickshank, James Alexander. Ensign, 10th October, 1840; lieutenant, 29th April, 1842. To 87th Foot, 1844.

Culpeper, Charles A. H. Bishop. Ensign, 12th May, 1869; lieutenant, 26th July, 1871. Retired, 1874.

Curling, Henry. From 25th and 30th Foot. Lieutenant, 6th January, 1832. To half-pay, 30th December, 1834.

Dalrymple, G. H. Paymaster, 1840 to 1856. Accidentally killed at Piræus, 12th June, 1856, by the falling of his house. He was buried outside the town of Piræus, on the right of the road to Athens.

Dashwood, Charles Francis. From 92nd Highlanders. Captain, 12th June, 1869. Retired, 1870.

Dealtry, Hugh T. C. Ensign, 16th August, 1864. Served with the regiment in India. Retired, 6th March, 1869.

Dewell, Charles Goddard. Ensign, 8th June, 1852; lieutenant, 10th March, 1844; captain, 17th November, 1857. **Served in Malta, Greece, Ionian Islands, and India, with the regiment. Retired, 22nd October, 1861.**

D'Eye, William Rust. Ensign, 13th May, 1853; lieutenant, 9th February, 1855; captain, 4th November, 1859. Served with the regiment in Malta, Greece, Ionian Islands, and India. To 92nd Highlanders, 1869.

Dickson, Edward John. Ensign, 27th September, 1839; lieutenant, 14th October, 1842. Served with the regiment in the Kaffir War of 1846–47, and had his horse shot under him, 21st May, 1846, when proceeding from Grahamstown to Fort Peddie. To half-pay, 30th April, 1850.

Dickson, David T. A. Second lieutenant, 22nd February, 1879. Served with the regiment during the latter part of the Zulu War. Died in Edinburgh, 1883. A tablet was erected to his memory by his brother officers in Stirling Church.

Divir, John Hawkins. Surgeon, 1830. Retired, 1840.

Dobie, James Henry. Ensign, 21st September, 1852; lieutenant, 5th September, 1854. Served in Malta, Greece, and Ionian Islands, with the regiment. Retired, 11th December, 1857.

Douglas, Sir William, K.C.B. From the 2nd battalion 84th Foot. Captain, 27th of June, 1798. In 1804 he was one of the four officers selected to raise a certain number of men for the regiment, for which service he was promoted lieutenant-colonel, 2nd August, 1804. Commanded the 91st from 1808 to the day of his death. Was present at the actions of Roleia and Corunna (medal). Served in the ill-fated Walcheren Expedition in 1809, where he contracted the fever which the British troops suffered so much from, and from the effects of which he never recovered. Was present at the actions of Pyrenees, Nivelle, Nive, Orthes (wounded), Toulouse (wounded slightly). Was in the reserve with the 91st at Waterloo, and in the march to Paris. Promoted colonel in army, 4th June, 1814. Received gold medal, and made a Knight Companion of the Bath. Died at Valenciennes, 23rd August, 1818, where he was buried.

Douglas, Robert. Assistant-surgeon, 1803; surgeon, 1805. Was present at Waterloo. To half-pay, 1821.

Ducat, Dugald, P.W. Ensign, 24th February, 1814; lieutenant, 5th May, 1822; captain, 4th August, 1828; major, 2nd July, 1841. Served in the Peninsular War from August, 1813, to its close; was present at the battles of Nivelle, Nive, Orthes, and Toulouse. Present at Waterloo and the storming of Cambray. Served in South Africa with the 1st battalion in 1842, until October of that year, when he assumed command of the reserve battalion. Died at Colesberg, South Africa, in 1844.

Duke, Roger. Ensign, 25th April, 1816; lieutenant, 14th February, 1823. To half-pay, 29th September, 1825.

Dunbar, Penrose John. Ensign, 8th December, 1848. To 32nd Foot, 1849.

Eddie, William Cruickshank. Assistant-surgeon, 1826. To Cape Mounted Riflemen, 1841.

Edmonstone, Charles Henry. From 21st Foot, 1830. Lieutenant, 12th April, 1833. To 81st Foot, 1837.

Egan, Carberry. From 9th garrison battalion. Lieutenant, 19th May, 1808. Served with the regiment during the second visit to the Peninsula. Was present at Waterloo (1822).

Elkington, Arthur. Ensign, 28th January, 1859. Served in India with the regiment. To Commissariat Department, 21st April, 1863.

Elrington, Thomas Gerard. Ensign, 29th July, 1859. To 2nd Dragoon Guards, 1860.

Elwes, William Henry. Ensign, 14th May, 1801. Retired, 1803.

Enright, John. Assistant-surgeon, 1801. To Light Dragoons, 1803. Returned to 91st, 1808. To 94th Foot, 1810.

Enzinger, John. From 1st garrison battalion. Lieutenant, 8th June, 1815. To half-pay, 25th February, 1816.

Erskine, Henry. From Scotch Brigade. Captain, 16th June, 1801. To 1st Foot, 1804.

Evans, Richard Henry. From half-pay, 39th Foot. Lieutenant, 7th September, 1820. Died, 1822.

Ewing, William. From 64th Foot. Lieutenant, 30th December, 1834 (1839).

Fairfowl, John. Paymaster, 1809. Died, 1821.

Fallowfield, Hugh Gordon. Ensign, 23rd October, 1867; lieutenant, 28th May, 1870. Was on the guard of honour, and carried the colour at the wedding of H.R.H. Princess Louise with the Marquis of Lorne, 21st March, 1871. Captain, 15th March, 1879. Served in the Zulu War of 1879; was present at the battle of Ginginhlovo and relief of Ekowe (medal with clasp). Was invalided home shortly afterwards. Appointed adjutant of the Royal Renfrew Militia, 27th May, 1881.

Farmer, John Charles. From 76th Foot. Lieutenant, 9th August, 1821 (1822).

Fenwick, Thomas Lisle. From 81st Foot. Lieutenant, 13th September, 1810. Served with the regiment during the second visit to the Peninsula. Was present at Waterloo. To half-pay, 71st Foot, 8th August, 1816.

Ferguson, P. B. T. Ensign, 6th May, 1795. Retired, 1797.

Ferguson, Archibald. Quarter-master, 1810. Retired, 1816.

Ferguson, George. Quarter-master, 1826 (1837).

Ferrier, James. Lieutenant, 29th March, 1794. To Scotch Brigade, 6th May, 1795.

Ferrier, Lorne. Lieutenant, 24th May, 1794 (1797).

Finch, Roger. From 1st garrison battalion (Ireland). Captain, 13th August, 1807. To half-pay, 8th garrison battalion (Ireland), 1810.

Fitzgerald, Edward. Ensign, 27th July, 1795 (1797).

Fitzgerald, Ormond. Ensign, 6th January, 1843. Served in the reserve battalion through the Kaffir War of 1846. Lieutenant, 30th April, 1847. To 86th Foot, 17th December, 1847.

Fitz Gerald, John. Paymaster, 1868. To 13th Hussars, 16th September, 1873.

Footner, Edward. Assistant-surgeon, 1871. To Medical Department, 1876.

Forbes, David. Ensign, 8th October, 1829; lieutenant, 23rd November, 1832; captain, 24th July, 1835; major, 14th April, 1846; brevet lieutenant-colonel, 28th May, 1853. Served with the reserve battalion and received the brevet for his services in the Kaffir Wars of 1846-47 and 1851-52-53 (medal), mentioned in despatches. Retired on full pay, 1855, as colonel.

Forbes, James. Ensign, 14th March, 1834. To the 11th Regiment, 1837.

Forrest, John. Surgeon, 1848. To staff, 21st May, 1850. Had previously served in the expedition against the Rajah of Kolapore in 1827, also against the insurgent Boers beyond the Orange River, South Africa, in 1845, and in the Kaffir War of 1846.

Forster, Benjamin. From 46th Foot. Lieutenant, 24th November, 1814. To half-pay, 1815.

Foskey, Richard Webb. Ensign, 23rd April, 1823; lieutenant, 10th September, 1825. Retired, 1829.

Fowler, Donald G. M. Lieutenant, 13th June, 1874. Served in the Zulu War of 1879; was present at the battle of Ginginhlovo, relief of Ekowe, and subsequent operations (medal with clasp).

Frank, Philip. Assistant-surgeon, 1855. Served in the Service Companies until the 28th March, 1856, when he was posted to the Depôt. To half-pay, 1st May, 1856.

Fraser, Donald. Ensign, 18th April, 1800 (1802).

Fraser, William. Lieutenant, 30th September, 1819; captain, 28th September, 1824; major, 13th July, 1826. Was present at Waterloo. Promoted lieutenant-colonel, unattached, 1831.

Fraser, John. From 53rd Foot, with which he had served in the Peninsula from August, 1811, to the end of the war, including the siege and capture of the fortified convents at, and the battle of, Salamanca; siege of the castle of Burgos; battles of Vittoria, Pyrenees, Nivelle, and Toulouse. Severely wounded at Pampeluna, 26th July, 1813. Captain 91st, 17th August, 1832. To major, half-pay, unattached, 15th April, 1842.

Fraser, Thomas. Second lieutenant, 22nd January, 1879. Served in the Zulu War of 1879, was present at the battle of Ginginhlovo, on which occasion he carried the Queen's colour; relief of Ekowe and subsequent operations (medal with clasp). Lieutenant, 8th April, 1880. Served at Mauritius with a detachment of the regiment.

Fry, John William. From 86th Foot, 1864, with which he served with the Central India Field Force under Sir Hugh Rose, in 1857-58, and had been present at the actions of Kooneh, all the operations before Calpee, from the 15th to the 22nd May; battle of Golowlie, capture of the town and fortress of Calpee, battle of Morar, battle before, and capture of, the town and fortress of Gwalior; commanded three companies of the 86th Foot, and captured a battery of three guns on the heights before Gwalior, and turned them on the enemy; also present at the taking of Pourie (medal with clasp). Captain, 29th February, 1863. To 88th Foot, 1869.

Gage, Hodson. Ensign, 12th November, 1812. To 60th Foot, 7th November, 1813.

Galbreath, George. Paymaster, 1800 (1808).

Gamble, Robert. Ensign, 15th July, 1814. To half-pay, 25th February, 1816.

Gard, William Goskwyck. From military train. Lieutenant, 27th July, 1866. To 91st, 1869. Captain, 24th December, 1873. Appointed adjutant to the Inverness-shire Volunteers, 23rd December, 1878.

Garland, William. From half-pay, 4th Foot. Lieutenant, 30th October, 1805. To Royal Corsican Rangers, 20th June, 1811.

Gibbons, Frederick. From half-pay, 26th Foot. Captain, 21st January, 1819. To 95th Foot, 1st December, 1823.

Gillies, James. Was promoted quarter-master from sergeant-major, 29th October, 1873. Served in the Zulu War of 1879, was present at the battle of Ginginhlovo and subsequent operations (medal with clasp).

Glass, Henry E. Ensign, 17th March, 1854. To 37th Foot, 1855.

Glegg, Berkenhead. From 49th Foot. Major, 17th August, 1797. To half-pay, 91st, 1810.

Goff, Gerald Lionel Joseph. Sub-lieutenant, 10th March, 1875; lieutenant, 10th March, 1875 (antedated). Served during the Zulu War of 1879; was present at the battle of Ginginhlovo, relief of Ekowe, and subsequent operations (medal with clasp).

Goldsworthy, Walter T. From 8th Hussars. Captain, 28th October, 1864. Had previously served in Oude with the Volunteer Cavalry of Havelock's column in 1857, and was present at the actions of Oonao and Busseerutgunje, and re-capture of Busseerutgunje; for these services he received a commission in the 8th Hussars; served in Rajpootana and Central India, on the staff and with the 8th Hussars throughout the campaign of 1858-59, including the siege of Kotah, re-occupation of Chondeyree, battle of Kotah ke Serai (as aide-de-camp to Brigadier Smith), capture of Gwalior (as aide-de-camp to Sir Hugh Rose), siege and capture of Pourie, actions of Koondrye and Boordah, and brigade-major in the Rajpootana Field Force, which appointment he held from the fall of Gwalior in June, 1858, to the end of the war (several times mentioned in despatches, medal with clasp). Served throughout the Abyssinian Expedition on the staff as brigade major of cavalry, and was present at the taking of Magdala (twice mentioned in despatches, medal, and promoted to major, unattached, without purchase). Major, 11th December, 1866. To half-pay, 30th September, 1868. Subsequently assistant-adjutant and quarter-master-general for Cork District. Sat as member of Parliament for Hammersmith.

Gordon, Theodore. Assistant-surgeon, 1804. To half-pay, 1809.

Gordon, Bertie Edward Murray. Ensign, 26th October, 1832; lieutenant, 24th July, 1835; captain, 23rd April, 1841. Was in command of troops on board the *Abercrombie Robinson* when wrecked in Table Bay, Cape of Good Hope, for which he was subsequently granted £100 per annum pension for meritorious service. Served in the Kaffir War of 1846-47. Major, 13th October, 1848; brevet lieutenant-colonel, 30th September, 1855; lieutenant-colonel, 31st August, 1858. Served in Greece and India with the regiment. Colonel, 31st August, 1860. Retired on half-pay, 28th January, 1870, having commanded the regiment for over twelve years. Died, 27th July, 1870.

Gordon, Gabriel. Colonel, 19th April, 1837, to 7th August, 1855. Had served previously in the 60th, at Martinique and Guadaloupe (medal with clasp).

Gordon, John. Quarter-master, 1841; ensign, 22nd January, 1847; adjutant, 22nd January, 1847; lieutenant, 27th December, 1849. Assegaied in action near Fort Hare, December, 1850, whilst saving the life of Lieutenant Borthwick, who was wounded, by placing him on his own charger.

Gordon, W. George Conway. Ensign, 9th June, 1849; lieutenant, 30th December, 1850; adjutant, 30th December, 1850, to 18th May, 1854; captain, 12th May, 1854. Served with the regiment at the Cape (Kaffir War) and in the Ionian Islands. Died, 21st September, 1858.

Gordon, William. Assistant-surgeon, 1855. Served in Greece with the regiment. To staff, 1856.

Gore, Hon. Charles, **K.C.B., K.H., P.W.** Had served previously with the 43rd in the Peninsula in July, 1811, and was present as one of the storming party of Fort San Francisco at the investment of Ciudad Rodrigo; also at the siege and storming of that fortress and of Badajoz, battle of Salamanca, as aide-de-camp to Sir Andrew Barnard; and in a similar capacity to Sir James Kempt in the battles of Vittoria, the Nivelle, the Nive (9th, 10th, and 11th December), Orthes, and Toulouse. He was also in the action of San Milan, capture of Madrid, storming of the heights of Vera, bridge of Yanzi, and all the skirmishes of the light division, from 1812 to the close of the war in 1814; after which he accompanied Sir James Kempt with the troops sent to Canada under his command; returned to Europe in time for the campaign of 1815, and was first and principal aide-de-camp to Sir James Kempt, and present at the battles of Quatre Bras (horse shot) and Waterloo (three horses shot), and capture of Paris. Received the war medal with nine clasps. Colonel of the 91st, 8th August, 1855, to 8th March, 1861. To 8th Foot, 9th March, 1861. Subsequently governor of Chelsea Hospital. Died, 4th September, 1869.

Gould, **Francis Augustus.** From half-pay (staff). Captain, 8th June, 1826. To half-pay, 7th September, 1832.

Gouldon, Francis **Attenbury.** From 93rd Foot. Lieutenant, 5th November, 1836. Retired, 1839.

Græme, Laurence. From half-pay, 33rd Foot. Captain, 16th January, 1826. Retired, 1834.

Grant, David **Macdowall.** Ensign, 2nd March, 1820. Died, 1823.

Grant, Gregory. Ensign, 4th August, 1837. Died at Nairn, in Scotland, February, 1839.

Grant, William. From sergeant-major to ensign, 13th August, 1858; lieutenant, 12th November, 1860; adjutant, 20th February, 1865, to 28th January, 1870; captain, 1871. Was on board the *Abercrombie Robinson* when wrecked in Table Bay, Cape of Good Hope, in 1842. Served with the regiment in the Kaffir War of 1846–47, including all the actions in the Amatola Mountains and Tambookieland Expedition beyond the Orange River in 1848, and action with and defeat of the insurgent Boers at Boemplaats. In the Kaffir War of 1850 and 1853. Present in every action in the Amatolas and Waterkloof in which the 91st were engaged (medal). Served in the Ionian Islands and India with the regiment. Was lieutenant of the guard of honour at the marriage of H.R.H. Princess Louise and the Marquis of Lorne, 21st March, 1871. Retired, 1874.

Gray, Henry. Ensign, 12th October, 1815. To half-pay, 25th February, 1816.

Green, Thomas. Ensign, 1st September, 1854. Served in Greece with the regiment. Retired, 19th June, 1857.

Gregorson, Donald. Ensign, 19th November, 1794; lieutenant, 18th March, 1795; captain, 3rd August, 1804; major, 30th April, 1812. To half-pay, 31st Foot, 9th November, 1815.

Gregorson, A. Assistant-surgeon, 1809. Died, 1810.

Gregg, Henry William. Ensign, 21st January, 1853; lieutenant, 10th November, 1854; captain, 28th September, 1858. Served at the Cape and in India with the regiment. Commanded the guard of honour at the wedding of H.R.H. Princess Louise with the Marquis of Lorne, 21st March, 1871. Brevet-major, 5th July, 1872. Died, 1874.

Gun, William. From 56th Foot. Captain, 7th June, 1810. Served with the regiment in the Peninsular War, at Orthes (wounded). To 56th Foot, 3rd May, 1821.

Gurney, William Prescod. Ensign, 17th February, 1854; lieutenant, 6th July, 1855; captain, 12th November, 1860. Served in Malta, Greece, Ionian Islands, and India, with the regiment; also in the Zulu War of 1879, was present at the battle of Ginginhlovo, relief of Ekowe, and subsequent operations (medal with clasp). Brevet-major, 28th September, 1873; major, 19th January, 1876. Died, 28th January, 1880, at Mauritius (where he commanded a detachment of the 91st), of fever, and from the effects of an illness contracted in the field during the Zulu campaign.

Gurney, Francis Prescod. Ensign, 25th July, 1865. Served in India with the regiment. Lieutenant, 31st January, 1870; captain, 14th April, 1875. Retired, 1878. Captain in reserve of officers.

Guthrie, Robert. Ensign, 3rd December, 1794 (1795).

Hacket, John George. Ensign, 25th January, 1839; lieutenant, 2nd July, 1841. Retired, 25th July, 1845.

Hadaway, Samuel M. Surgeon, 1843 to 1847.

Hall, Thomas E. A. Ensign, 2nd September, 1853; lieutenant, 5th June, 1855; captain, 11th May, 1860. Served at the Cape, Corfu, and India with the regiment. To 49th Foot, 9th March, 1861.

Hamilton, Francis. From 40th Foot. Lieutenant, 2nd November, 1809. To 3rd Ceylon Regiment, 1813.

Hamilton, Henry. Ensign, 15th December, 1857; lieutenant, 4th November, 1859. Served in the Ionian Islands and India with the regiment. Retired, 23rd March, 1866.

Hanson, William. Ensign, 26th December, 1806; lieutenant, 17th May, 1808. To 6th Dragoon Guards, 14th July, 1808.

Harding, Frederick. Ensign, 7th August, 1840; lieutenant, 15th April, 842. Died, 11th April, 1845.

Harvey, Charles Lacon. Ensign, 5th March, 1858; lieutenant, 10th July, 1860; captain, 23rd October, 1867. Served in India with the regiment. To 71st Highland Light Infantry, 16th September, 1868, p. s. c., 1870. Subsequently served on the staff in the Zulu War of 1879. Has received the Royal Humane Society's Medal for saving life.

Hawkins, George Palmer. From 3rd West India Regiment. Lieutenant, 20th May, 1824; captain, 15th May, 1827. To half-pay, 25th May, 1827.

Hawkshaw, T. S. From 31st Foot. Major, 1st June, 1815. To half-pay, 20th June, 1816.

Hay, David. Ensign, 12th April, 1799; lieutenant, 29th August, 1801; captain, 25th February, 1804. Retired, 1808.

Hay, William. From 67th Foot. Captain, 1st December, 1823; major, 3rd February, 1825. To half-pay, lieutenant-colonel, 10th January, 1826.

Hay, Charles Murray. Colonel 91st, 9th March, 1861, to 4th July, 1864.

Head, John. Ensign, 15th December, 1840; lieutenant, 19th November, 1842. To 29th Foot, 1847.

Hearne, Henry Thomas. From half-pay, West India Regiment. Captain, 14th November, 1826. Retired, 1830.

Heartszoak, Henry. Paymaster, 1823. Died, 1830.

Henderson, John. Assistant-surgeon, 1808. Died, 1812.

Henry, ——. Ensign, 9th June, 1814; adjutant, 1814 to 1816. To half-pay, 25th February, 1816.

Henry, Richard. Assistant-surgeon, 1861. Had served in India in 1857–59 (medal with clasp). To staff, 1865.

Heywood, James. Ensign, 1811. To 21st Light Dragoons, 9th June, 1812.

Hibbert, Francis Gordon. Ensign, 5th April, 1851; lieutenant, 23rd November, 1852; captain, 8th June, 1855. Served at the Cape (Kaffir War), wounded, 4th March, 1852, and in Greece with the regiment. To Royal Canadian Rifles, 15th June, 1857.

Hinton, William Cecil. Ensign, 22nd October, 1861. Served in India with the regiment. Lieutenant, 16th August, 1864. Retired, 1869.

Hollway, Charles. Ensign, 7th July, 1857; lieutenant, 28th September, 1858. Was staff-officer to Major Patterson, commanding the field force directed on Mooltye and Baitool, 27th March, 1859.

Captain, 10th April, 1866. Served in the Ionian Islands, India, and at the Cape, with the regiment. Brevet-major, 31st December, 1878; major, 21st June, 1879. To half-pay, 8th December, 1880.

Home, **Francis.** Ensign, 4th June, 1807; lieutenant, **10th August,** 1808. To 81st Foot, 13th September, 1810.

Hood, **James.** Ensign, 28th August, 1807; lieutenant, 3rd August, 1809. Served with the regiment in the Peninsular War, at Toulouse (wounded). Present at Waterloo. To the 2nd Royal Veteran Battalion, 25th December, 1821.

Hornsby, William **Wilson.** From half-pay. Lieutenant, 3rd December, 1829. Retired, 1840.

Horsburgh, David Knox. Ensign, 13th July, 1847; lieutenant, 4th May, 1849. Retired, 1850.

Horsley, **Nicholas.** Ensign, 18th March, 1813; lieutenant, 5th October, 1815. Served in Holland, was wounded and taken prisoner at Bergen-op-Zoom. To half-pay, 25th February, 1816. Subsequently appointed to the 38th Foot, 9th August, 1833.

Howard, **Robert Henry.** Ensign, 12th October, 1841; lieutenant, 13th January, 1845; captain, 28th April, 1852. Served throughout Kaffir War, 1846-47, with the reserve battalion. Returned to England with the 1st battalion in 1848. Retired, 8th June, 1855.

Hughes, John. Ensign, 29th April, 1824. To 92nd Foot, 13th September, 1827.

Hughes, Richard. From half-pay, 3rd West India Regiment. Lieutenant, 8th April, 1825. Died, 1826.

Hugo, Thomas. From 100th Foot. Captain, 22nd July, 1813. To half-pay, 25th February, 1816.

Jameson, Thomas Rose. Surgeon, 1851. To Medical Department, 1854.

Jennings, **Edmund William.** From 36th Foot. Lieutenant, 12th May, 1841; adjutant, 27th January, 1843, to 1848. Died, 7th July, 1848, in England, at Haslar.

Johnston, **Charles.** From 8th garrison battalion. Captain, 6th December, 1810. To 71st Foot, 10th December, 1812.

Johnston, **Henry F. Campbell.** Sub-lieutenant, 5th June, 1875; lieutenant, 5th June, 1877. Served during the Zulu War of 1879; was present at the battle of Ginginhlovo and relief of Ekowe (medal with clasp); was invalided home shortly afterwards. Served at Mauritius with a detachment of the regiment.

Jones, Robert Powell. Ensign, 19th June, 1857; lieutenant, 31st August, 1858. Served in the Ionian Islands and India with the regiment. Died, 24th February, 1864, at Punagurh, India.

Kemm, Henry Cæsar. Ensign, 7th September, 1858; lieutenant, 22nd October, 1861. Served in India with the regiment. Retired, 1870.

Kenny, John. From 56th Foot. Captain, 9th November, 1830. Retired, 1832.

Kerr, Arthur Percy. From the 51st Foot, with which he had served in the Burmah campaign from February, 1853, to the end of the war (medal). Captain, 14th December, 1855. Retired, 1858.

King, Fielder. From 84th Foot. Major, 2nd March, 1796. Served with the regiment at the Cape of Good Hope, being in command part of the time. To Cape Regiment, 1801.

King, Thomas Fraser. Ensign, 14th September, 1870; lieutenant, 1st November, 1871. To 49th Foot, 1872. Served subsequently with the 49th in Egypt.

Kirk, James Buchanan. From the 89th Foot as major to the 91st, 29th January, 1870. Was appointed to command the 91st in January, 1876. Was unable to proceed with the regiment to the Zulu War, in 1879, owing to a tumour having formed in his right foot, from the effects of which he subsequently died. Was placed on half-pay and appointed to the Intelligence Department, 21st June, 1879. Died, 1880.

Knox, Robert Spencer. Ensign, 16th May, 1808; lieutenant, 2nd January, 1812. Served with the regiment during its second visit to the Peninsula. Was present at Waterloo. To half-pay, 25th March, 1817.

Kysh, John Anthony. Paymaster, 1856. Served in Greece, Ionian Islands, and India with the regiment. To 109th Foot, 16th September, 1868.

Lamert, Matthew. Surgeon, 8th July, 1827. To half-pay, 1830.

Lamont, Norman, K.H., P.W. Ensign, 26th August, 1813; lieutenant, 3rd September, 1818; captain, 7th April, 1825; major, 2nd December, 1831. Served in the Peninsular campaign of 1813–14; present at the Pyrenees, Nivelle, Nive, Orthes, Toulouse, Waterloo, storming of Cambray, and capture of Paris. Died, 1845, at Fort Beaufort, South Africa (in command of the reserve battalion).

Lamont, John. Ensign, 20th October, 1846. Retired, 1848.

Lane, Thomas T. Ensign, 19th August, 1851; lieutenant, 1st January, 1854; captain, 14th December, 1855. Served throughout the Kaffir War of 1852–53 (medal), and was in India with the regiment. Retired, 23rd October, 1857.

Lavers, Robert Gresley. Ensign, 27th August, 1804; lieutenant, 31st October, 1805; captain, 8th January, 1818. Served in Jamaica with the regiment. Retired, 24th July, 1835.

Lavers, Robert Frederick Augustus. Ensign, 20th May, 1842. Was on board the *Abercrombie Robinson* when wrecked in Table Bay, Cape of Good Hope, 1842. To Cape Rifles, 1847.

Lennox, Lord Frederick. Ensign, 3rd September, 1818. Was appointed aide-de-camp to the commander of the forces in Canada. To 62nd Foot, 21st January, 1819.

Levingstone, Donald. Ensign, 27th June, 1805. Retired, 1806.

Lind, Lawrence. Ensign, 9th June, 1814. Was present at Waterloo. To half-pay, 25th November, 1816.

Lindsay, Henry. From Colonel Ward's Regiment. Lieutenant, 1st July, 1795. To 69th Foot, 9th July, 1803. Served subsequently at Waterloo, where he was badly wounded.

Lindsay, Martin George Thomas. From 78th Foot. Lieutenant-colonel, 8th April, 1842. Had served in Holland in 1814 and 1815, and was present at the bombardment of Antwerp. Commanded the troops on the *Abercrombie Robinson* transport in 1842, but was not on board when she was wrecked. Commanded the 1st battalion from October, 1842, until he retired in October, 1848, having served with his regiment throughout the wars of 1846–47.

Ling, John Theodore. From 4th Light Dragoons, with which he served in the Punjaub campaign of 1848–49, including the action at Ramnuggur (with the charging squadrons), battles of Chillianwallah and Goojerat, crossing of the Chenab, the Jhelum, and the Indus, surrender of the Sikh army at Rawul Pindee, and pursuit of the Afghans to Peshawur (medal and two clasps). Served towards the close of the Eastern campaign of 1855–56, with the local rank of major, as commandant of the 7th Regiment of Albanian Cavalry. Captain, 16th October, 1855. To 2nd Dragoon Guards, 1858. Died, 1860.

Livingstone, Duncan. Ensign, 25th August, 1814. To half-pay, 25th February, 1816.

Lloyd, Frederick. Ensign, 21st July, 1825; lieutenant, 26th August, 1829. Retired, 1830.

Lloyd, Craven. Ensign, 25th July, 1845; lieutenant, 13th July, 1849; captain, 14th October, 1851. Served in the Kaffir Wars of 1846–47 and 1851–52 with the reserve battalion. Retired, 1852. Died, 1855.

Lloyd, Cecil. Ensign, 9th February, 1864. Served in India with the regiment. Retired, 1869.

Loraine, Alexander. From 9th Foot. Lieutenant-colonel, 25th June, 1801. Became deputy-governor of Southsea Castle, 1809.

Lorimer, C. Ensign, 26th August, 1804. To West India Regiment, 1805.

Lorimer, William. Assistant-surgeon, 1815. To half-pay, 1816.

Love, Edward Missenden. From 28th Foot. Lieutenant, 17th August, 1838; captain, 20th December, 1842. Retired, 1849.

Lovett, G. W. Molyneux. Ensign, 27th April, 1820; lieutenant, 30th November, 1824. Commanded a detachment at Turks Island, Bahamas, in 1824. Served with the regiment in Jamaica for a short time. To half-pay, 30th Foot, 6th January, 1832.

Lowrie, Robert. Ensign, 3rd October, 1798; lieutenant, 10th May, 1799. Was one of the four officers selected to raise a number of men for the regiment in 1804, for which service he was promoted captain, 26th October, 1804. Served with the regiment during the Peninsular War; was severely wounded at Sauroren, 28th July, 1813, from the effects of which he died, 23rd November, 1813. A tablet was erected to his memory in St. Martin's Church, Lincoln, by his brother officers as a mark of their esteem. When St. Martin's Church was rebuilt in 1874, the tablet was removed to the new building.

Lucas, Samuel H. Lieutenant, 25th April, 1806; captain, 22nd January, 1809. Retired, 1810.

Macay, George. Ensign, 25th April, 1799. Retired, 1802.

Macbean, Alfred. From 64th Foot. Lieutenant, 24th July, 1823. Served with the regiment in Jamaica. Captain, 22nd March, 1827. Died, 9th June, 1828.

Macbeth, Hugh Mackay. Assistant-surgeon, 1858. To Royal Artillery, 1865.

Macdonald, Donald. Captain, 31st March, 1803. Served in the Peninsular War with the regiment. Killed at Badajos, March, 1812.

Macdonald, Æneas. Ensign, 30th May, 1805 (1806).

Macdonald, John. Major, 29th November, 1821; lieutenant-colonel, 23rd September, 1824, to 15th August, 1827. Subsequently made a K.C.B.

MacDonald, Dangan J. MacGregor. Ensign, 9th October, 1869; lieutenant, 28th October, 1871; captain, 25th May, 1879. Served in the Zulu War of 1879; was present at the battle of Ginginhlovo, relief of Ekowe, and subsequent operations (medal with clasp). Served at Mauritius with a detachment of the regiment in 1880.

Macdougall, Colin. Ensign, 12th October, 1809; lieutenant, 19th July, 1813. Served with the regiment during its second visit to the Peninsula, at Orthes (wounded), (1815).

Macdougall, John. Ensign, 27th August, 1807; lieutenant, 15th June, 1809. Served in the regiment through the Peninsular War. With the 2nd battalion in Holland. Was present at Waterloo. To half-pay, 39th Foot, 7th September, 1820.

MacDougall, John. Ensign, 1808 (1808).

MacDugald, Donald. Ensign, 18th March, 1795. To 33rd Foot, 1796.

Macfarlane, Andrew Angus. Lieutenant, 26th October, 1804; captain, 10th September, 1812. To half-pay, 25th February, 1816.

Macfarlane, Peter. Ensign, 23rd May, 1811; lieutenant, 23rd July, 1813. Served with the regiment during its second visit to the Peninsula, present at Pyrenees (wounded). To half-pay, 25th March, 1817.

Machin, David Vaus. Ensign, 3rd September, 1812. Served in Holland, wounded and taken prisoner at Bergen-op-Zoom. Lieutenant, 27th July, 1814. To 46th Foot, 24th November, 1814.

Mackenzie, Alexander Watson. Ensign, 6th October, 1848; lieutenant, 6th December, 1850. Served in the Kaffir War of 1851–52, and succeeded to the command of the patrol at Goga, when Major Wilmot, R.A., was killed. Captain, 17th February, 1854. Retired, 9th February, 1855.

Mackenzie, John. Ensign, 7th January, 1803; lieutenant, 11th August, 1804. To paymaster, 95th Foot, 1805.

Maclagen, David. Assistant-surgeon, 1807 to 1811.

Maclaine, Murdock. Ensign, 29th November, 1833. To 4th Foot, 1837.

Maclean, Allen. Ensign, 1797 (1798).

Maclean, Andrew. Served at the Cape with the regiment, afterwards as sergeant-major through the Peninsular War, at Waterloo, Cambray, and occupation of Paris. Promoted lieutenant and quartermaster, 1821. In 1825, being specially recommended by Sir Charles Rowan, he was appointed superintendent of the London Metropolitan police, in which post he served many years, ultimately retiring to Boulogne on a pension of £120 a year, where he died in 1869.

Maclean, George. Ensign, 5th February, 1818. To half-pay, 88th Foot, 22nd March, 1821.

Maclean, James. Ensign, 16th August, 1797; lieutenant, 18th April, 1800; captain, 19th June, 1806. To half-pay, 91st, 1813.

Macnab, Robert. From half-pay, 88th Foot. Lieutenant, 13th February, 1794. Served with the regiment at the Cape of Good Hope. Captain, 25th September, 1801; major, 25th December, 1804. Mentioned in General Craig's despatches of 19th August, 1796, for services at Saldanha Bay. On leaving the regiment became an inspecting officer for recruiting. Retired, 1813.

MacNeal, D. Lieutenant, 18th April, 1794; captain, 11th December, 1800. One of the four officers selected to raise a certain number of men in 1804, for which he received promotion. Major, 1st August, 1811; lieutenant-colonel, 3rd September, 1818. Served with the regiment during the Peninsular War, present at the Pyrenees (wounded), medal with clasp. Received the gold medal for his gallant conduct in command of the light companies of the Highland Brigade, sixth division, at Sauroren, on the 28th and 30th July, 1813, when he was promoted lieutenant-colonel in the army. Retired in 1824.

MacNeal, John. Lieutenant, 20th April, 1794. To 18th Foot, 19th July, 1803.

Macneil, Archibald (of Colonsay). Ensign, 18th August, 1804; lieutenant, 15th August, 1805; adjutant, 15th June, 1809, to 1813; captain, 25th November, 1813. To half-pay, 25th February, 1816. Subsequently served in the Forfar Militia.

Macneil, Roderick, P.W. From 84th Foot. Had served in Sir John Moore's retreat, and subsequently at Walcheren in 1809; in Swedish Pomerania, in 1813; in Holland, in 1814, including the attack on Bergen-op-Zoom. Served also in the campaign of 1815, including the battle of Waterloo. Lieutenant-colonel, 91st, 1842, but never served with the regiment, as he exchanged to the 78th Foot.

Macpherson, John. Ensign, 20th October, 1843; lieutenant, 6th October, 1848. Served in the reserve battalion in the Kaffir War of 1846–47; fort adjutant at Beaufort, South Africa, 1849; became paymaster at the depôt. Retired, 1853.

Macpherson, Robert. Ensign, 14th May, 1853; lieutenant, 25th May, 1855. To 92nd Highlanders, 25th January, 1856.

Macqueen, Mal. Potter. Ensign, 18th April, 1851; lieutenant, 23rd April, 1853; captain, 7th September, 1855. Served in Malta and Greece with the regiment. Retired, 1860.

Macrae, James Charles. Lieutenant, 23rd March, 1809. Retired, 1812.

Mainwaring, Edward George. Ensign, 9th April, 1847; lieutenant, 13th April, 1849. Was present at the affair at Boemplaats, 29th August, 1848. Served in the Kaffir War, 1850. Captain, 24th August, 1852. To Cape Mounted Rifles, 1854.

Manners, Douglas Ernest. Ensign, 18th April, 1845. Served in the Kaffir War of 1846–47 with the regiment. To 63rd Foot, 18th May, 1849.

Marshall, Robert. From 14th battalion of reserve. Lieutenant, 11th October, 1804; captain, 17th October, 1805. Retired, 1814.

Marshall, John. Ensign, 14th May, 1808; lieutenant, 23rd November, 1809; captain, 20th February, 1823; brevet-major, 28th June, 1838. Served with the regiment in the Peninsular War. Was present at Roleia, Vimiero, and advance into Spain; action at Lugo and Corunna; expedition to Walcheren, 1809; at Vittoria, Pyrenees (wounded), Nivelle, Nive, investment of Bayonne, Orthes (wounded severely), and Pampeluna (wounded). To half-pay, 16th February, 1838. Received the war medal with seven clasps. Died in London, 1859.

Marshall, John McLean. Assistant-surgeon, 1858. Served in India with the regiment. To staff, 1861.

Maurice, Atherton Powys. Ensign, 19th March, 1861; lieutenant, 19th February, 1864. Served in India with the regiment, from which place he was invalided home. Died at sea, 15th October, 1865.

McArthur, Duncan. Ensign, 16th August, 1797; lieutenant, 19th March, 1801. To half-pay, 1803.

McCallum, Arthur Edward. From Madras Native Army. Captain, 12th June, 1869 (1870).

M'Cullum, ——. Quarter-master, 1804 to 1808.

McDonald, Robert. Ensign, 25th November, 1802; lieutenant, 10th August, 1804; adjutant, 25th November, 1802, to 14th June, 1809 (1812).

McDonald, Angus. Ensign, 14th August, 1805; lieutenant, 26th August, 1807. To paymaster, 95th Foot, 1810.

McDonald, John. Ensign, 18th May, 1809; lieutenant, 30th April, 1812. Served in Holland at Bergen-op-Zoom (wounded). Was present at Waterloo. To half-pay, 25th March, 1817.

McDougall, John. Captain, 18th February, 1794; major, 1st August, 1804 (1808).

McDougall, Colin. Ensign, 5th January, 1809 (1809).

McDougall, Colin. Ensign, 12th August, 1805; lieutenant, 16th January, 1806. Served with the regiment during its first visit to the Peninsula, remained in Portugal when the regiment returned to England in 1808, when he served in the company formed of 91st men left in hospital. Killed at Talavera in 1809.

McDugald, Hugh. Ensign, 4th June, 1812; lieutenant, 14th April, 1814. Served in Holland, erroneously reported killed at Bergen-op-Zoom (was evidently left for dead on the battle-field). To half-pay, 25th February, 1816.

McGregor, Hugh. From 79th Foot. Captain, 2nd July, 1812. To half-pay, 25th March, 1817.

McInroy, William. Ensign, 10th September, 1828; lieutenant, 8th October, 1829; captain, 29th November, 1833. To half-pay, 17th August, 1838.

McInroy, James. Ensign, 2nd July, 1841; lieutenant, 8th July, 1843. Was on board the *Abercrombie Robinson* when wrecked in 1842. Retired, 21st March, 1845.

McIntosh, Phineas. From 109th Foot. Lieutenant, 30th September, 1796. Retired, 1799.

McIntyre, Malcolm. Ensign, 28th September, 1804. To West India Regiment, 27th November, 1806.

McIntyre, David. From the 79th Foot. Lieutenant, 20th March, 1806; captain, 9th March, 1809. Served with the regiment in the Peninsular War. Killed at Nive, 9th December, 1813.

McIntyre, Thomas Giddy. Ensign, 10th February, 1820; lieutenant, 15th February, 1823. Died, 18th October, 1828, in Jamaica.

McIntyre, Hugh D. Second-lieutenant, 14th January, 1880. Subsequently went to the Indian Staff Corps.

McKay, William. Quarter-Master, 1855. To half-pay, 27th July, 1856, and appointed to depôt battalion at Chatham.

McKenna, John. Ensign, 29th April, 1813. Retired, 1815.

McKenzie, George. Ensign, 12th January, 1805 (1806).

M'Lachlan, Allan. Ensign, 11th February, 1794; lieutenant, 18th March, 1795 (1803).

McLachlan, Andrew. Ensign, 10th April, 1806; lieutenant, 14th May, 1808. Was present at Waterloo. Captain, 2nd May, 1822. Died, 1822.

McLachlan, George M. Assistant-surgeon, 1812. Was present at Waterloo. To half-pay, 7th June, 1821.

McLaren, Duncan. Ensign, 28th August, 1801; lieutenant, 25th June, 1803; captain, 18th December, 1806. To 25th Foot, 10th October, 1811.

McLaren, Alexander D. Ensign, 3rd June, 1812; lieutenant, 31st March, 1814. To half-pay, 25th February, 1816. Retired, 1839.

McLaren, George. Assistant-surgeon, 1835. Died, 1842.

McLean, Allan. Ensign, 7th August, 1806; lieutenant, 15th May, 1808. Served with the regiment in their first visit to the Peninsula; was present at Pyrenees (wounded, 28th July, from the effects of which he died, 24th November, 1813).

McLeod, Donald. Ensign, 9th August, 1804. To 95th Foot, 1805.

McLeod, Francis W. Blake. Ensign, 28th August, 1829; lieutenant, 4th October, 1833. To 35th Foot, 10th June, 1836.

McLeod, Norman Bernes. Ensign, 23rd December, 1831. Retired, 1835.

McMahon, William. Ensign, 28th August, 1804; lieutenant, 10th April, 1806. To 96th Foot, 9th September, 1813.

McMurdo, Charles Baird. Ensign, 8th January, 1829; lieutenant, 8th February, 1831. Died at St. Helena, aged 26, on the 30th July, 1838, from an injury received in his knee which resulted in lockjaw. A tablet was erected to his memory in the church at James Town, St. Helena.

McNeil, Roderick. Lieutenant, 19th July, 1810. To 60th Foot, 5th January, 1815.

McPherson, Allan. From 71st Foot. Lieutenant, 10th February, 1794; adjutant, 10th February, 1794, to 11th December, 1800; captain, 20th May, 1799. To 6th garrison battalion, 1803.

McPherson, Angus. From 18th Foot. Captain, 20th October, 1825. Retired, 1829.

Meade, Augustus. From half-pay, Royal Regiment of Malta. Major, 28th February, 1812. Served with the regiment in the Peninsular War at Toulouse (wounded). Retired, 1818.

Melvin, Alfred James. Ensign, 13th October, 1841; lieutenant, 19th May, 1845. Served in the Kaffir War of 1846–47, and was killed in action, **31st December,** 1850, near Fort Cox, South Africa.

Metcalfe, Henry Christopher. Ensign, 29th April, 1842; lieutenant, 25th July, 1845. Served in the Kaffir War, 1846–47, with the 1st battalion; honourably mentioned for his conduct at Tyumie Post, 19th April, 1846. Transferred to the reserve battalion in 1851. Retired, 1851.

Middlemas, William Hume. Lieutenant, 28th February, 1874. Served in South Africa with the regiment.

Middlemore, Robert Frederick. Ensign, 13th November, 1835; lieutenant, 12th July, 1839; captain, 19th May, 1845. Served in the latter part of the Kaffir War of 1846–47, also in that of 1851–53 (medal), in the reserve battalion, and was present in every affair the battalion was engaged in during these wars. To half-pay, 9th November, 1855.

Middleton, John. Ensign, 5th January, 1809. To 95th Foot, 1809.

Mill, William Macdonald. Ensign, 17th April, 1842. To Cape Rifles, 30th April, 1847.

Miller, John. Quarter-master, 1821. Died 1822.

Mills, William Salmon. Ensign, 31st January, 1863. Served with the regiment in India. Lieutenant, 10th April, 1866; captain, 24th September, 1873. Served in the Zulu War, 1879; was present at the battle of Ginginhlovo, relief of Ekowe, and subsequent operations (medal with clasp). Commanded a detachment of the regiment at St. Helena in 1880–81.

Morgan, Nathaniel. Surgeon, 1839. Retired, 1843.

Mules, Alfred Philip. Ensign, 20th May, 1864; lieutenant, 12th June, 1869. Served in India with the regiment. Captain, 28th May, 1870. Retired, 1871.

Munro, William. Ensign, 12th February, 1794; lieutenant, 18th March, 1795. To 42nd Foot, 1803.

Munro, William. Assistant-surgeon, 1844. Served with the 91st through the Kaffir War, 1846–47. To Medical Department, 1851.

Munro, Donald. Quarter-master. Had served with the 72nd Highlanders in the Crimea, from the 13th June, 1855, including the expedition to Kertch, siege and fall of Sebastopol (medal with clasp, and Turkish medal). Served at the siege and capture of Kotah on the 30th March, 1858 (medal with clasp). To 91st, 24th January, 1865. Served in India with the regiment (1871).

Murdock, James C. Ensign, 18th June, 1806; lieutenant, 28th May, 1807; captain, 29th November, 1810. Was present at Waterloo. To half-pay, 1819.

Murphy, Miah. W. Surgeon, 1854. Had previously served with the 80th Foot during the Burmese War of 1852–53, and was present at the taking of Prome; also present as staff-surgeon to the Bengal Division with Sir J. Cheape's force at Donabew, and wounded at the attack on the enemy's stockade, 19th March, 1853 (medal). Served in Malta, Greece, Ionian Islands, and India, with the regiment. To staff, 1864.

Murray, Sir John, Bart. Lieutenant, 23rd May, 1805 (1806).

Murray, Thomas. Ensign, 15th May, 1808; lieutenant, 11th July, 1811. Served with the regiment during its second visit to the Peninsula. Was present at Waterloo. Captain, 30th November, 1824. Died, 1826.

Murray, John. From 71st Foot. Captain, 11th December, 1812. To half-pay, 25th February, 1816.

Murray, Peter. From sergeant-major, 2nd battalion 19th Foot. Quarter-master, 1861. Was on board the *Abercrombie Robinson*, when wrecked in Table Bay, Cape of Good Hope, in 1842. Served with the regiment at the Cape (Kaffir War) and in India. To 72nd Foot, 1865.

Noden, Francis. Paymaster, 1805. Retired, 1809.

Norman, William Frederick. Ensign, 6th November, 1846. Served in the Kaffir War of 1846–47 with the regiment. Lieutenant, 7th June, 1850 (1854).

Obbard, Edward K. From the London Militia. Ensign, 8th July, 1856; lieutenant, 13th August, 1858. Served in the Ionian Islands and India with the regiment. Died at Omerapore, 24th April, 1860.

O'Callaghan, Cornelius. Ensign, 2nd July, 1829. To 49th Foot, 23rd December, 1831.

O'Doherty, Theobald. From half-pay, 40th Foot. Captain, 28th June, 1821 (1825).

O'Donel, Hugh J. Assistant-surgeon, 1814. Served with the regiment in Holland, taken prisoner at Bergen-op-Zoom. To half-pay, 1818.

Ogilvie, William. Lieutenant, 31st December, 1794. To 4th Foot, 1798.

O'Hara, Walter. Ensign, 9th March, 1809. Retired, 1810.

O'Keefe, Edward B. H. Ensign, 14th January, 1797. To 71st Foot, 1798.

O'Leary, John. Ensign, 27th June, 1811; lieutenant, 6th October, 1813. To half-pay, 25th March, 1817.

Olivey, Walter Rice. Ensign, 14th February, 1851; lieutenant, 29th October, 1852. To 12th Foot, 1856.

O'Neal, John. Assistant-surgeon, 13th April, 1852. Served in Greece and India with the regiment. Surgeon to the staff, 5th May, 1859.

Onslow, Richard C. Ensign, 12th June, 1835; lieutenant, 25th January, 1839. Retired, 1842.

Orde, James. Captain, 29th April, 1795 (1802). Died, 1850.

Ormerod, S. Nicholas. Ensign, 12th May, 1808; lieutenant, 9th March, 1809; captain, 31st March, 1814. Served with the regiment during its second visit to the Peninsula; present at Alverez, 25th May, 1812; also at Pyrenees (wounded, 28th July). To half-pay, 25th February, 1816.

Ormiston, John Andrew. Ensign, 3rd October, 1811; lieutenant, 29th July, 1813. Served with the regiment during its second visit to the Peninsula, present at Pyrenees (wounded, 28th July). To half-pay, 25th March, 1817. Died, 1838.

Osborne, Eric Willoughby. Ensign, 10th April, 1866. To 1st West India Regiment, 8th June, 1867.

O'Sullivan, George Lidwell. From 33rd Foot. Captain, 91st, 1st April, 1875. Served in the Zulu War of 1879; was present at the battle of Ginginhlovo and subsequent operations (medal with clasp).

Oswald, Robert. From 35th Foot. Captain, 8th September 1802. To 35th Foot, 25th May, 1803.

Ottley, Benjamin Wynne. From half-pay, 27th Foot. Major, 4th December, 1806; lieutenant-colonel, 2nd January, 1812. Served in the Peninsular War; was present at Roleia, Vimiero, and Corunna; in the expedition to Walcheren; and in Holland, where he was wounded and taken prisoner at Bergen-op-Zoom. To half-pay, 21st October, 1816.

Owgan, Joseph. Ensign, 16th April, 1842; lieutenant, 21st March, 1845. Served in the Kaffir War of 1846-47, and subsequently against rebel Boers across the Orange River, including the affair at Boemplaats, 29th August, 1848. Retired, 1851.

Passingham, R. Townshend. Ensign, 1st June, 1860; lieutenant, 21st June, 1864. Served in India with the regiment. Retired, 9th March, 1867.

Paterson, James. From sergeant-major to quarter-master, 1847. Served with the regiment at St. Helena and the Cape (Kaffir War); in Greece, Ionian Isles, and India. To half-pay as captain, 9th April, 1861. Died, 1862.

Paterson, Stanley. Second-lieutenant, 9th July, 1879. Served in South Africa.

Paton, James. Ensign, 30th December, 1813. Was present at Waterloo. Lieutenant, 27th April, 1820. Retired, 1828.

Paton, John. Ensign, 23rd February, 1839. To 1st West India Regiment as lieutenant, 9th October, 1840. Returned to the 91st in 1842. Retired, 1847.

Patterson, William Thomas Laird. Ensign, 22nd February, 1839; lieutenant, 12th October, 1841. Served in the Kaffir War of 1846–47 (medal). Captain, 20th April, 1849; major, 14th December, 1855. Served in India with the regiment. Commanded a field force sent in the direction of Mooltye and Baitool to capture Tantia Topee, 27th March, 1859. Lieutenant-colonel, 12th November, 1860; colonel, 12th November, 1865. To half-pay, 14th January, 1869. Subsequently assistant-adjutant and quarter-master-general for the Cork district.

Pearce, James. Ensign, 23rd January, 1812. Retired, 1813.

Peile, Richard Spier. Assistant-surgeon, 1850. Died, 1853.

Pennington, J. M. Ensign, 26th December, 1837; lieutenant, 9th October, 1840. Commanded a detachment of the regiment at Boemplaats, 29th August, 1848 (mentioned in despatches). Captain, 7th May, 1850. Served in the Kaffir War of 1851–52. Retired, 1852.

Penton, John. From 84th Foot, with which he had served in the Indian Campaign of 1857–58; joined Havelock's force at Cawnpore, present at the actions of Mungawar and Alumbagh, headed a party which stormed and took possession of a gate through which the relieving force had to pass on its way to the Residency of Lucknow, commanded a company in the sortie of the 29th September, when a number of guns were taken, and at the storming of the Hirn Khannan he extricated the commanding officer, Major Willis, from a mine pit, while exposed to a heavy fire from three points, and was the first in through the breach; present with Outram's force at the Alumbagh; at the fall of Lucknow commanded three companies of the 84th Foot at the storming of Kaisabagh; served with Lugard's column, and present in the actions of the 17th and 26th of April, relief of Azimghur, and pursuit of Koer Sing (medal with two clasps and a year's service). Major in 91st, 5th April, 1864. To 89th Foot, 1870.

Perkins, Augustus Frederick. Ensign, 9th February, 1855; lieutenant, 27th November, 1857. Served with the regiment in Greece and Ionian Islands. Was staff officer to Major Savage, commanding a field force in the Baitool district, 22nd April, 1859. Retired, 21st June, 1864.

Philips, James. Lieutenant, 1st October, 1794. To Coldstream Guards, 1795.

Pickwick, Charles Henry S. Ensign, 4th May, 1849; lieutenant, 11th April, 1851. Served in the Kaffir War, 1851 (wounded, 27th June). Retired, 1852.

Pike, Francis. From 92nd Highlanders. Lieutenant, 7th October, 1855; captain, 21st April, 1862. Served in Greece, Ionian Islands, and India, with the regiment. To 86th Foot, 22nd March, 1864.

Fox-Pitt, William Augustus Lane. Second-lieutenant, 22nd February, 1879. Served in the latter part of the Zulu War, 1879 (medal with clasp). To the Grenadier Guards in 1880, with which he served in Egypt.

Power, Robert. Ensign, 17th September, 1812; lieutenant, 5th January, 1815. To 73rd Foot, 8th February, 1816.

Power, William John. Surgeon, 1846. Had previously served with the 7th Dragoon Guards in the expedition against the insurgent Boers at the Cape of Good Hope in 1845, and in the Kaffir War of 1846-47—the latter part of which as surgeon of the reserve battalion 91st. Died in England, 7th September, 1849.

Prevost, William. Ensign, 9th March, 1867. Served with the regiment in India. Lieutenant, 13th May, 1870; captain, 2nd March, 1878. Served in the Zulu War of 1879; was present at the battle of Ginginhlovo and relief of Ekowe (medal with clasp). Was invalided home shortly afterwards. To the Commissariat and Transport Staff Department, 1st July, 1880.

Purcell, John. Quarter-master, 1871. Had previously served with the 65th Foot throughout the New Zealand wars, from May, 1847, including actions at Wanganui, skirmish at St. John's Bush in 1847; attack and capture of Pah at Kotai, expedition to Warea, attack and capture of Pahs, 20th to 30th April, expedition to Kilukihi, attack and capture of Pahs, 11th and 12th October, sapping operations to Rifle Pits at Huirangi in 1860; action at Huirangi, sapping operations at Rifle Pits and Pah at Pukiangiori with repulse of sortie, storm and capture of Rifle Pits and Pah at Rangiori, attack and capture of Rangiawhia and Huirini, in 1864 (medal) (1874).

Rae, Edward James Somers. Ensign, 29th April, 1847; lieutenant, 28th December, 1849; captain, 5th of June, 1855. Served in the Kaffir War of 1851-52 (commanded a levy of Fingoes); also served in Greece and India with the regiment. Retired, 4th November, 1859.

Rawstorne, John George. From 62nd Foot, with which he had served in the Peninsula from August, 1813, to the end of the war, and was present at the battle of Orthes. Captain, 10th October, 1838. Joined 91st in 1842. Served in the Kaffir War, 1846-47 (medal); was wounded at Block Drift, April, 1846. Commanded a detachment of 91st under Sir Harry Smith in 1848 against the Boers. Served in Greece with 91st. To 17th Foot, 1858.

Read, C. C. Assistant-surgeon, 1853. To 1st Grenadier Guards, 1854.

Reid, Thomas. From 76th Foot. Captain, 26th August, 1804. To 33rd Foot, 20th August, 1807.

Reid, Francis. Surgeon, 1849 to 1851.

Rendell, William Jasper. Surgeon, 1867. Had previously served with the 41st and 55th Foot at the siege and fall of Sebastopol, from the 10th of March, 1855 (medal and clasp, and Turkish medal). Served in India during the mutiny of 1857–59; present in medical charge of two batteries of Royal Artillery at the action of Secundra (medal). Served with the 55th Foot on the Bhootan Expedition in 1865 (1868).

Richardson, Charles James. Second-lieutenant, 22nd January, 1879; lieutenant, 10th April, 1880. Served in the Zulu War in 1879; was present at the battle of Ginginhlovo, on which occasion he was in charge of the regimental colour, relief of Ekowe, and subsequent operations (medal with clasp).

Richardson, Robert Walsh. From 63rd Foot. Captain, 1st January, 1824. Retired, 1825.

Ricketts, Fred Walter. Ensign, 17th September, 1850. Served in the Kaffir War of 1850–51 with the regiment. Was dangerously wounded in action on the Waterkloof heights, 14th October, 1851; succumbed to his wounds, 8th November, 1851.

Rivarola, Count George. Ensign, 16th September, 1845. To 26th Foot, 1847.

Rivers, James. From 3rd Royal Veteran Battalion. Captain, 8th April, 1825. Served in Jamaica with the regiment. Major, 22nd July, 1830. Retired, 4th October, 1833.

Robbins, George Blakemore. From 80th Foot. Lieutenant, 3rd February, 1872. Served in the Zulu War of 1879; was present at the battle of Ginginhlovo, relief of Ekowe, and subsequent operations (medal with clasp). Served at Mauritius in 1880 with a detachment of the regiment.

Roberton, Alexander. Ensign, 9th January, 1812; lieutenant, 25th November, 1813. To half-pay, 25th February, 1816.

Roberts, Henry H. Ensign, 6th January, 1860. Killed by accidentally falling into a well, on the 28th August, 1861, at Kamptee, India.

Roberts, William. Assistant-surgeon, 1805 to 1807.

Robertson, Edward Lovett. Ensign, 11th January, 1833; lieutenant, 14th November, 1835. To 2nd Dragoon Guards, 10th June, 1836.

Robertson, George Francis. Ensign, 23rd April, 1858. To 3rd Grenadier Guards, 1859.

Robertson, James. Assistant-surgeon, 1822 to 1830.

Robertson, John. From 60th Foot. Captain, 8th June, 1796 (1804).

Robeson, **James**. Ensign, 7th November, 1822. Died, 1825.

Robley, **Horatio Gordon**. From half-pay, 68th Foot, with which regiment he served in the New Zealand War of 1864 to 1866, and was present at the attack on Gate Pah (medal). To 91st as captain in 1871; major, 28th January, 1880. Served at Mauritius and in South Africa with the regiment, being in command of the detachment of the 91st at the former place.

Rogers, **James Thomas**. Ensign, 4th May, 1860; lieutenant, 3rd May, 1864. Served in India with the regiment. Captain, 19th August, 1873. Served in the Zulu War of 1879; was present at the battle of Ginginhlovo (medal with clasp). Was invalided home shortly after. Appointed adjutant of the Renfrew Militia, 10th January, 1880. Retired in May, 1881.

Rolfe, **Henry Robert**. Ensign, 4th July, 1860. Served in India with the regiment. Died at Jubbulpore of remittent fever, after an illness of eleven days, 1864.

Ross, **Archibald**. From 19th Light Dragoons. Captain, 12th September, 1811. Served in the Peninsular War, and was attached to the Portuguese service at Vittoria (medal). Retired, 1820.

Russell, John. From 2nd Foot. Lieutenant, 11th May, 1808. Served with the regiment during its second visit to the Peninsula. Was present at Waterloo. To half-pay, 25th February, 1816.

Rutherford, John. Ensign, 7th November, 1811; lieutenant, 7th October, 1813. To half-pay, 25th February, 1816. Died, 23rd July, 1833.

Sargent, **Samuel Tomkins**. Ensign, 18th May, 1849. To 51st Foot, 8th March, 1850.

Saunders, **John Alexander**. Ensign, 30th April, 1847 (1849).

Savage, **Henry J.** Ensign, 5th June, 1835; lieutenant, 11th May, 1838; captain, 8th July, 1843. Served against the Boers in 1845, and in the Kaffir War of 1846–47. Brevet-major, 20th June, 1854; major, 31st August, 1858. Served with the regiment at Corfu and India. Commanded a field force in the Baitool district, April, 1859. Brevet lieutenant-colonel, 19th June, 1860. To 84th Foot, 28th October, 1864.

Sayer, William. Ensign, 22nd January, 1807; lieutenant, 28th April, 1808 (1809).

Schank, **Henry Alexander**. Ensign, 14th January, 1871; lieutenant, 1st November, 1871. Served in the Zulu War; was present at the battle of Ginginhlovo and subsequent operations (medal with clasp). To 71st Highland Light Infantry, 10th April, 1880.

Served in Egypt. Attached to the 74th Highlanders in 1882. Died of consumption at Brighton, 1886.

Scott, ——. Quarter-master, 1808 to 1810.

Scott, James. Surgeon, 1809 to 1810.

Scott, George. Ensign, 26th April, 1810; adjutant, 26th April, 1810, to 23rd October, 1821; lieutenant, 21st July, 1813. Served in Holland with the 2nd battalion at Bergen-op-Zoom (wounded and taken prisoner). Was present at Waterloo. To half-pay, 1821.

Scott, James. Ensign, 27th July, 1814. To half-pay, 25th February, 1816.

Scott, William Glendonwyn. Ensign, 30th March, 1832; lieutenant, 12th June, 1835; captain, 22nd February, 1839. Served throughout the Kaffir War of 1846–47 with the reserve battalion, and part of the same as deputy-adjutant and quarter-master-general to the first division. Returned to England with the 1st battalion in 1848. Brevet-major, 15th September, 1848. Served in Greece with the regiment. Retired, 1856.

Scott, John Alexander. Assistant-surgeon, 1865 to 1869. Served in India with the regiment.

Sears, Samuel Montague. From 11th battalion of reserve. Captain, 2nd August, 1804. To 8th Royal Veterinary Battalion, 20th June, 1805.

Shaw, Charles. Lieutenant, 7th November, 1801. To 17th Foot, 17th May, 1803.

Sheddon, Thomas. Lieutenant, 8th April, 1825. Retired, 1829.

Shinkwin, Thomas. Ensign, 9th November, 1809. Retired, 1811.

Sinclair, Hon. Alexander E. G. From 26th Foot. Lieutenant, 9th April, 1847. Retired, 1850.

Sitwell, Harold Cooper. From 88th Foot. Had previously served at General Windham's actions with the Gwalior Contingent at Pandoo Nuddee on the 26th November, and at Cawnpore on the 27th and 28th November, 1857, and subsequent defence of Cawnpore. Served with the 9th Lancers at the battle of Cawnpore on the 6th December, pursuit and action at Seraighat, 9th December, action at Kalee Nuddee, and re-occupation of Futtehgur, capture of Meangunge, siege of Lucknow and subsequent operations, the summer campaign, including the attack on the fort of Rooyah, action at Allagunge, battle of Bareilly, actions of the 18th and 24th May, at Shahjehanpore, and pursuit to Mohumdee (medal with clasp). Captain, 16th July, 1864. Joined the 91st in 1869. Brevet-major, 1st October, 1877; lieutenant-colonel, 2nd March, 1878. Retired, 2nd March, 1878.

Smith, William. Ensign, 28th June, 1810; lieutenant, 21st July, 1813. Served with the regiment during its second visit to the

Peninsula. Was present at Waterloo. To half-pay, 27th April, 1817. Died at Dumfries, 1840.

Smith, **Alexander**. Lieutenant, 30th August, 1810. Served with the regiment during its second visit to the Peninsula. Was present at Waterloo. To half-pay, 42nd Foot, 30th September, 1819.

Smith, **Andrew**. Ensign, 14th April, 1814. Was present at Waterloo. Lieutenant, 5th December, 1822. Died, 1823.

Smyth, John Selby. Ensign, 12th April, 1850; lieutenant, 16th September, 1851. Retired, 1853.

Snodgrass, John James. From 52nd Foot, with which he served in the Peninsular and Burmese Wars, and was present at Waterloo. Captain, 22nd December, 1825; major, 14th November, 1826. To half-pay, 1826. Subsequently deputy-quarter-master-general at Halifax, Nova Scotia, where he died in 1841.

Somerset, Lord Arthur. From 7th Foot. Captain, 2nd October, 1806. To 19th Light Dragoons, 12th September, 1811.

Spraight, George. Ensign, 16th March, 1850. To 31st Foot, 1852.

Spearman, **Horace Ralph**. Ensign, 18th December, 1857; lieutenant, 25th April, 1860. Served in the Ionian Islands and India with the regiment. To Bengal Staff Corps, 4th December, 1866.

Sprot, **John**. From half-pay, 83rd Foot, with which he had served under General Woodburn in the affair at Aurungabad in 1857 (medal); afterwards served as acting executive engineer of the Rajpootana field force, and received the commendation of General Roberts, commanding, and of the Bombay Government, for his "great energy and ability" in the construction of barracks for the European troops at Neemuch. Major, 22nd January, 1867. To 91st, the 31st July, 1869. Commanded the regiment from the 29th January, 1870, to the 19th January, 1876. To half-pay, 1876. On leaving the regiment was appointed assistant-adjutant and quarter-master-general North British District, and subsequently commanded a brigade depôt.

Squirl, William. Prior to entering the British army, served as a lieutenant in the Austrian service under Marshal Radetski, in the campaign of 1848–49, and was present at the battles of Montarra and Novarra (wounded), and subsequently at the siege of Leghorn. Ensign, 11th May, 1849; lieutenant, 8th July, 1851. Served with the regiment during the Kaffir War of 1850–53 (medal). Adjutant, 19th May, 1854, to 1856. To recruiting service, 15th March, 1856. Served in the Ionian Islands and India with the regiment. Captain, 5th March, 1858. To half-pay, 12th July, 1869.

Stanton, William Barron. Ensign, 28th January, 1848; lieutenant, 16th August, 1850; captain, 23rd November, 1852. Retired, 1854.

St. Clair, James L. C. Ensign, 23rd September, 1871; lieutenant, 1st November, 1871; adjutant, 1st December, 1875, to 31st December, 1880. Served in the Zulu War of 1879; was present at the battle of Ginginhlovo (where he had a narrow escape of being shot, a bullet having passed through his helmet) and the relief of Ekowe. Was invalided home in July (medal with clasp). Captain, 1st October, 1880.

Stein, Robert. Ensign, 19th October, 1840; lieutenant, 15th April, 1842. Retired, 6th October, 1848.

Steuart, William. Ensign, 16th January, 1804; lieutenant, 6th June, 1805; captain, 17th April, 1806. Was present at Waterloo. Major, 12th August, 1819. Died, 1825.

Stevenson, George N. From 83rd Foot. Captain 91st, 28th October, 1871. Served in the Zulu War of 1879; was present at the battle of Ginginhlovo, relief of Ekowe, and subsequent operations (medal with clasp).

Stewart, Robert. Ensign, 31st October, 1805; lieutenant, 13th May, 1808; captain, 27th April, 1820. Served with the regiment in the Peninsular War; wounded at Pyrenees, 28th February, 1813. Was present at Waterloo. Retired, 1823.

Stewart, James. Quarter-master, 1807 to 1821. Was present at Waterloo.

Stewart, Archibald. Ensign, 30th March, 1815. To half-pay, 25th February, 1816. Retired, 1st April, 1833.

Stewart, Malcolm. Ensign, 27th July, 1815. To half-pay, 25th February, 1816.

Stewart, Allan W. From 82nd Foot. Ensign, 26th October, 1855 (1857).

St. George, Thomas Baldwin. Captain, 1st August, 1804 (1804).

Stokes, F. Fraser. Ensign, 11th May, 1838. Died, 1841.

Stow Kenyon, Frederick M. From Military Train. Ensign, 3rd January, 1865. To 91st, 1870. To 19th Hussars, 1871. Subsequently commanded the 5th Dragoon Guards.

Streatfield, John. From 71st Foot. Lieutenant, 8th August, 1816. To half-pay, 25th March, 1817.

Stuart, James. From 7th Foot. Captain, 15th February, 1794; major, 22nd December, 1794 (1795).

Stuart, Duncan. Ensign, 18th March, 1795; lieutenant, 20th May, 1799. Was one of the four officers selected in 1804 to raise a certain number of men for the regiment, for which service he was promoted captain (1809).

Stuart, Hugh. Ensign, 18th March, 1795; lieutenant, 25th October, 1797; adjutant, 11th December, 1800, to 24th November, 1802. Retired, 1803.

Stuart, Charles. Ensign, 19th May, 1808; lieutenant, 16th January, 1812. Served with the regiment during their second visit to the Peninsula. Was present at Waterloo. To half-pay, 25th March, 1817.

Stuart, William. Assistant-surgeon, 1842 to 1843.

Stubbs, John H. E. Assistant-surgeon, 1842 to 1843. Was on duty on board the *Abercrombie Robinson* when wrecked in Table Bay, Cape of Good Hope, in 1842.

Summers, John. Surgeon, 1865. Served in India with the regiment. To staff, 1867.

Sutherland, James Milford. From 53rd and 42nd Regiments. Captain, 27th August, 1804; major, 10th September, 1812. To half-pay from 1817 to 1828. Lieutenant-colonel, 16th August, 1827. Served with the regiment in Jamaica. Retired, 1831.

Sutherland, Alexander. Lieutenant, 13th December, 1809 (1813).

Sweny, John Charles. Ensign, 12th December, 1850; lieutenant, 24th August, 1852; captain, 9th February, 1855. Served in Malta, Greece, and India with the regiment. Retired, 5th April, 1864.

Swinton, John. From 65th Foot. Captain, 25th May, 1803 (1806).

Sword, Alexander. Ensign, 28th January, 1813; lieutenant, 2nd March, 1815. Served with the regiment during the latter part of its second visit to the Peninsula. Was present at Waterloo. To half-pay, 25th February, 1816.

Taylor, John. Ensign, 30th July, 1812; lieutenant, 14th July, 1814. Served with the regiment during its second visit to the Peninsula, at Orthes (wounded). To half-pay, 25th February, 1816.

Teale, Charles Shipley. Ensign, 7th April, 1825; lieutenant, 10th December, 1827. To 4th Foot, 1837.

Thom, George. Ensign, 15th April, 1842; lieutenant, 14th April, 1846; adjutant of the reserve battalion, 1845. Served in the Kaffir War of 1846-47. Honourably mentioned in general orders for his conduct in April, 1846. Retired, 1847.

Thomas, Lloyd H. Ensign, 17th October, 1851; lieutenant, 17th February, 1854; captain, 13th August, 1858. Served through the Kaffir War of 1851-52, and was in every action in the Waterkloof in which the 91st were engaged (medal). Served in the Ionian Islands and India with the regiment. Exchanged to the 63rd Foot, 6th November, 1863. Died, 1864.

Thorburn, Charles James. Ensign, 5th April, 1864; lieutenant, 13th July, 1867. Served in India with the regiment. Captain, 28th

May, 1870. To 83rd Foot, 1871. Subsequently adjutant of the Banffshire Rifle Volunteers.

Thornhill, Henry. Ensign, 4th October, 1833 (1834).

Thornhill, John. Ensign, 5th April, 1827; lieutenant, 10th September, 1828; captain, 8th February, 1831. Retired, 1841.

Tingcombe, John Macleod. Ensign, 7th December, 1855; lieutenant, 23rd July, 1858; captain, 1st April, 1870. To 72nd Foot, 1870. Subsequently served with the 72nd in the advance by the Kurum Valley under General Sir Frederick Roberts, V.C., and was present at the battle of Charasiah, in the Afghan War of 1878-79. Died at Chelsea Hospital while holding the appointment of Captain of Invalids, June, 1890. A tablet to his memory was erected at Chelsea Hospital by his brother officers of the 72nd and 91st.

Tottenham, Arthur Ely H. Sub-lieutenant and lieutenant, 1st February, 1873. Served in the Zulu War of 1879; was present at the battle of Ginginhlovo and relief of Ekowe (medal with clasp). Was invalided home shortly afterwards.

Traill, William. Assistant-surgeon, 1861. Served in India with the regiment. Died, 1871.

Trimmer, William. Ensign, 18th November, 1813. Served with the regiment during the latter part of its second visit to the Peninsula. Was present at Waterloo. Lieutenant, 2nd March, 1820. To 38th Foot, 9th August, 1821.

Truter, D. Ensign, 29th January, 1799. Retired, 1803.

Truter, J. M. Ensign, 30th August, 1801; lieutenant, 6th August, 1802. To the Ramsay Regiment of Infantry, 3rd April, 1806.

Upperton, George. Ensign, 27th February, 1862; lieutenant, 23rd October, 1867. Served in India with the regiment. To half-pay, 15th August, 1868.

Ussher, John Theophilus. From 22nd Foot, with which he served in the campaign of 1844-45 in the Southern Mahratta country, and was present at the investment and capture of the forts of Panulla and Powughur. To 91st as lieutenant, 14th April, 1846. To 87th Foot, 1854.

Veitch, Henry. From 57th Foot. Major, August, 1795. Retired, 1796.

Vereker, C. Ensign, 15th June, 1826. To 27th Foot, 2nd March, 1827.

Voyle, Francis R. C. Ensign, 9th October, 1863. Served in India with the regiment. To Bengal Staff Corps, 1869.

Wade, Walter O. Ensign, 10th March, 1854; lieutenant, 27th November, 1857; adjutant, 27th November, 1857, to 19th February,

1865. Served in Greece, Ionian Islands, and India, with the regiment. Retired, 13th July, 1867.

Walker, Alexander. Ensign, 8th February, 1831. To 11th Dragoons, 11th July, 1833.

Wallace, Houston. Ensign, 11th October, 1804. To 14th Light Dragoons, 27th August, 1805.

Walsh, James. From 34th Foot. Captain, 28th August, 1804; major, 3rd September, 1818. Served with the regiment during its first visit to the Peninsula; was left behind sick in Portugal in 1808, and commanded the company formed of men left in hospital; was actively employed in the operations which led to the capture of Oporto in 1809; was present at the battle of Talavera, on the 27th July, 1809, when he was taken prisoner, but managed eventually to effect his escape in August, and after suffering great privations, rejoined the army under the Duke of Wellington. Served with the regiment at Toulouse, where he was wounded. Was present at Waterloo. Retired in 1825.

Warburton, Augustus. From 57th Foot. Major, 18th December, 1806. Appointed Inspecting Field Officer of the Canadian Militia, 7th August, 1811.

Ward, John. Ensign, 8th April, 1816; lieutenant, 8th September, 1828. Served at St. Helena with the regiment. Was present when Napoleon's body was exhumed, in 1840. Captain, 15th April, 1842. Wrecked in the *Abercrombie Robinson* in 1842. Served in the Kaffir War of 1846-47; appointed commandant of Fort Beaufort in 1847, during the absence of the lieutenant-governor. Major, half-pay, 12th April, 1850.

Ware, Charles. From sergeant-major. Ensign, 21st October, 1862; lieutenant, 23rd March, 1866. Served in Malta, Greece, Ionian Islands, and India, with the regiment. Captain, 1st April, 1870. To half-pay, 17th May, 1870.

Warlock, Aaron. From half-pay. Captain, 2nd December, 1831. Died, 1832.

Warren, J. Sandham. Had previously served in the campaign on the Sutlej (medal) in 1845, and was attached to the 53rd, and with them in the engagements at Buddiwal and Aliwal; was present with his own regiment, the 73rd Bengal Native Infantry, at the battle of Sobraon. Also engaged with the Cape Mounted Rifles in the action against the Boers at Boemplaats, in 1848. Captain, 21st May, 1850. Retired, 1854.

Warren, Lionel Smith. Ensign, 23rd November, 1852. To 65th Foot, 1853.

Watson, Robert. Assistant-surgeon, 1854. Served in Greece, Ionian Islands, and India, with the regiment. To staff, 1861.

Wesley, Robert Butt. Ensign, 12th November, 1858; lieutenant, 21st April, 1862. Served in India with the regiment. Retired, 16th August, 1864.

West, Thomas. Lieutenant, 4th April, 1800 (1802).

Wetenhall, William Marsden. Ensign, 23rd September, 1824. To 31st Foot, 1825.

White, Henry John. Ensign, 2nd February, 1838. Retired, 1839.

Whitle, Robert. Ensign, 28th April, 1847; lieutenant, 20th April, 1849 (1852).

Will, Andrew. Ensign, 1808 (1808).

Williamson, Donald. Ensign, 24th April, 1823; lieutenant, 17th November, 1825 (1828).

Wilson, Alexander. Second-lieutenant, 22nd February, 1879. Served through the latter part of the Zulu War of 1879 with the regiment (medal with clasp). Served at Mauritius with a detachment of the 91st in 1880.

Wood, Henry. Ensign, 17th August, 1852; lieutenant, 19th May, 1854; captain, 23rd July, 1858. Served in Malta, Greece, and India, with the regiment. Major, 29th January, 1870. Retired, 1873.

Wright, Edward W. C., C.B. Ensign, 21st December, 1832; lieutenant, 13th November, 1835; captain, 2nd July, 1841. Served during the Kaffir War of 1846–47, as aide-de-camp to Major-General Hare (medal). Was senior surviving officer of the troops embarked in the *Birkenhead*, and for his heroic conduct on the night of the 26th February, 1852, he was promoted to the brevet rank of major, and awarded a pension of £100 per annum for "distinguished services," and subsequently promoted to rank of lieutenant-colonel for "service in the field." Became deputy-inspector of the reserve forces. Died, 26th August, 1871.

Wyllie, Frederick. Second-lieutenant, 22nd February, 1879. Served through latter part of the Zulu War of 1879 with the regiment (medal with clasp). Subsequently transferred to the Madras Staff Corps.

Wymer, Reginald. From 34th Foot. Ensign, 21st August, 1867. To 91st, 1870. Retired, 1871.

Young, John. Ensign, 16th August, 1804; lieutenant, 13th August, 1805; captain, 6th October, 1813. To half-pay, 25th February, 1816.

Young, William H. Surgeon, 1811. Was present at Waterloo. To half-pay, 1816.

Yarborough, Charles Cook, C.B. From 15th Foot, 5th April, 1833. Captain, 4th January, 1833; major, 19th May, 1845.

Served in the Kaffir Wars of 1846–47 and 1851–52–53. Became lieutenant-colonel, and commanded the reserve battalion from the 13th October, 1848. Wounded at the affair at the Waterkloof, 4th March, 1852. Was appointed Companion of the Bath for his services in the Kaffir Wars (medal). To half-pay, 29th January, 1856, as colonel.

THE END.

PRINTED BY WILLIAM CLOWES AND SONS, LIMITED,
LONDON AND BECCLES.

D. & Co.

www.ingramcontent.com/pod-product-compliance
Lightning Source LLC
Chambersburg PA
CBHW030424300426
44112CB00009B/842